MUSIC
CRITICISM

AN ANNOTATED GUIDE
TO THE LITERATURE

Harold J. Diamond

The Scarecrow Press, Inc.
Metuchen, N.J., & London
1979

Library of Congress Cataloging in Publication Data

Diamond, Harold J   1934–
   Music criticism.

   Bibliography: p.
   Includes indexes.
   1. Music—History and criticism—Bibliography.
2. Musical criticism—Bibliography. I. Title.
ML113.D5   016.78'09   79–22279
ISBN 0–8108–1268–1

To Ellen

CONTENTS

PREFACE

Music Criticism will serve as an aid to students seeking critical and analytic material on musical compositions. Though aimed specifically at the undergraduate student and serious musical amateur, many of the listings deal with complex musical works. These listings are, of necessity, on an advanced level and will prove useful to graduate students as well.

This is a selected list of readily available books and periodicals, chosen and annotated to lead the student beyond the popular and accessible commentary usually found in "Concertgoers' Companions" and record jacket notes. Because all the listed material has been traced and seen, the user should not encounter misleading entries, bibliographic dead ends or items difficult to obtain.

Doctoral dissertations and works in languages other than English are excluded. Articles that deal with editorial problems, or contain a high proportion of subjective, descriptive commentary are avoided unless they have some redeeming virtue. Some music of broad popular appeal is poorly represented in the critical literature, perhaps owing to a lack of interest among those writing on a high critical or analytic plane. However, controversies rage over seldom heard works and heated discussions over a few measures of a Bartok Quartet or Webern Symphony are typical. For this reason, Rimsky-Korsakov's Scheherazade is not included, but an intense discussion of Delius' Piano Concerto is.

The work is arranged by musical form, as follows:

Solo Works: Compositions for solo instrument without accompaniment. The chapter is mainly devoted to keyboard music, which is self-accompanying. However, the relatively scant literature for unaccompanied violin, violoncello and other instruments is represented.

vii

Operas: The musical aspects of opera. Entries emphasizing plot are included only if needed to clarify the music. Overtures can be found under Orchestral.

Vocal Music: Compositions for the voice, exclusive of opera. Songs, as well as choral works with and without accompaniment, are found here.

Orchestral Music: Compositions utilizing full orchestra, exclusive of symphonies. Operatic overtures, tone-poems, and ballet music occupy this category.

Concertos: Compositions in the concerto form, or bearing the title "concerto."

Chamber Music: Compositions using small instrumental forces. The range from solo instrument sonatas with accompaniment to works for 15 instruments is covered in this category.

Symphonies: Compositions in classical symphonic form, or bearing the title "Symphony" or "Sinfonia."

Because Music Criticism is arranged by form, the user who does not know the form of the composition will need to consult either the composer or the title index. However, a warning is in order. Music Criticism has drawn material from many general sources. Rather than discuss each composition in a clearly identifiable section, these sources often discuss many pieces together to support an overall musical observation, such as the composer's tonality, rhythmic characteristics or other traits. As a result, Debussy's L'Isle Joyeuse is not found in the index, but is discussed in some of the many books listed under Debussy, "Piano Music-- General" in the Solo Works section. Therefore, the index serves only as a partial guide to the contents. Because the Essay and General Literature Index, as well as other Scarecrow guides have utilized the same "General Works" category with success, users should not be inconvenienced. Music Criticism has the added feature of annotating its listings, which should reduce the chance of any confusion.

Composers are listed alphabetically in each chapter. The subheadings under each composer begin with the most general and increase in specificity until the titles of individual pieces appear. Titles of compositions and spellings of composers' names are in forms familiar to English-speaking readers. Tchaikovsky is not spelled Chaikovskii and Haydn's

Seasons is not given in the original German. Because The Rite of Spring and Le Sacre du Printemps are equally familiar titles, both are found here.

A judgment had to be made as to which cut-off points in musical history to observe, in order to serve the best interests of the intended user. Pre-Bach music seems to attract critical commentary intended more for the specialist. However, the earliest composer represented in this work is Machaut (1300-1377) because undergraduate music majors are required to deal with enough of Machaut's intricacies to make easy access to analytic materials on him most welcome. Advanced discussions on 20th century music are also included, because simple commentary on most 20th century music does not seem to exist. Also, contemporary music is a regular part of the college and university curriculum. There may well be compositions missing that obviously qualify for inclusion. As explained earlier, a lack of sufficient and appropriate analytic literature is one reason for the absence of some titles. However, it is not beyond possibility that appropriate titles have been overlooked despite all efforts. I can only regret their absence now and include them in later editions.

The periodical indexes (RILM and the Music Index) were scanned systematically up to 1978. The search was selective, passing over many articles that were inappropriate or obviously difficult to obtain. Because the Music Index thins out and its coverage becomes irregular before 1960, pre-1960 periodical listings do not usually appear in Music Criticism. However, if a composition attracted an abundance of analytic information, the search was extended to pre-1960 volumes. It was also felt that the older the listing, the more difficult it becomes to obtain. Though the search through the periodical indexes, as described, was systematic, the search on the actual library shelves, leafing through volumes for appropriate nuggets was doomed from the start to be a precarious procedure. Therefore, knowledgeable readers may notice the absence of a favorite book containing just the kind of analytic treatment meant for this work. Since a truly complete listing seemed unrealistic from the outset, all efforts were channeled into the selection of as many appropriate listings as necessary to achieve a high level of usability. Future editions will benefit from any constructive criticism directed to this first attempt of its kind.

Special thanks are due to the Herbert H. Lehman
College of the City University of New York and its Library
and to the Music Division of The New York Public Library.

                                    Harold J. Diamond
Hastings-on-Hudson
New York, 1978

CHAPTER I: SOLO WORKS

BACH, CARL PHILIPP EMANUEL, 1714-1788

Keyboard Music--General

Barford, Philip. The Keyboard Music of C. P. E. Bach.
New York: October House, 1966, 186p. Thorough treatment of Bach's total output for keyboard. Historical perspective and relationship to the sonata principle empha-
sized. Musical examples.

Rondos for Piano

Cole, Malcolm Stanley. "Rondos, proper and improper, "
Music & Letters 51:4 (Oct. 1970), 388-399. Shows how
Bach departed from normal rondo structure. Musical ex-
amples.

Rondo Espresivo for Piano

Agay, D. "The search for authenticity, " Clavier 14:8 (1975),
29-31. Speculations on the compositional history of
Bach's Rondo. Musical examples.

Solfegietto

Dumm, R. "Piano footnotes: an analytic-interpretive lesson
on C. P. E. Bach's 'Solfegietto, '" Clavier 2:3 (1963), 21-
23. Brief analytic remarks with a view towards performance. Music for entire piece included.

BACH, JOHANN SEBASTIAN, 1685-1750

Solo Works--General

Geiringer, Karl. Johann Sebastian Bach. New York: Oxford University Press, 1966, pp. 211-310. Excellent

1

overview of the organ, clavier and violin works. Much
specific information and individual analyses. Musical examples.
Schweitzer, Albert. J. S. Bach. 2 vols. English translation by Ernest Newman. London: Breitkopf & Hartel,
1911, I, pp. 265-400. To be used with caution because
of the age of the research. However, much useful information on specific works for the student. Musical examples.

Keyboard Music--General

Little, M. E. "The contribution of dance steps to musical
analysis and performance: 'La Bourgogne,'" Journal of
the American Musicological Society 28:1 (1975), 112-123.
In-depth discussion of Bach's use of French dance structures. Advanced level.
Matthews, Denis, ed. Keyboard Music. New York: Praeger, 1972, pp. 68-101. Summary by Charles Rosen of
Bach's keyboard achievement. Historical perspective,
stylistic traits and analytic remarks on individual pieces.
Musical examples.
Rueb, P. K. "Handel's keyboard suites: a comparison
with those of J. S. Bach," American Music Teacher 20:5
(1971), 33-36. A comparison of stylistic characteristics
in the Handel suites with those of Bach's keyboard suites.
No musical examples.
Terry, Charles Sanford. The Music of Bach: An Introduction. New York: Dover, 1963, pp. 12-42. Background
and highlights of Bach's output for keyboard. An overview rather than analyses of specific works. Musical
examples.

Organ Music--General

Eickhoff, H. J. "Bach's chorale-ritornello forms," Music
Review 28:4 (1962), 257-276. Examines formal principles
used in chorales. Musical examples.
Gehring, P. "Rhythmic character in Bach's organ music,"
American Music Teacher 19:1 (1969), 33-35+. The
sources of Bach's rhythmic ideas as seen in the vocal,
keyboard, violin and dance styles. No musical examples.
Grace, Harvey. The Organ Works of Bach. London: Novello, n.d., 319p. Thorough overview with critical and
analytic comments. Musical examples.
Keller, Hermann. The Organ Works of Bach. Translated
from the German by Helen Hewitt. New York: Peters,

1967, 312p. Detailed annotated catalog of all Bach's organ works. Though intended for the specialist, the annotations provide information that can be understood by undergraduates and amateurs. Musical examples.

Sonatas and Partitas for Violin, Unaccompanied

Ulrich, Homer. "The nationality of Bach's solo-violin partitas, " in Glowacki, John, ed. Paul A. Piske: Essays in His Honor. Austin: University of Texas, 1966, pp. 96-102. Examination of the formal structure and speculation on Bach's use of French and English forms. No musical examples.

Art of the Fugue

Tovey, Donald Francis. Essays in Musical Analysis: Chamber Music. London: Oxford University Press, 1956, pp. 75-92. Thorough analysis with musical examples.

Chorale Preludes

Tusler, Robert L. The Style of Bach's Chorale Preludes. New York: Da Capo, 1968, 75p. Thorough treatment including background, organs, style and ornamentation. Musical examples.

English Suites for Harpsichord

Cameron, R. "Bach's six English Suites, " Music Journal 32 (July 1974), 6-7. Background and brief descriptive remarks. No discussion of individual works in detail. No musical examples.

Fantasy & Fugue in G Minor, Organ, S. 542

Tischler, Hans. The Perceptive Music Listener. Englewood Cliffs, N. J.: Prentice-Hall, 1955, pp. 101-103. Condensed analysis to be used with score in hand.

French Suite (Harpsichord) no. 5, G major

Nallin, Walter E. The Musical Idea. New York: Macmillan, 1968, pp. 154-157. Brief analysis with musical examples.

Goldberg Variations

David, H. T. "Bach form--ground plans ('Goldberg Variations')," Bach 1:1 (1970), 15-16. Illustrates key, thematic, textural and formal relationships.
Ehle, R. C. "Comments on the 'Goldberg variations,'"
American Music Teacher 19:2 (1969), 20-22. Analytic
comments with musical examples.
Jandy, O. "Rhythmic symmetry in the 'Goldberg Variations,'" Musical Quarterly 52:2 (1966), 204-208. Reveals
mathematical symmetry Bach imposed on the music as a
numerological game. Musical examples.
Tovey, Donald Francis. Essays in Musical Analysis:
Chamber Music. London: Oxford University Press,
1956, pp. 28-73. Thorough background discussion with
full analysis. Musical examples.

Inventions

Herford, J. "Bach's model of 'good' inventions," Bach 2:4
(1971), 10-14. Bach's method in his use of themes.
Musical examples.
Vassar, J. B. "The Bach two-part inventions: a question
of authorship," Music Review 33:1 (1972), 14-21. Analytic examination with a view to Bach's collaboration with
his son on the inventions. Musical examples.

Invention no. 1, C major

Walton, Charles W. Basic Forms in Music. Port Washington, N.Y.: Alfred Publishing Co., 1974, pp. 148-150.
Condensed analysis with full musical quotation. No score
needed.
Zabrack, H. "The inventions were meant to be teaching
pieces," Clavier 13:8 (1974), 28-30. Performance observations with analytic insights. Full musical example.

Invention no. 6, E major

Schroeder, C. F. "Piano lesson: Two-part invention no. 6
in E major by Johann Sebastian Bach," Clavier 3:4 (1964),
27-30. Remarks for performance with analytic observations. Complete musical examples.

Partita no. 1, B♭ for Harpsichord, S. 825

Lambert, A. "A dance suite--the Bach Partita in B♭,"
Clavier 8:1 (1969), 13-22. Analysis with complete musical example.

Partita no. 2, D minor, Violin Unaccompanied: Chaconne,
S. 1004

Cantrell, B. "Three B's--Three chaconnes, " Current Musicology 12 (1971), 63-66+. Analysis with musical examples.
Leichtentritt, Hugo. Musical Form. Cambridge, Mass. :
Harvard University Press, 1959, pp. 312-314. Condensed
breakdown of variation structure. Musical examples.
Walton, Charles W. Basic Forms in Music. Port Washington, N. Y. : Alfred Publishing Co. , 1974, pp. 105-109.
Condensed analysis with musical examples.

Partita no. 3 for Violin Unaccompanied: Gavotte en Rondeau,
S. 1006

Nallin, Walter E. The Musical Idea. New York: Macmillan, 1968, pp. 208-210. Brief analysis with musical examples.

Passacaglia & Fugue, Organ, C minor, S. 582

Leichtentritt, Hugo. Musical Form. Cambridge, Mass. :
Harvard University Press, 1959, pp. 311-312. Brief,
but condensed analytic romarks. Musical examples.
Mulbury, D. "Bach's passacaglia in c minor, " Bach 3:2
(1972), 14-27; 3, 12-20; 4, 17-21. Background and ante-
cedents. Sets the work in historical perspective as a
form. Musical examples.
Tischler, Hans. The Perceptive Music Listener. Englewood Cliffs, N. J. : Prentice-Hall, 1955, pp. 211-214.
Descriptive and analytical with musical examples.
Walton, Charles W. Basic Forms in Music. Port Washington, N. Y. : Alfred Publishing Co. , 1974, pp. 101-105.
Condensed analytic outline with musical examples.

Suite no. 3 for Violoncello Unaccompanied: Sarabande,
S. 1009

Schenker, Heinrich. "The Sarabande of J. S. Bach's Suite
no. 3 for unaccompanied violoncello, BWV 1009, " in The
Music Forum, New York: Columbia University Press,
1970, III, pp. 274-282. In-depth "Schenkerian" analysis
for the advanced student only. Musical examples.

Suite no. 6 for Violoncello Unaccompanied, D major, S. 1012

Tischler, Hans. The Perceptive Music Listener. Engle-

wood Cliffs, N. J. :   Prentice-Hall, 1955, pp. 108-110.
Brief analysis.   Musical examples.

Well-Tempered Clavier--General

Elder, D.   "Jorg Demus," Clavier 6:1 (1967), 20-27.
Demus' general remarks for performance.   Stylistic and
analytic remarks.   Musical examples.
Fuller-Maitland, John A.   The '48': Bach's Wohltemper-
erirtes Clavier.   New York: Books for Libraries Press,
1970, 2 Vols.   Lightweight discussion on all 48 preludes
and fugues.   Musical examples.
Gray, Cecil.   The Forty-Eight Preludes and Fugues of J. S.
Bach.   London: Oxford University Press, 1952, 148p.
Thorough overview with analytic insights.   Musical exam-
ples.
Keller, Hermann.   The Well-Tempered Clavier by Johann
Sebastian Bach.   Translated by Leigh Gerdine.   New
York: Norton, 1976, 207p.   Thorough discussion and
analyses of the entire Well-Tempered Clavier.   Musical
examples.
Leichtentritt, Hugo.   Musical Form.   Cambridge, Mass. :
Harvard University Press, 1959, pp. 302-308.   Overview,
highlighting different types of preludes with analytic re-
marks.   Musical examples.

Well-Tempered Clavier--Book I

Fugue no. 1, C major

Greenberg, B.   "Bach's C major fugue (WTC I); a subjective view," In Theory Only 2 (Jun-Jul. 1976), 13-17.
Intensive analysis for the advanced.   Musical examples.

Fugue no. 2, C minor

Bryant, C. M.   "Can he understand a fugue?" Clavier 4:3
(1965), 26-31.   Analysis for performance.   Complete
musical example.

Fugue no. 8, E♭ minor

Davie, Cedric Thorpe.   Musical Structure and Design.   New
York: Dover, 1966, pp. 164-165.   Bar-by-bar analysis
to be used with score in hand.
DeYoung, L.   "Fugue: the treatment of thematic materials,"
Clavier 7:7 (1968), 37-40.   Analysis with complete musi-
cal examples.

Preludes 1 & 2

Herford, J. "The C major and c minor preludes of the
'Well-Tempered Clavier,' Book I," Bach 4:2 (1973), 17-
24. Analysis and comparison for the advanced student.
No musical examples.

Prelude no. 2, C minor

Wagner, E. "Analyzing a Bach prelude," Clavier 8:7 (1969),
35-38. Performer's analysis with complete musical example.

Prelude and Fugue no. 8, E♭ minor

Tischler, Hans. The Perceptive Music Listener. Englewood Cliffs, N. J.: Prentice-Hall, 1955, pp. 103-105.
Condensed analysis to be used with score in hand.

Prelude no. 10, E minor

David, H. T. "Bach analyses," Bach 2:2 (1971), 18-19.
Analysis. No musical examples.

Prelude no. 21, B♭ major

Bryant, C. M. "Becoming a well-tempered musician,"
Clavier 11:8 (1972), 27-30. Performer's notes with
analytic observations. Complete musical example.
Schachter, Carl. "Bach's fugue in B♭ major, 'Well-Tempered Clavier,' Book I, no. XXI," in The Music Forum,
N. Y.: Columbia University Press, 1973, III, pp. 239-
267. In-depth analysis. Advanced. Musical examples.

Well-Tempered Clavier--Book II

Fugue no. 3, C minor

Walton, Charles W. Basic Forms in Music. Port Washington, N. Y.: Alfred Publishing Co., 1974, pp. 156-158.
Condensed analysis with full musical quotation. No score
needed.

Fugue no. 5, D major

Walton, Charles W. Basic Forms in Music. Port Wash-

ington, N. Y. :   Alfred Publishing Co. , 1974, pp. 151-154.
Condensed analysis with full musical quotation.   No score
needed.

Fugue no. 6, D minor

Walton, Charles W.   Basic Forms in Music.   Port Washington, N. Y. :   Alfred Publishing Co. , 1974, pp. 154-156.
Condensed analysis with full musical quotation.   No score
needed.

Fugue no. 9, E major

Davie, Cedric Thorpe.   Musical Structure and Design.   New
York: Dover, 1966, pp. 162-164.   Bar-by-bar analysis
to be used with score in hand.

Fugue no. 12, F minor

Davie, Cedric Thorpe.   Musical Structure and Design.   New
York: Dover, 1966, pp. 161-162.   Bar-by-bar analysis
to be used with score in hand.

BALAKIREV, MILY, 1837-1910

Piano Music--General

Garden, Edward.   Balakirev: A Critical Study of His Life
and Music.   New York: St. Martin's, 1967, pp. 216-244.
Thorough discussion and analysis of all the piano works.
Musical examples.

BARBER, SAMUEL, 1910-

Piano Music--General

Broder, Nathan.   Samuel Barber.   New York: Schirmer,
1954, pp. 68-73.   Brief mention of the smaller works,
but more detailed study of the Sonata, op. 26.   Musical
examples.
Fairleigh, J. P.   "Serialism in Barber's solo piano works, "
Piano Quarterly 18:72 (1970), 13-17.   Shows fusion of
serial and tonal elements as a compositional device.
Musical examples.

Piano Sonata, op. 26

Chittum, D. "The synthesis of materials and devices in
nonserial counterpoint," Music Review 31:2 (1970), 123-
135. Analytic insights. Advanced. Musical examples.
Tischler, Hans. The Perceptive Music Listener. Englewood Cliffs, N.J.: Prentice-Hall, 1955, pp. 276-281.
Analysis with musical examples.

BARTOK, BELA, 1881-1945

Piano Music--General

Stevens, Halsey. The Life and Music of Béla Bartók. New
York: Oxford University Press, 1953, pp. 109-140.
Thorough overview of the piano works with remarks on
specific pieces. Musical examples.
Weismann, John. "Bartók's piano music," in Béla Bartók:
A Memorial Review, Oceanside, N.Y.: Boosey &
Hawkes, 1950, pp. 60-71. Thorough descriptive com-
mentary of all the piano works. No musical examples.

15 Hungarian Peasant Songs

Dumm, R. "A Bartók ballad from Fifteen Hungarian Peasant Songs," Clavier 15:3 (1976), 33-37. Performer's
analysis. Full musical quotation.

Mikrokosmos

Elkin, B. "'Mikrokosmos'; an analysis of three pieces by
Bartók," Music in Education 28:308 (1964), 167. "Free
variations," "From the Diary of a Fly," and the second
of "Six Dances in Bulgarian Rhythm" analyzed briefly.
No musical examples.
Franklin, A. "Comments on Béla Bartók's 'Mikrokosmos,'"
Music Teacher 50 (June 1971), 9+. Background and analytic commentary. No musical examples.
Suchoff, B. "Béla Bartók's contributions to music education," Tempo 60 (Winter 1961-1962), 37-43. Analytic and
critical remarks. Musical examples.
Suchoff, B. "History of Béla Bartók's 'Mikrokosmos,'"
Journal of Research in Music Education 7:2 (1959), 185-
196. Historical background. Not a discussion of the
music.

Mikrokosmos, Vol. VI

Bryant, C. M. "The music lesson," Clavier 5:4 (1966),
33-36. Analytic remarks with view towards performance.
Complete musical example provided.

BEETHOVEN, LUDWIG VAN, 1770-1827

Piano Music--General

Arnold, Denis and Nigel Fortune, eds. The Beethoven Companion. London: Faber & Faber, 1971, pp. 68-193.
Thorough overview of Beethoven's solo piano output.
Clear discussion of influences with many analytic insights
into specific works. Musical examples.
Matthews, Denis, ed. Keyboard Music. New York:
Praeger, 1972, pp. 168-185. Background, historical
perspective, stylistic traits and critical observations on
specific works. Musical examples.
Ringer, Alexander L. "Beethoven and the London pianoforte
school," in Lang, Paul Henry, ed. The Creative World
of Beethoven. New York: Norton, 1971, pp. 240-256.
Clear demonstration of the influence of London pianoforte
school composers on Beethoven in his piano compositions.
Musical examples.
Rosen, Charles. "The piano as the key to 'late Beethoven,'"
Stereo Review 24 (June 1970), 69-71. Beethoven's approach to keyboard writing and how he viewed the piano
as a medium for his compositions. No musical examples.
Scherman, Thomas K. and Louis Biancolli, eds. The
Beethoven Companion. New York: Doubleday, 1972, 1230
p. Program-note treatment intended for interested amateurs or students. No musical examples. Discussion of
individual works accessible through table of contents.

Piano Sonatas--General

Blom, Eric. Beethoven's Pianoforte Sonatas Discussed.
New York: Da Capo, 1968, 251p. Analyses of all the
sonatas. Musical examples.
Brendel, Alfred. "Beethoven: form and psychology," Music
& Musicians 19 (June 1971), 20-24. General remarks on
style and composition procedure with analytic observations.
Burk, John N. The Life and Works of Beethoven. New
York: Modern Library, 1943, 415-454. Very brief
program-note type commentary on each of the sonatas.
Musical examples.

Cooper, Martin. Beethoven: The Last Decade, 1817-1827.
London: Oxford University Press, 1970, pp. 145-220.
Thorough examination of the later sonatas. Of interest
to the layman and scholar. Musical examples.
Dale, Kathleen. Nineteenth-Century Piano Music: A Hand-
book for Pianists. London: Oxford University Press,
1954, 320p. Highlights stylistic traits and unique contri-
bution to the literature of the piano. Form, harmony and
other musical aspects discussed in relation to style.
Locate discussion of individual works through index.
Ferguson, Donald N. Piano Music of Six Great Composers.
Plainview, N. Y.: Books for Libraries, 1947, pp. 39-123.
Descriptive, critical and analytic commentary, showing
stylistic growth of the composer. Many useful general
remarks on sonata form, as well. Musical examples.
Matthews, Denis. Beethoven Piano Sonatas. (BBC Music
Guides). Seattle: University of Washington, 1969. 56p.
Discussion of all the sonatas, showing Beethoven's devel-
opment as a composer. For layman and professional.
Reti, Rudolph. Thematic Patterns in Sonatas of Beethoven.
New York: Macmillan, 1967, 204p. Advanced analyses,
breaking structural elements down to their essentials.
Musical examples.
Tovey, Donald Francis. A Companion to Beethoven's Piano-
forte Sonatas. London: The Associated Board of the
Royal Schools of Music, 1931, 284p. Bar-by-bar analyses
of all the sonatas. Musical examples.

Bagatelle no. 2, op. 126, G minor

Dumm, R. "The inner meaning: an analytic-interpretive
lesson," Clavier 2:1 (1963), 22-25. Analytic remarks
with a view towards performance. Musical example given
in its entirety.

Diabelli Variations, op. 120

Geiringer, Karl. "The structure of Beethoven's 'Diabelli
Variations,'" Musical Quarterly 50:4 (1964), 496-503.
Analysis with chart of structure. No musical examples.
Leichtentritt, Hugo. Musical Form. Cambridge, Mass.:
Harvard University Press, 1959, pp. 98-103. Analytic
discussion displaying Beethoven's variation techniques.
Musical examples.
Porter, D. H. "The structure of Beethoven's 'Diabelli
Variations,' op. 120," Music Review 31:4 (1970), 295-
301. Intense analysis. No musical examples.

Tovey, Donald Francis. Essays in Musical Analysis:
Chamber Music. London: Oxford University Press, 1956,
pp. 124-136. Critical observations and analysis with
musical examples.

Piano Sonata no. 1, op. 2, F minor

Walton, Charles W. Basic Forms in Music. Port Washington, N. Y.: Alfred Publishing Co., 1974, pp. 52-56.
Condensed analysis with full musical quotation. No score
needed. Second movement only.

Piano Sonata no. 3, op. 2, C major

Walton, Charles W. Basic Forms in Music. Port Washington, N. Y.: Alfred Publishing Co., 1974, pp. 65-76.
Condensed analysis with full musical quotation. No score
needed. Last movement only.

Piano Sonata no. 4, op. 7, E♭ major

Kamien, R. "Chromatic detail in Beethoven's piano sonata
in E♭ major, op. 7," Music Review 35:2 (1974), 149-156.
Intense analysis with musical examples.

Piano Sonata no. 7, op. 10, D major

Imbrie, Andrew. "'Extra' measures and metrical ambiguity
in Beethoven," in Tyson, Alan, ed. Beethoven Studies.
New York: Norton, 1973, pp. 45-54. Advanced analysis
focusing on rhythmic characteristics. Musical examples.

Piano Sonata no. 8, op. 13, C minor, "Pathétique"

Davie, Cedric Thorpe. Musical Structure and Design. New
York: Dover, 1966, pp. 50-51. Bar-by-bar analysis of
the slow movement as an example of rondo form. To be
used with score in hand.
Nallin, Walter E. The Musical Idea. New York: Macmillan, 1968, pp. 185-186. Brief analysis with musical examples.
Newman, W. S. "K. 457 and op. 13--two related master-
pieces in C minor," Music Review 28:1 (1967), 38-44.
Demonstrates influence of Mozart's piano sonata in c minor, K. 457 on Beethoven's "Pathétique" sonata. Musical
examples.

Piano Sonata no. 12, op. 26, A♭ major

Davie, Cedric Thorpe. Musical Structure and Design. New
   York: Dover, 1966, pp. 133-135. Bar-by-bar analysis
   to be used with score in hand.

Piano Sonata no. 17, op. 31, D minor, "Tempest"

Misch, Ludwig. Beethoven Studies. Norman: University of
   Oklahoma Press, 1953, pp. 39-53. Analytic considera-
   tions on a sonata that deviates from traditional form.
   Musical examples.

Piano Sonata no. 19, op. 49, G minor

Walton, Charles W. Basic Forms in Music. Sherman Oaks,
   Calif. : Alfred Publishing Co. , 1974, pp. 168-174. Condensed analysis outline with full musical quotation. No
   score needed. First movement only.

Piano Sonata no. 21, op. 53, C major, "Waldstein"

Chavez, C. "Anatomic analysis: Beethoven's 'Waldstein'
   op. 53, " Piano Quarterly 21:82 (1973), 17-19. Full dia-
   grammatic analysis. Musical examples.
Crain, A. J. "Problems in the Beethoven literature, "
   Clavier 9:1 (1970), 30-36. Performer's analysis with
   musical examples.
Davie, Cedric Thorpe. Musical Structure and Design. New
   York: Dover, 1966, pp. 51-52. Bar-by-bar analysis to
   be used with score in hand. Rondo movement only.
Leichtentritt, Hugo. Musical Form. Cambridge, Mass. :
   Harvard University Press, 1959, p. 118. Condensed anal-
   ysis. No musical examples. Finale only.
Rosen, Charles. The Classical Style: Haydn, Mozart,
   Beethoven. New York: Viking Press, 1971, pp. 396-399.
   Critical observations on stylistic features on an intermedi-
   ate level. Musical examples.
Schramm, H. "Beethoven's 'Waldstein' and 'Appassionata'
   sonatas, " Piano Quarterly 19:73 (1970), 18-19. Analytic
   remarks focusing on the "new" romantic traits. No
   musical examples.

Piano Sonata no. 22, op. 54, F major

Elder, D. "Alfred Brendel talks about Beethoven, " Clavier
   12:9 (1973), 10-20. General remarks on Beethoven's

style in the sonatas and specific analytic remarks on op.
54. Musical examples.

Piano Sonata no. 23, op. 57, F minor, "Appassionata"

Tischler, Hans. The Perceptive Music Listener. Englewood Cliffs, N. J.: Prentice-Hall, 1955, pp. 268-272.
Analysis with musical examples.

Piano Sonata no. 29, op. 106, B♭ major, "Hammerklavier"

Leichtentritt, Hugo. Musical Form. Cambridge: Harvard
University Press, 1959, pp. 326-339. Exhaustive, in-
tense analysis with musical examples.
Newman, W. S. "Some 19th-century consequences of
Beethoven's 'Hammerklavier Sonata' opus 106," Piano
Quarterly 17:67 (1969), 12-18. Traces influence of
"Hammerklavier" on certain composers especially Mendel-
ssohn and Brahms. Musical examples.
Rosen, Charles. The Classical Style: Haydn, Mozart,
Beethoven. New York: Viking Press, 1971, pp. 409-434.
Analysis on a high level. Only for the advanced student.
Musical examples.

Piano Sonata no. 30, op. 109, E major

Bliss, R. "Late Beethoven, playing Sonata op. 109,"
Clavier 15:1 (1976), 19-22. For the performer, but use-
ful here for its analytic view. Musical examples.
Davie, Cedric Thorpe. Musical Structure and Design. New
York: Dover, 1966, 135-137. Bar-by-bar analysis to be
used with score in hand. Last movement only.
Forte, Allen. The Compositional Matrix. New York:
Music Teachers National Association, 1961; New York:
Da Capo Press, 1974, 95p. The entire book devoted to
an analysis and examination of the sketches. Not for the
beginner. Musical examples.
Kerman, Joseph. Listen. second edition. New York:
Worth Publishers, 1976, pp. 200-205. Analysis with
musical examples. For the student.

Piano Sonata no. 31, op. 110, A♭ major

Ashforth, A. "The relationship of the sixth in Beethoven's
piano sonata, op. 110," Music Review 32:2 (1971), 93-101.
Intense analysis on advanced level. Musical examples.
Misch, Ludwig. Beethoven Studies. Norman: University of

Oklahoma Press, 1953, pp. 54-75. Analytic insights on an advanced level. Musical examples.

Piano Sonata no. 32, op. 111, C minor

Rosen, Charles. The Classical Style: Haydn, Mozart, Beethoven. New York: Viking Press, 1971, pp. 441-444. Analytic observations on the opening measures of this sonata. Musical examples.

Variations for Piano, C minor

Cantrell, B. "Three B's--three chaconnes," Current Musicology 12 (1971), 67-69. Analysis with musical examples.
Davie, Cedric Thorpe. Musical Structure and Design. New York: Dover, 1966, pp. 123-126. Bar-by-bar analysis to be used with score in hand.
Kochevitsky, G. "Beethoven's 32 variations in c minor," Clavier 6:6 (1967), 37-43+. Performance notes with descriptive and analytic commentary. Musical examples.
Leichtentritt, Hugo. Musical Form. Cambridge, Mass.: Harvard University Press, 1959, pp. 104-106. Analysis, displaying Beethoven's variation techniques. No musical examples.

Variations for Piano, op. 34, F major

Tischler, Hans. The Perceptive Music Listener. Englewood Cliffs, N. J.: Prentice-Hall, 1955, pp. 215-217. Descriptive and analytical with musical examples. Focuses on variation form.

Variations for Piano, op. 35, E♭ major (Eroica Variations)

Tovey, Donald Francis. Essays in Musical Analysis. 6 Vols. London: Oxford University Press, 1909, Vol. VI, pp. 31-35. Analysis intended for student. Musical examples.

BERG, ALBAN, 1885-1935

Piano Sonata op. 1

Matthews, Denis ed. Keyboard Music. New York: Praeger, 1972, pp. 327-328. Brief critical and analytic discussion. Musical examples.

Redlich, H. F. Alban Berg: The Man and His Music.
London: John Calder, 1957, pp. 47-49. Brief analysis.
Musical examples.

BIZET, GEORGES, 1838-1875

Piano Music--General

Dean, Winton. Bizet. London: Dent, 1948, pp. 115-121.
Critical overview of Bizet's keyboard output. Musical
examples.

BORODIN, ALEXANDER, 1833-1887

Piano Music--General

Abraham, Gerald. Borodin: The Composer and His Music.
London: William Reeves, n. d. , pp. 146-159. Descrip-
tive overview of Borodin's small output for the keyboard.
Dianin, Serge. Borodin. Translated from the Russian by
Robert Lord. London: Oxford University Press, 1963,
pp. 247-256. Descriptive and analytic commentary.
Musical examples.

BOULEZ, PIERRE, 1925-

Piano Music--General

Matthews, Denis, ed. Keyboard Music. New York:
Praeger, 1972, pp. 340-345. Critical and analytic discussion with musical examples.

Piano Sonata no. 1

Peyser, Joan. Boulez. New York: Schirmer Books, 1976,
pp. 39-42. Brief descriptive, background, and analytic
remarks. Musical examples.

Piano Sonata no. 2

Peyser, Joan. Boulez. New York: Schirmer Books, 1976,
pp. 47-52. Background, description and analytic remarks.
Musical examples.

Piano Sonata no. 3

Ligeti, G. "Some remarks on Boulez' 3rd piano sonata,"
Die Reihe 5 (1961), 56-58. Analytic discussion. No
musical examples.
Maw, N. "Boulez and tradition," Musical Times 103 (March
1962), 162-164. Brief descriptive and analytic remarks.
No musical examples.

BRAHMS, JOHANNES, 1833-1897

Organ Music--General

Gotwals, Vernon. "Brahms and the organ," Music (A. G. O.)
4 (April 1970), 38-55. Thorough survey of Brahms' organ works. Descriptive and analytic commentary with
musical examples.

Piano Music--General

Dale, Kathleen. Nineteenth-Century Piano Music: A Handbook for Pianists. London: Oxford University Press,
1954, 320p. Highlights the stylistic traits and unique
contribution to the literature of the piano. Form, harmony and other musical aspects discussed in relation to
style. Locate discussion of individual works through
index.
Evans, Edwin. Handbook to the Pianoforte Works of
Johannes Brahms. London: William Reeves, n. d. 327p.
Useful for its thorough, descriptive and analytic remarks,
despite antiquated language and concepts. Musical examples.
Fairleigh, James P. "Neoclassicism in the later piano
works of Brahms," Piano Quarterly 58 (Winter 1966-
1967), 24-26. Advanced discussion of Brahms' neoclassic
tendencies.
Ferguson, Donald N. Piano Music of Six Great Composers.
Plainview, N. Y. : Books for Libraries, 1947, pp. 251-
318. Descriptive and critical commentary showing stylistic development. Musical examples.
Geiringer, Karl. Brahms: His Life and Work. second
edition. New York: Oxford University Press, n. d. ,
pp. 205-221. Background, descriptive and critical commentary. No musical examples.
Matthews, Denis, ed. Keyboard Music. New York:
Praeger, 1972, pp. 198-208. Background, critical ob-

servations, historical perspective, stylistic traits and
influences.   Musical examples.
Niemann, Walter. Brahms. Translated from the German
by Catherine Alison Phillips. New York: Knopf, 1935,
pp. 213-250. Descriptive and critical commentary on
Brahms' piano works. No musical examples.
Schauffler, Robert Haven. The Unknown Brahms. New
York: Dodd, Mead, 1936, pp. 356-371. Descriptive and
critical remarks. Musical examples.

Ballade, op. 10, no. 1, D major

Fiske, Roger. "Brahms and Scotland," Musical Times
109:1510 (Dec. 1968), 1106-1110. Discusses Brahms'
settings of Herder's translations of Scottish Ballads in
his simple "folk song" style. Three of these were converted into piano music. Musical examples.

Capriccio, op. 116, no. 7, D minor

Bryant, C. M. "Catching the temperament of a Brahms
'Caprice,'" Clavier 8:4 (1969), 29-33. Performer's
analysis with complete musical example.

Intermezzo, op. 117, no. 1, E♭ major

Fiske, Roger. "Brahms and Scotland," Musical Times
109:1510 (Dec. 1968), 1106-1110. Discusses Brahms'
settings of Herder's translations of Scottish ballads in
his simple "folk song" style. Three of these were converted into piano music. Musical examples.

Intermezzo, op. 117, no. 2, B♭ minor

Zabrack, H. "Projecting emotion: a lesson on a Brahms
Intermezzo," Clavier 14:6 (1975), 27-34. Performer's
view of this popular intermezzo. Full musical example.

Intermezzo, op. 117, no. 3, C♯ minor

Davie, Cedric Thorpe. Musical Structure and Design. New
York: Dover, 1966, pp. 46-48. Bar-by-bar analysis to
be used with score in hand.

Intermezzo, op. 119, no. 1, B minor

Newbould, Brian. "A new analysis of Brahms's Intermezzo

in B minor, op. 119, no. 1," Music Review 38:1 (Feb. 1977), 33-43. Thorough, intense analysis for the advanced student. Musical examples.

Intermezzo, op. 119, no. 2, E minor

Dumm, R. "Playing one of the intermezzos: a performer's analysis," Clavier 13:2 (1974), 29-32. Analysis with full musical quotation.

Piano Sonatas 1, 2, 3

Kirby, F. E. "Brahms and the piano sonata," in Glowacki, John, ed., Paul A. Piske: Essays in His Honor. Austin: University of Texas, 1966, pp. 163-180. Thorough analyses and historical perspective. Musical examples.

Piano Sonata, op. 1, C major

Fiske, Roger. "Brahms and Scotland," Musical Times 109:1510 (Dec. 1968), 1106-1110. Discusses Brahms' settings of Herder's translations of Scottish ballads in his "folk song" style. Three of these were converted into piano music. Musical examples.
Newman, W. S. "Some 19th century consequences of Beethoven's 'Hammerklavier sonata' opus 106," Piano Quarterly 17:68 (1969), 14-15. Traces influences of "Hammerklavier Sonata" on other composers, especially Mendelssohn and Brahms. Musical examples.

Piano Sonata, op. 5, F minor

Sutton, W. "Brahms: Sonata in F minor, op. 5," Music Teacher 52 (Aug. 1973), 12-13. Brief analytic remarks. No musical examples.

Rhapsodies for Piano, op. 79

Smith, E. "Brahms: Two rhapsodies for piano, op. 79," Music Teacher 55 (May 1976), 13-14. Brief analytic remarks. No musical examples.

Variations on a Theme by Handel

Tovey, Donald Francis. Essays in Musical Analysis: Chamber Music. London: Oxford University Press, 1956, pp. 167-172. Critical observations and analytic insights. Musical examples.

Variations on a Theme by Paganini

Tovey, Donald Francis.   Essays in Musical Analysis:
Chamber Music.   London: Oxford University Press, 1956,
pp. 172-185.   Critical observations and analytic insights.
Musical examples.

Variations on a Theme by Schumann

Crowder, L.   "Brahms' early tribute to the Schumanns, "
Clavier 5:7 (1966), 18-25.   Descriptive and analytic overview with background remarks.   Musical examples.

Waltzes

Gruber, A.   "Some viewpoints on Brahms: understanding
rhythm in the piano music, " Clavier 13:2 (1974), 9-13.
Analytic insights on rhythm.   Musical examples.

BYRD, WILLIAM, 1543-1623

Keyboard Music--General

Fellowes, Edmund H.   William Byrd.   London: Oxford
University Press, 1936, pp. 201-221.   Historical significance and descriptive commentary.   Musical examples.

CHABRIER, EMMANUEL, 1841-1894

Piano Music--General

Cortot, Alfred.   French Piano Music.   Translated by Hilda
Andrews.   London: Oxford University Press, 1932,
pp. 140-177.   Descriptive overview with observations on
Chabrier's style.   No musical examples.
Myers, Rollo.   Emmanuel Chabrier and His Circle.   London: Dent, 178 pp.   Background, descriptive and critical
commentary.   Musical examples.   Individual pieces must
be looked up in index.

CHOPIN, FREDERIC, 1810-1849

Piano Music--General

Bidou, Henri.   Chopin.   Translated by Catherine Alison

Phillips. New York: Knopf, 1927, 267p. Mainly a life of Chopin; however, many useful analyses along the way. Lack of index to compositions makes it difficult to use. Musical examples.

Dale, Kathleen. Nineteenth-Century Piano Music: A Handbook for Pianists. London: Oxford University Press, 1954, 320p. Highlights stylistic traits and unique contribution to the literature of the piano. Form, harmony and other musical aspects discussed in relation to style. Locate discussion of individual works through index.

Einstein, Alfred. Music in the Romantic Era. New York: Norton, 1947, pp. 213-220. Some specific works mentioned, but mainly a portrait of Chopin and his art with comparisons to Schumann. No musical examples.

Elder, D. "A conversation with Artur Rubinstein," Clavier 8:6 (1969), 14-20. Stylistic and interpretive insights. Musical examples.

Ferguson, Donald N. Piano Music of Six Great Composers. Plainview, N. Y. : Books for Libraries, 1947, pp. 213-249. Descriptive and critical commentary with analytic insights. Musical examples.

Hedley, Arthur. Chopin. London: Dent, 1974, 214p. Descriptive, critical and analytic commentary aimed at informed amateur. Easy to read style. Musical examples.

Higgins, T. "Tempo and character in Chopin," Musical Quarterly 59:1 (1973), 106-120. Chopin's use of metronome indications. Some discussion of individual character of works. Musical examples.

Huneker, James. Chopin: The Man and His Music. New York: Scribner's, 1900; reprint, n. d. , Scholarly, 415p. Thorough discussion of Chopin's output, but beware the age and subjectivity of the writing. Musical examples.

Kelley, Edgar Stillman. Chopin the Composer. New York: Schirmer, 1913, 190p. Thorough analytic discussions with excellent index to works. Musical examples.

Longyear, Roy M. Nineteenth Century Romanticism in Music. Englewood Cliffs, N. J. : Prentice-Hall, 1969, pp. 88-94. Intended for student. Overview with descriptive and critical remarks. Musical examples.

Matthews, Denis, ed. Keyboard Music. New York: Praeger, 1972, pp. 213-230. Background, historical perspective, innovations, stylistic traits with discussion of specific pieces. Musical examples.

Riedel, Johannes. Music of the Romantic Period. Dubuque, Iowa: William C. Brown, 1969, pp. 116-122. Intended for beginning student. Brief descriptive remarks on Chopin's stylistic traits. Musical examples.

Walker, Alan, ed. The Chopin Companion. New York:
     Norton, 1966, 312 p. Very useful for analyses of indi-
     vidual works. Thorough, with musical examples and good
     index.
Weinstock, Herbert, ed. Chopin: The Man and His Music.
     New York: Knopf, 1959, 336p. Thorough discussion of
     the life and the music. Good index. Musical examples.

Ballade no. 1 in G minor

Kerman, Joseph. Listen. second edition. New York:
     Worth Publishers, 1976, pp. 232-233. Brief analysis
     with musical examples. For the student.

Etudes

Tovey, Donald Francis. Essays in Musical Analysis:
     Chamber Music. London: Oxford University Press,
     1956, pp. 155-163. Critical observations on Etudes,
     op. 25, no. 7, 12 and Méthode des Méthodes, nos. 1 & 3.

Etude in F major, op. 25, no. 3

Salzer, Felix. "Chopin's Etude in F major, opus 25, no.
     3: the scope of tonality," in The Music Forum, Vol. 3;
     New York: Columbia University Press, 1970, pp. 281-
     290. In-depth analysis, according to the "Schenker"
     method. For the advanced student only. Musical exam-
     ples.

Fantaisie impromptu, op. 66, C♯ minor

Davie, Cedric Thorpe. Musical Structure and Design. New
     York: Dover, 1966, pp. 45-46. Bar-by-bar analysis to
     be used with score in hand.

Impromptu, op. 36, F♯ major

Tovey, Donald Francis. Essays in Musical Analysis:
     Chamber Music. London: Oxford University Press, 1956,
     pp. 163-166. Critical observations and analytic insights.
     Musical examples.

Mazurka, op. 7, no. 1, B♭ major

Dumm, R. "Piano footnotes on Chopin's Mazurka, op. 7,
     no. 1," Clavier 4:1 (1965), 33-35. Notes for perform-

ance.   Close descriptive commentary.   Complete musical
example.

Nocturne in C♯ minor, op. 27, no. 1

Dumm, R.   "Piano footnotes; an analytic-interpretative lesson on Chopin's Nocturne in C-sharp minor (posthumous), "
Clavier 3:1 (1964), 27-30.   Remarks for performance.
Some analytic observations.   Music for entire piece given.
Salzer, Felix.   "Chopin's Nocturne in C♯ minor, opus 27,
no. 1, " in The Music Forum.   New York: Columbia
University Press, 1970, III, pp. 283-297.   In-depth analysis, according to the "Schenker" method.   For the advanced student only.   Musical examples.

Nocturne, op. 37, no. 1, G minor

Davie, Cedric Thorpe.   Musical Structure and Design.   New
York: Dover, 1966, p. 44.   Condensed bar-by-bar analysis
to be used with score in hand.

Piano Sonata no. 3, op. 58, B minor

Sutton, W.   "Chopin: Sonata in B minor, op. 58, " Music
Teacher 52 (July 1973), 13+.   Brief analytic remarks.
No musical examples.

Polonaise Fantaisie op. 61

Payne, D.   "Achieving the effect of freedom in musical
composition, " Piano Quarterly 20:78 (1971-1972), 12-14+.
Analytic remarks with musical examples.

Preludes op. 28

Higgins, Thomas, ed.   Chopin, Preludes, Op. 28 (Norton
Critical Scores).   New York: Norton, 1974, 99p.   Historical background, analysis, criticism with full musical
quotation.

Prelude, op. 28, no. 1, C major

Talley, H.   "Take it apart--put it together; a key to the
study and mastery of music, demonstrated through analysis of a Chopin Prelude, " Clavier 3:4 (1964), 31-33.
Analysis for performance.   Music for entire piece given.

Prelude, op. 28, no. 2, A minor

Meyer, Leonard B. Emotion and Meaning in Music.
  Chicago: University of Chicago Press, 1956, pp. 93-97.
  Analysis with musical examples. This analysis may also
  be found in Higgins, Thomas, ed. Chopin, Preludes, Op.
  28 (Norton Critical Scores). New York: Norton, 1973,
  pp. 76-79.

Prelude, op. 28, no. 4, E minor

Clark, F. and D. Kraehenbuel. "An interpretive analysis
  of Chopin's Prelude in E minor," American Music Teacher 12:5 (1963), 16-17+. Analytic remarks for the performer. Musical examples.

CLEMENTI, MUZIO, 1752-1832

Piano Music--General

Dale, Kathleen. Nineteenth-Century Piano Music: A Handbook for Pianists. London: Oxford University Press,
  1954, 320p. Highlights stylistic traits and unique contribution to the literature of the piano. Form, harmony
  and other musical aspects discussed in relation to style.
  Locate discussion of individual works through index.
Ehle, R. "The writer of sonatas," Clavier 9:8 (1970), 17+.
  Background, influences and critical comments on specific
  works. Musical examples.
Plantinga, Leon. Clementi: His Life and Music. London:
  Oxford University Press, 1977, 346p. Thorough treatment of all his works with analytic insights. Clementi's
  influences on other composers discussed. Musical examples.
Plantinga, L. "Clementi, virtuosity, and the 'German manner,'" Journal of the American Musicological Society
  25:3 (1972), 303-330. Clementi's contributions to idio-
  matic keyboard writing. Influences on Clementi discussed.
  Musical examples.

Piano Sonatas--General

Pauly, Reinhard G. Music in the Classic Period. second
  edition. Englewood Cliffs, N. J. : Prentice-Hall, 1973,
  pp. 121-123. Brief remarks on stylistic traits with mention of a few specific sonatas. Musical examples.

Etudes

Ganz, F. "Clementi: a ladder to Parnassus," Clavier 9:8
    (1970), 16+. Brief critical and descriptive commentary.
    Musical examples.

Piano Sonata, op. 8, no. 1, G minor

Bloch, J. "A forgotten Clementi sonata," Piano Quarterly
    21:79 (1972), 24-31. Overview of Clementi's piano sonata
    output. Full musical example.

Preludes and Cadences, op. 19

Badura-Skoda, Eva. "Clementi's 'musical characteristics'
    opus 19," in Landon, H. C. Robbins, Studies in Eight-
    eenth Century Music. New York: Oxford University
    Press, 1970, pp. 53-67. Examination of Clementi's
    deliberate parodies of musical styles. Musical examples.

Sonatina for Piano, op. 36, no. 5, C major

Walton, Charles W. Basic Forms in Music. Port Wash-
    ington, N. Y. : Alfred Publishing Co. , 1974, pp. 175-177.
    Condensed analysis outline with full musical quotation.
    No score needed.

                    COPLAND, AARON, 1900-

Piano Music--General

Smith, Julia. Aaron Copland. New York: Dutton, 1955,
    336p. Full background and analytic commentary. Musi-
    cal examples.
Young, D. "The piano music," Tempo 95 (Winter 1970-
    1971), 15-22. Describes the Variations, Piano Sonata,
    and Fantasy, showing sharp stylistic differences.

Piano Fantasy

Fisher, F. "Contemporary American style: how three
    representative composers use the 'row,'" Clavier 14:4
    (1975), 34-37. Copland's use of the tone row in this
    piece. No musical examples.

Piano Variations

Berger, Arthur. Aaron Copland. New York: Oxford
University Press, 1953, pp. 42-48. Brief background
and analytic remarks. Musical examples.

COUPERIN, FRANCOIS, 1668-1733

Keyboard Music

Mellers, Wilfred. Francois Couperin and the French Classical Tradition. New York: Roy Publishers, 1951, 412p.
Critical and analytic commentary with musical examples.

CRAMER, JOHANN BAPTIST, 1771-1858

Piano Music--General

Dale, Kathleen. Nineteenth-Century Piano Music: A Handbook for Pianists. London: Oxford University Press,
1954, 320p. Highlights stylistic traits and unique contribution to the literature of the piano. Form, harmony and
other musical aspects discussed in relation to style.
Locate discussion of individual works through index.

DEBUSSY, CLAUDE, 1862-1918

Piano Music--General

Cortot, Alfred. French Piano Music. Translated by Hilda
Andrews. London: Oxford University Press, 1932,
pp. 1-36. Descriptive overview with some observations
on Debussy's style. No musical examples.
Dawes, Frank. Debussy's Piano Music (BBC Music Guides).
London: British Broadcasting Corporation, 1969, 63p.
General introduction covering all the works for one and
two pianos. Considers the composer's harmonic innovations and influence that shaped his music. Musical examples.
Ferguson, Donald N. Piano Music of Six Great Composers.
Plainview, N. Y. : Books for Libraries, 1947, pp. 319-
344. Descriptive and critical overview. Musical examples.
Lockspeiser, Edward. Debussy. London: Dent, 1951,

pp. 143-162.   Critical overview of all Debussy's keyboard output.   Many analytic insights.   Musical examples.
Lockspeiser, Edward.   Debussy; His Life and Music.   New
York: Macmillan, 1962, 2 vols.   A definitive work treating all aspects of Debussy's art.   Index to musical compositions an excellent key to finding individual works.
Musical examples.
Long, Marguerite.   At the Piano with Debussy.   Translated
by Olive Senior-Ellis.   London: Dent, n. d.   112p.   A
pianist's observations on Debussy's piano music.   Descriptive and critical commentary with a view towards
performance.   Musical examples.
Matthews, Denis, ed.   Keyboard Music.   New York:
Praeger, pp. 272-280.   Overview with observations on
style and influences.   Musical examples.
Nichols, Roger.   Debussy.   London: Oxford University
Press, 1973, 86p.   An analytic work, but difficult to use
because of the lack of an index.   Useful, nevertheless.
Musical examples.
Raynor, J.   "The piano music of Claude Debussy," Music
in Education 34:341 (1970), 26-27; 342, 80-82; 343, 154-
155.   Brief analytic remarks on some representative
pieces.   Musical examples.
Schmitz, E. Robert.   The Piano Works of Claude Debussy.
New York: Duell, Sloan & Pearce, 1950, 236p.   Thor-
ough review, both descriptive and analytic.   No musical
examples.
Thompson, Oscar.   Debussy: Man and Artist.   New York:
Dover, 1965, pp. 247-275.   Excellent critical and descriptive commentary.   Not analytic.   Musical examples.
Whittall, A.   "Tonality and the whole-tone scale in the
music of Debussy," Music Review 36:4 (1975), 261-271.
Intense analysis on advanced level.   Musical examples.

Children's Corner Suite

Nallin, Walter E.   The Musical Idea.   New York: Macmillan, 1968, pp. 270-273.   Brief analytic discussion with
musical examples.

Preludes

Freundlich, Irwin.   "Random thoughts on the preludes of
Claude Debussy," Piano Quarterly 22:87 (1974), 17-18+.
Also in Current Musicology 13 (1972), 48-57.   Analytic
discussion of all the preludes with mention of their literary allusions.   Musical examples.

Preludes, Bk. I: La Cathédral Engloutie

Dumm, R. "Lesson on a Debussy prelude," Clavier 6:9
(1967), 18-25.   Performance notes with descriptive and
analytic observations.   Complete musical example provided.

Preludes, Book I: Minstrels

Bryant, C. M. "Surprise adds humor to a piano piece,"
Clavier 6:1 (1967), 42-45.   Performance notes with descriptive and analytic observations.   Musical examples.

Preludes, Bk. II: Brouillards

Schnebel, D. "Brouillards'--tendencies in Debussy," Die
Reihe 6 (1964), 33-39.   Analytic discussion.   Musical
examples.

DOWLAND, JOHN, 1562-1626

Solo Lute Music--General

Poulton, Diana.   John Dowland: His Life and Works.
Berkeley: University of California Press, 1972, pp. 94-
180.   Full discussion of background and style.   Musical
examples.

DUKAS, PAUL, 1865-1935

Piano Music--General

Cortot, Alfred.   French Piano Music.   Translated by Hilda
Andrews.   London: Oxford University Press, 1932,
pp. 178-208.   Descriptive overview with observations on
Dukas' style.   No musical examples.

DVORAK, ANTONIN, 1841-1904

Piano Music--General

Dale, Kathleen.   Nineteenth-Century Piano Music: A Handbook for Pianists.   London: Oxford University Press,
1954, 320p.   Highlights stylistic traits.   Form, harmony

and other musical aspects discussed in relation to style.
Locate discussion of individual works through index.
Fischl, Viktor, ed. Antonin Dvořák: His Achievement.
Westport, Conn.: Greenwood Press, 1970, pp. 127-133.
Critical overview of Dvořák's piano writing. No discussion of individual works. No musical examples.
Robertson, Alec. Dvořák. London: Dent, 1947, pp. 104-110. Brief critical commentary on Dvořák's small piano output. Musical examples.

FALLA, MANUEL DE, 1876-1946

Fantasia Bética

Demarquez, Suzanne. Manuel de Falla. Philadelphia:
Chilton, 1968, pp. 109-118. Background and analysis.
No musical examples.

FAURE, GABRIEL, 1845-1924

Piano Music--General

Cortot, Alfred. French Piano Music. Translated by Hilda
Andrews. London: Oxford University Press, 1932,
pp. 109-139. Descriptive overview with observations on
Fauré's style. No musical examples.
Matthews, Denis, ed. Keyboard Music. New York:
Praeger, 1972, pp. 265-268. Stylistic traits, influences
and mention of specific pieces. Musical examples.
Suckling, Norman. Fauré. London: Dent, 1951, pp. 120-152. Overview of Fauré's piano works showing influences
and style with critical evaluations. Musical examples.
Vuillermoz, Emile. Gabriel Fauré. Translated by Kenneth
Schapin, Philadelphia: Chilton, 1969, 265p. Thorough
overview of Fauré's piano works. Critical and descriptive
commentary. No musical examples.

Improvisations for Piano, op. 84, no. 5

Dumm, R. "A Fauré improvisation," Clavier 15:4 (1976),
20-23. Performer's analysis. Full musical example.

FIELD, JOHN, 1782-1837

Piano Music--General

Branson, David. John Field and Chopin. London: Barrie
& Jenkins, 1972, 216p. Focus is Field's influence on
Chopin. Traces similarities through the music. Very
thorough. Musical examples.
Dale, Kathleen. Nineteenth-Century Piano Music: A Handbook for Pianists. London: Oxford University Press,
1954, 320p. Highlights stylistic traits and unique contribution to the literature of the piano. Form, harmony and
other musical aspects discussed in relation to style.
Locate discussion of individual works through index.
Piggot, Patrick. The Life and Music of John Field: 1782-
1837. Berkeley: University of California Press, 1973,
287p. Thorough critical and analytic treatment with background information. Shows Field's influence on other
composers, notably Chopin. Musical examples.

FRANCK, CESAR, 1822-1890

Keyboard Music--General

Davies, Laurence. Franck. London: Dent, 1973, pp. 63-
83. Critical and analytic observations. Musical examples.
Demuth, Norman. César Franck. London: Dennis Dobson,
1949, pp. 95-122; 143-155. Critical and analytic observations. Musical examples.
Horton, John. César Franck. London: Oxford University
Press, 1948, pp. 19-28. Critical and analytic remarks
on some of Franck's piano and organ solos. Musical
examples.
Vallas, Leon. César Franck. Translated by Hubert Foss.
New York: Oxford University Press, 1951, 283p. Description and critical commentary with background. No
musical examples.

Organ Music--General

Nordgren, Q. R. "A study in chromatic harmony," American Music Teacher 15:4 (1966), 20-21. Advanced discussion of Franck's harmonic idiom. Musical examples.
Peters, Flor. "César Franck's organ music," Musical
Times 113 (April 1972), 395+; (May 1972), 499-500. Dis-

cussion of registration used on Franck's organ with men-
tion of many of the organ works. No musical examples.
Peters, Flor. "The organ works of César Franck," Music
(A. G. O.) 5 (August 1971), 22-27+; (Sept. 1971), 40-42.
Overview with description and analytic comments on
specific works. Musical examples.

Piano Music--General

Cortot, Alfred, French Piano Music. Translated by Hilda
Andrews. London: Oxford University Press, 1932,
pp. 37-107. Descriptive overview with observations on
Franck's style. No musical examples.

GERSHWIN, GEORGE, 1898-1937

Piano Music--General

Goodfriend, James. "Is Gershwin classical or popular?"
Stereo Review 31 (Sept. 1973), 79-80. Some opinions on
a continuing controversy.

Preludes for Piano

Schwartz, Charles. Gershwin: His Life and Music. Indian-
apolis, Ind. : Bobbs-Merrill, 1973, pp. 324-327. Analytic insights with musical examples.

GRIEG, EDVARD, 1843-1907

General

Abraham, Gerald, ed. Grieg: A Symposium. Norman:
University of Oklahoma, 1940, pp. 45-70. Thorough overview of Grieg's total piano output, covering specific
pieces. Stylistic traits, description, critical commentary
and analytic insights are covered.
Dale, Kathleen. Nineteenth-Century Piano Music: A Handbook for Pianists. London: Oxford University Press,
1954, 320p. Highlights stylistic traits and unique contribution to the literature of the piano. Form, harmony
and other musical aspects discussed in relation to style.
Locate discussion of individual works through index.
Finck, Henry T. Grieg and His Music. New York: Dodd,
Mead, 1922, pp. 204-224. Beware the age of this work

(actually 1909) and the rhapsodic, subjective commentary.
However, useful for the student seeking any information
on Grieg's style or on individual pieces. No musical
examples.
Horton, John. Grieg. London: Dent, 1974, pp. 136-148.
Brief critical overview with musical examples. Mainly
the piano works.
Matthews, Denis, ed. Keyboard Music. New York:
Praeger, 1972, pp. 297-300. Brief critical summation
with musical examples.

Lyric Pieces, op. 12, no. 2

Tilens, N. A. & others. "Teacher's roundtable," American
Music Teacher 19:5 (1970), 34-35+. Analysis for performer. No musical examples.

GRIFFES, CHARLES TOMLINSON, 1884-1920

Piano Music--General

Maisel, Edward M. Charles T. Griffes. New York: Da
Capo, 1972, 347p. Mostly a life of Griffes, but a few
very thorough analyses. Locate individual compositions
through index. Musical examples.

HANDEL, GEORGE FRIDERIC, 1685-1759

Keyboard Music--General

Abraham, Gerald, ed. Handel: A Symposium. London:
Oxford University Press, 1954, pp. 233-247. Thorough
overview, discussing form and style with critical appraisals.
Best, T. "Handel's keyboard music," Musical Times 112
(Sept. 1971), 845-848. An annotated listing of Handel's
keyboard works with some critical commentary. Musical
examples.
Matthews, Denis, ed. Keyboard Music. New York:
Praeger, 1972, pp. 101-107. Brief overview of Handel's
keyboard output by Charles Rosen. Handel's place in the
art of keyboard writing, stylistic traits, and critical observation on some pieces. Musical examples.

Harpsichord Suites--General

Lang, Paul Henry. George Frideric Handel. New York:
   Norton, 1966, pp. 657-660. Brief remarks on background
   and style with critical remarks. No musical examples.
Rueb, P. K. "Handel's keyboard suites: a comparison
   with those of J. S. Bach," American Music Teacher 20:5
   (1971), 33-36. A comparison of stylistic characteristics
   with Bach's keyboard suites. No musical examples.
Streatfield, R. A. Handel. New York: Da Capo, 1964,
   pp. 327-328. Brief critical remarks. No musical examples.
Young, Percy M. Handel. London: Dent, 1961, pp. 116-
   119. Descriptive and critical commentary. Musical examples.

HAYDN, FRANZ JOSEPH, 1732-1809

Piano Music--General

Hughes, Rosemary. Haydn. London: Dent, 1962, pp. 139-
   146. Critical and analytic commentary for the student.
   Musical examples.
Landon, H. C. Robbins. Haydn: Chronicle and Works.
   Vol. III (Haydn in England, 1791-1795). Bloomington:
   Indiana University Press, 1976, pp. 437-452. Critical
   and analytic with musical examples.
Matthews, Denis, ed. Keyboard Music. New York:
   Praeger, 1972, pp. 108-141. Background, historical
   perspective, stylistic traits, critical and analytic observa-
   tions on specific pieces. Musical examples.
Radcliffe, Philip. "Keyboard Music," in The New Oxford
   History of Music (Vol. VII; The Age of Enlightenment).
   London: Oxford University Press, 1973, pp. 596-602.
   Brief overview, highlighting important stylistic character-
   istics. Musical examples.

Piano Sonatas--General

Brown, A. P. "The structure of the exposition of Haydn's
   keyboard sonatas," Music Review 36:2 (1975), 102-129.
   Thorough analyses focusing on the exposition. Musical
   examples.
Geiringer, Karl. Haydn: A Creative Life in Music.
   Berkeley: University of California, 1968, 434p. Brief
   critical remarks. Use index to locate comments on individual works. Musical examples.

Landon, H. C. Robbins. Essays on the Viennese Classical
Style: Gluck, Haydn, Mozart, Beethoven. London:
Barrie & Rockliff, 1970, pp. 44-67. Thorough overview,
showing stylistic traits. Critical remarks with musical
examples.

Pauly, Reinhard G. Music in the Classic Period. second
edition. Englewood Cliffs, N. J. : Prentice-Hall, 1973,
pp. 110-113. Brief overview of stylistic traits with
specific sonatas discussed in some detail. Musical examples.

Piano Sonata no. 37, D major

Bryant, C. M. "Claiming our musical heritage, " Clavier
8:3 (1969), 35-39. Performer's analysis with complete
musical example. First movement only.

Piano Sonata no. 52 in E♭

Tovey, Donald Francis. Essays in Musical Analysis:
Chamber Music. London: Oxford University Press,
1956, pp. 93-105. Analysis with musical examples.

HINDEMITH, PAUL, 1895-1963

Organ Music--General

Gibson, E. C. "A study of the major organ works of Paul
Hindemith, " Diapason 62 (Feb. 1971), 22-24. Describes
basic stylistic features with complete analyses of the five
organ works.

Organ Sonatas--General

Milner, A. "The organ sonatas of Paul Hindemith, " Musical Opinion 87 (June 1964), 533+. Brief critical overview with musical examples.

Piano Music--General

Matthews, Denis, ed. Keyboard Music. New York:
Praeger, 1972, pp. 330-332. Brief critical overview.
Musical examples.

Organ Sonata no. 1

Gibbs, A. "Organ music of our century, " Musical Times

105 (Feb. 1964), 134-135. Descriptive and analytic remarks with musical examples.

Organ Sonata no. 3

Trevor, C. H. "Hindemith's Third Sonata," Musical Times
102 (Jan. 1961), 44-45. Brief descriptive commentary
from a performance standpoint. Musical examples.

Piano Sonata no. 2

Bryant, C. M. "Neo-classicism; antique style with a modern twist," Clavier 7:1 (1968), 21-23. Background and
analysis. Musical examples.

IVES, CHARLES EDWARD, 1874-1954

Piano Music--General

Hinson, M. "The solo piano music of Charles Ives (1874-
1954)," Piano Quarterly 23:88 (1974-1975), 32-35. De-
scriptive and analytic overview. No musical examples.
McCrae, E. "The piano music," Music Educators Journal
61 (Oct. 1974), 53-57. Brief descriptive and analytic
remarks. Musical examples.
Matthews, Denis, ed. Keyboard Music. New York:
Praeger, 1972, pp. 353-355. Brief critical appraisal.
Musical examples.
Wuellner, G. S. "The smaller piano works of Charles Ives,"
American Music Teacher 22:5 (1973), 14-16.

Piano Sonata no. 2, "Concord"

Burk, J. M. "Ives' innovations in piano music," Clavier
13:7 (1974), 14-16. Good capsule commentary on Ives'
new musical ideas and devices. Musical examples.
Clark, S. R. "The element of choice in Ives' 'Concord
Sonata,'" Musical Quarterly 60:2 (1974), 167-186. An
examination of the performance latitude allowed by Ives.
Musical examples.
Cowell, Henry & Sidney. Charles Ives and His Music. New
York: Oxford University Press, 1955, pp. 190-201.
Analysis with musical examples.
Fisher, F. "Ives' 'Concord Sonata,'" Piano Quarterly 24:92
(1975-1976), 23-27. Background and analytic remarks.
Musical examples.

Hansen, Peter S. An Introduction to Twentieth Century
  Music. second edition. Boston: Allyn & Bacon, 1967,
  pp. 82-84. Good descriptive commentary showing Ives'
  intentions. For the beginning student. Musical examples.
Perry, Rosalie Sandra. Charles Ives and the American
  Mind. Kent, Ohio: Kent State University Press, 1974,
  137p. Analytic comments and Ives' methods discussed
  throughout book. No index to locate those portions dealing with 'Concord' sonata. Musical examples.

Piano Study no. 22

Dumm, R. "Performer's analysis of an Ives piano piece,"
  Clavier 13:7 (1974), 21-25. Exactly as the title states.
  Full musical quotation.

Variations on America (Organ)

Buechner, A. "Ives in the classroom; a teaching guide to
  two compositions," Music Educators Journal 61:2 (1974),
  64-70. Analysis and background. Musical examples.

KUHNAU, JOHANN, 1660-1722

Biblical Sonata

Nallin, Walter E. The Musical Idea. New York: Macmillan, 1968, pp. 371-374. Brief analysis with musical examples.

LISZT, FRANZ, 1811-1886

Organ Music--General

Bakken, H. "Liszt and the organ," Diapason 60 (May 1969),
  27-29. Analysis of major organ compositions. Musical
  examples.
Searle, Humphrey. "Liszt's organ music," Musical Times
  112:1540 (June 1971), 597-598. A discussion of Liszt's
  original works and transcriptions for organ. Musical
  examples.
Sutter, M. "Liszt, and his role in the development of 19th
  century organ music," Music (A. G. O.) 9 (Jan. 1975),
  35-39. Liszt's contribution to organ music discussed.

Piano Music--General

Beckett, Walter. Liszt. London: Dent, 1963, pp. 83-108.
Descriptive and critical commentary intended for the intelligent layman and student. Musical examples.
Dale, Kathleen. Nineteenth-Century Piano Music: A Hand-
book for Pianists. London: Oxford University Press,
1954, 320p. Highlights stylistic traits and unique contri-
bution to the literature of the piano. Form, harmony
and other musical aspects discussed in relation to style.
Locate discussion of individual works through index.
Einstein, Alfred. Music in the Romantic Era. New York:
Norton, 1947, pp. 209-212. Specific works not discussed
in detail, but Liszt's romantic impulse well portrayed.
No musical examples.
Matthews, Denis, ed. Keyboard Music. New York:
Praeger, 1972, pp. 243-253. Background, historical
perspective, critical observations and capsule commen-
taries on many pieces. Musical examples.
Pisk, Paul A. "Elements of impressionism and atonality
in Liszt's last piano pieces," Radford Review 23:3 (Sum-
mer 1969), 170-176. Structural and harmonic analyses
of seven piano pieces (written in or after 1880) in which
Liszt experimented with new devices.
Searle, Humphrey. The Music of Liszt. New York:
Dover, 1966, 207p. Overview of Liszt's piano works.
Critical and analytic with musical examples.
Walker, Alan, ed. Franz Liszt: The Man and His Music.
New York: Taplinger, 1970, pp. 79-201. Thorough overview of all Liszt's works for piano, including the trans-
criptions. Critical, descriptive and analytic, with musi-
cal examples.

Années de pèlerinage

Kirby, F. E. "Liszt's pilgrimage," Piano Quarterly 23:09
(1975), 17-21. Background and analytic observations on
the Années de pèlerinage. No musical examples.

Bagatelle sans tonalité

Dumm, R. "Liszt lives," Piano Quarterly 17:66 (1968-
1969), 22-23+. Descriptive commentary with musical
examples.

Fantasia Quasi Sonata

Robert, W. "Après une Lecture de Dante, (Fantasia Quasi

Sonata) of Liszt," Piano Quarterly 23:89 (1975), 22-24+.
The symbolism of the sonata. Musical examples.

Sonata in B minor

Longyear, R. M. "Liszt's B minor sonata: precedents for
a structural analysis," Music Review 34:3-4 (1973), 198-
209. Advanced analysis with musical examples.
Longyear, Rey M. Nineteenth-Century Romanticism in
Music. Englewood Cliffs, N. J.: Prentice-Hall, 1969,
pp. 108-112. Brief, but complete analysis. Chart and
musical examples.
Longyear, R. M. "The text of Liszt's B minor sonata,"
Musical Quarterly 60:3 (1974), 435-450. Background and
textual problems considered, but many analytic insights
along the way. Musical examples.
Sutton, W. "Liszt: Piano sonata in B minor," Music
Teacher 52 (Sept. 1973), 16-17. Brief analytic remarks.
No musical examples.

Transcendental Etudes

Banowetz, J. "Liszt, 'Etudes d' Exécution Transcendente,'"
American Music Teacher 20:3 (1971), 18-19+. Background
and descriptive commentary. No musical examples.

MACDOWELL, EDWARD, 1861-1908

Piano Sonatas--General

Kaiserman, D. "Edward MacDowell--the 'Celtic' and
'Eroica' piano sonatas," Music Journal 24 (Feb. 1966),
51+. Descriptive commentary with background. For the
performer. No musical examples.

MEDTNER, NIKOLAI, 1880-1951

Piano Sonata, op. 22, G minor

Truscott, H. "Medtner's sonata in G minor, op. 22,"
Music Review 22:2 (1961), 112-123. Full analysis with
musical examples.

MENDELSSOHN, FELIX, 1809-1847

Solo Works--General

Jacob, Heinrich Eduard. Felix Mendelssohn and His Times. Westport, Conn.: Greenwood Press, 1963, 356p. Descriptive and critical commentary. Musical examples. Piano and organ compositions.

Radcliffe, Philip. Mendelssohn. London: Dent, 1957, pp. 74-88. Descriptive and critical commentary for the student. Musical examples. Piano and organ compositions.

Werner, Eric. Mendelssohn. Translated from the German by Dika Newlin. London: Free Press of Glencoe, 1963. 545p. Background, critical remarks and analysis presented in an easy to read style. Individual works accessible through index. Musical examples.

Piano Music--General

Dale, Kathleen. Nineteenth-Century Piano Music: A Handbook for Pianists. London: Oxford University Press, 1954, 320p. Highlights stylistic traits and unique contribution to the literature of the piano. Form, harmony and other musical aspects discussed in relation to style. Locate discussion of individual works through index.

Songs Without Words

Duncan, J. L. "Words in defense of 'Songs Without Words,'" Music Educators Journal 56 (March 1970), 69-70+. Evaluative remarks. No musical examples.

Songs Without Words, op. 30, no. 6, F♯ minor

Walton, Charles W. Basic Forms in Music. Port Washington, N. Y.: Alfred Publishing Co., 1974, pp. 27-29. Condensed analysis with full musical quotation. No score needed.

MESSIAEN, OLIVIER, 1908-

Solo Works--General

Johnson, Robert Sherlaw. Messiaen. Berkeley: University of California Press, 1975, 221p. Thorough treatment of

Messiaen's total output. Not for the beginner. Musical
examples.
Nichols, Roger. Messiaen. London: Oxford University
Press, 1975, 79p. Messiaen's complex compositional
techniques explained. Since those seeking information on
Messiaen will probably be prepared for a technical discussion, this volume should be useful to them. Musical
examples.

Piano Music--General

Matthews, Denis, ed. Keyboard Music. New York:
Praeger, 1972, pp. 337-340. Critical and analytic remarks. Musical examples.

MOZART, WOLFGANG AMADEUS, 1756-1791

Keyboard Music--General

Blom, Eric. Mozart. London: Dent, 1956, pp. 262-274.
Critical appraisal of Mozart's works in this form.
Specific mention of the more important works. Musical
examples.
Einstein, Alfred. Mozart: His Character, His Work.
Translated by Arthur Mendel and Nathan Broder. London:
Oxford University Press, 1945, pp. 237-251. General
observations on Mozart's keyboard output. Some mention
of specific pieces from a stylistic point of view. Not
analytic. Musical examples.
Landon, H. C. Robbins and Donald Mitchell. The Mozart
Companion. New York: Norton, 1956, pp. 32-64.
Background and critical overview of Mozart's keyboard
output. Many specific works discussed. Musical examples.

Piano Music--General

Matthews, Denis, ed. Keyboard Music. New York:
Praeger, 1972, pp. 143-165. Background, historical
perspective, stylistic traits, and analytic remarks on
specific works. Musical examples.
Radcliffe, Philip. "Keyboard Music," in The New Oxford
History of Music. (Vol. VII; The Age of Enlightenment)
London: Oxford University Press, 1973, pp. 602-610.
Overview, highlighting important stylistic characteristics.
Musical examples.

Piano Sonatas--General

Elder, D. "Lili Kraus--on mastering Mozart," Clavier
10:4 (1971), 10-16. Performer's remarks on style in
Mozart. Critical observations on K. 332 and K. 333.
Kraus, Lili. "Making Mozart live," Clavier 10:5 (1971),
12-18. Notes for performance, but useful here for its
analytic remarks. Musical examples.
Pauly, Reinhard G. Music in the Classic Period. second
edition. Englewood Cliffs, N. J. : Prentice-Hall, 1973,
pp. 113-121. Brief overview of stylistic traits with
specific sonatas discussed in some detail. Musical examples.
Tobin, J. Raymond. Mozart and the Sonata Form. New
York: Da Capo, 1971, 156p. Bar-by-bar analyses of
each sonata. Since no musical examples are provided,
must be used with score.

Fantasy in C minor, K. 475

Rosen, Charles. The Classical Style: Haydn, Mozart,
Beethoven. New York: Viking Press, 1971, pp. 91-93.
Analytic observations on form and key relationships.
Musical examples.
Tischler, Hans. The Perceptive Music Listener. Engle-
wood Cliffs, N. J. : Prentice-Hall, 1955, pp. 207-209.
Descriptive and analytic with musical examples.

Piano Sonata no. 6, K. 284, D major

Walton, Charles W. Basic Forms in Music. Port Washington, N. Y. : Alfred Publishing Co. , 1974, pp. 174-175.
Brief analysis outline with full musical quotation. No
score needed. First movement only.

Piano Sonata no. 10, K. 309, C major

Bryant, C. M. "The music lesson: acquire sophistication
through Mozart," Clavier 9:9 (1970), 24-32. Performer's
analysis with musical examples.

Piano Sonata no. 12, K. 332, F major

Mason, W. "Melodic unity in Mozart's piano sonata, K.
332," Music Review 22:1 (1961), 28-33. Analysis showing melody to be the major unifying force in this work.
Musical examples.

Piano Sonata no. 14, K. 457, C minor

Newman, W. S. "K. 457 and op. 13--two related master-
pieces in c minor," Music Review 28:1 (1967), 38-44.
Shows Mozart's K. 457 as the true direct ancestor of
Beethoven's "Pathétique" Sonata. Musical examples.

Variations on "Ah, vous dirai-je, Maman" K. 300e (265)

Nallin, Walter E. The Musical Idea. New York: Macmillan, 1968, pp. 154-157. Brief analysis with musical examples.

MUSSORGSKY, MODEST, 1839-1881

Piano Music--General

Calvocoressi, M. D. Mussorgsky. London: Dent, 1946,
pp. 166-175. Background, descriptive and critical commentary. Musical examples.

Pictures at an Exhibition

Calvocoressi, M. D. Mussorgsky. Translated by A.
Eaglefield Hull. London: Kegan Paul, n. d., pp. 79-87.
Descriptive and critical commentary. Musical examples.
Kerman, Joseph. Listen. second edition. New York:
Worth Publishers, 1976, pp. 272-273. Background and
analysis for the student.
Matthews, Denis, ed. Keyboard Music. New York:
Praeger, 1972, pp. 309-310. Critical and analytic com-
ments. Musical examples.
Riesemann, Oskar von. Moussorgsky. New York: Knopf,
1929, pp. 290-293. Program-note type description. No
musical examples.
Tischler, Hans. The Perceptive Music Listener. Engle-
wood Cliffs, N. J. : Prentice-Hall, 1955, pp. 155-156.
Brief descriptive and analytic remarks. Musical examples.

NIELSEN, CARL, 1865-1931

Keyboard Music--General

Simpson, Robert. Carl Nielsen: Symphonist, 1865-1931.

London: Dent, pp. 153-163. Critical overview. No
musical examples.

POULENC, FRANCIS, 1899-1963

Piano Music--General

Davies, L. "The piano music of Poulenc," Music Review
33:3 (1972), 194-203. Overview of Poulenc's piano compositions, focusing on style with background remarks and
critical evaluation. Musical examples.
Kerner, W. K. "The piano music of Francis Poulenc,"
Clavier 9:3 (1970), 17-19. General remarks on style.
Very brief.

PROKOFIEV, SERGEI, 1891-1953

Piano Music--General

Nestyev, Israel V. Prokofiev. Stanford, Calif.: Stanford
University Press, 1960, 528p. Critical commentary.
Musical examples. Use index to locate specific works.

Piano Sonatas--General

Chaikin, L. "The Prokofieff sonatas: a psychograph,"
Piano Quarterly 22:86 (1974), 8-19. Analyses of all the
sonatas. Musical examples.
Roseberry, E. "Prokofiev's piano sonatas," Music & Musicians 19 (March 1971), 38-42+. Stylistic traits and analytic remarks both specific and general. Musical examples.

Piano Sonata no. 8, op. 84, B♭ major

Brown, M. A. "Prokofieff's Eighth piano sonata," Tempo
70 (Autumn 1964), 9-15. Analysis. Somewhat advanced.
Musical examples.

RACHMANINOFF, SERGEI, 1873-1943

Piano Music--General

Crociata, F. "The piano music of Sergei Wassilievitch
Rachmaninoff," Piano Quarterly 21:82 (1973), 27-33.

Capsule commentaries on many of the piano pieces.
Critical and descriptive with musical examples.
Culshaw, John. Rachmaninov: The Man and His Music.
New York: Oxford University Press, 1950, pp. 100-119.
Descriptive commentary and critical evaluations. Re-
marks on style. Musical examples.

Preludes

Slenczynska, Ruth. "Rachmaninoff's preludes," Clavier 2:6
(1963), 27-30. Discussion of the preludes from a performer's standpoint. Useful here for Rachmaninoff's remarks and descriptive commentary. Complete musical
examples.

RAMEAU, JEAN PHILIPPE, 1683-1764

Harpsichord Music--General

Girdlestone, Cuthbert. Jean-Philippe Rameau: His Life and
Work. New York: Dover, 1969, pp. 14-37. Descriptive
and critical commentary. Musical examples.

RAVEL, MAURICE, 1875-1937

Piano Music--General

Demuth, Norman. Ravel. London: Dent, 1956, pp. 46-82.
Critical and analytic remarks with musical examples.
Shows Ravel's stylistic development.
Matthews, Denis, ed. Keyboard Music. New York:
Praeger, 1972, pp. 280-285. Critical overview with dis-
cussion of influences. Musical examples.
Myers, Rollo H. Ravel: Life & Works. New York:
Thomas Yoseloff, 1960; Westport, Conn. : Greenwood,
1973, pp. 153-180. Descriptive and critical commentary.
Musical examples.
Nichols, Roger. Ravel. London: Dent, 1977, 199p.
Critical and analytic commentary. Musical examples.
Use index to locate discussion of individual works.
Orenstein, Arbie. Ravel: Man and Musician. New York:
Columbia University Press, 1975, 291p. Brief critical
sketches with analytic insights. No musical examples.
Use index to locate discussion of specific works.
Stuckenschmidt, H. H. Maurice Ravel: Variations on His

Life and Work. Translated from the German by Samuel
R. Rosenbaum. Philadelphia: Chilton, 1968, 271p.
Brief stylistic observations. No analyses. Use table of
contents or index to locate discussion of specific pieces.
No musical examples.

Minuet sur le nom d'Haydn

Montadon, B. "A Twentieth-century minuet," Clavier 11:2
(April 1972), 29-30. Performer's notes with analytic observations. Complete musical example.

Sonatine

Smith, E. "Ravel: Sonatine," Music Teacher 55 (March
1976), 13-15. Analysis with musical examples.

ROUSSEL, ALBERT, 1869-1937

Piano Music--General

Deane, Basil. Albert Roussel. London: Barrie and Rockliff, 1961, pp. 121-131. Descriptive and critical commentary. Musical examples.

SATIE, ERIK, 1866-1925

Piano Music--General

Fisher, F. "Erik Satie's piano music--a centenary survey,"
Clavier 5:5 (1966), 14-19. Background remarks with de-
scriptive overview of Satie's piano works. Complete
musical example provided.
Templier, Pierre-Daniel. Erik Satie. Translation by
Elena and David French. Cambridge, Mass.: The M.I.T.
Press, 1969, 127p. Descriptive and critical commentary.
No musical examples.

Embryons Desséchés no. 2

Fisher, F. "A lesson on Satie's 'Dessicated Embryo no.
2,'" Clavier 5:5 (1966), 25. Brief analytic description.
Complete musical example provided.

SCARLATTI, DOMENICO, 1685-1757

Harpsichord Music--General

Bogianchino, Massimo. The Harpsichord Music of Domenico
   Scarlatti. Translation from Italian by John Tickner.
   Rome: Edizioni de Santis, 1967, 138p. Background and
   full treatment of the music. Musical examples.
Kirkpatrick, Ralph. Domenico Scarlatti. Princeton, N.J.:
   Princeton University Press, 1953, 473p. The definitive
   work. Thorough, in-depth treatment. Musical examples.

Harpsichord Sonatas--General

Clark, J. "Domenico Scarlatti and Spanish folk music: a
   performer's re-appraisal," Early Music 4:1 (1976), 19-21.
   Relationship of the sonatas to Spanish folk music. No
   musical examples.

Sonata in D minor, Longo 370 or K. 10

Bryant, C. M. "Teach Scarlatti's music," Clavier 4:6
   (1965), 24-29. Stylistic traits and analysis. Complete
   musical example provided.

SCHOENBERG, ARNOLD, 1874-1951

Piano Music--General

Carpenter, P. "The piano music of Arnold Schoenberg,"
   Piano Quarterly 41 (Fall 1962), 26-31. Analytic with
   musical examples.
Carpenter, P. "The piano music of Arnold Schoenberg,"
   Piano Quarterly 42 (Winter 1962-1963), 23-29. Analytic
   with musical examples.
MacDonald, Malcolm. Schoenberg. London: Dent, 1976,
   pp. 157-166. Critical and analytic overview. Musical
   examples.
Matthews, Denis, ed. Keyboard Music. New York:
   Praeger, 1972, pp. 323-326. Brief critical summary.
   Musical examples.
Rosen, Charles. Arnold Schoenberg. New York: Viking
   Press, 1975, pp. 73-77; 79-81. Critical and analytic
   commentary. Clearly written. Musical examples.

Piano Pieces, op. 11

Hansen, Peter S. An Introduction to Twentieth Century
Music. second edition. Boston: Allyn & Bacon, 1967,
pp. 67-68. Descriptive commentary for the beginning
student. Musical examples.
Leichtentritt, Hugo. Musical Form. Cambridge, Mass.:
Harvard University Press, 1959, pp. 425-443. Exhaustive, intense analyses with musical examples.

Piano Pieces, op. 11, no. 1

Wittlick, G. "Interval set structure in Schoenberg's op. 11,
no. 1," Perspectives of New Music 13:1 (1974), 41-55.
Analysis for the very advanced student. Musical examples.
Leichtentritt, Hugo. Musical Form. Cambridge, Mass.:
Harvard University Press, 1959, 443-450. Thorough
analyses with musical examples.

Piano Pieces, op. 23, no. 1

Barkin, E. "Registral procedures in Schoenberg's op.
23/1," Music Review 34:2 (1973), 141-145. Use of
register as a structural device. Musical examples.
Graziano, John. "Serial procedures in Schoenberg's opus
23," Current Musicology 13 (1972), 58-63. Analysis with
musical examples.

Piano Pieces, op. 33A

Graebner, E. "An analysis of Schoenberg's Klavierstueck,
op. 33A," Perspectives of New Music 12:1-2 (1973-1974),
128-140. Analysis for the very advanced.

Sonata for Organ (Unfinished)

Watkins, G. E. "Schoenberg and the organ," Perspectives
of New Music 4:1 (1965), 119-135. Intense discussion for
the advanced student. Musical examples.

Variations on a Recitative for Organ, op. 40

Bibbs, A. "Schoenberg's 'Variations on a Recitative,'"
Musical Times 103 (March 1962), 184-185. Brief analy-
tic commentary. Musical examples.
Folts, M. "Arnold Schoenberg's 'variations on a recitative':

opus 40--an analysis," Diapason 65 (Sept. 74), 4-9.
Advanced analysis.   Musical examples.
Folts, M.   "Arnold Schoenberg's 'variations on a recitative'
for organ: opus 40--an analysis," Diapason 66 (March
1975), 7-10+.   Advanced analysis, continued.   Musical
examples.
Milner, A.   "Schoenberg's variations for organ," Organ
43:172 (1964), 179-187.   Analysis with musical examples.
Walker, J.   "Schoenberg's opus 40," Music (A. G. O.) 4 (Oct.
1970), 33-35+.   Analytic and editorial remarks.   No
musical examples.
Watkins, G. E.   "Schoenberg and the organ," Perspective of
New Music 4:1 (1965), 119-135.   Intense discussion for the
advanced student.   Musical examples.

SCHUBERT, FRANZ, 1797-1828

Piano Music--General

Abraham, Gerald, ed.   The Music of Schubert.   New York:
Norton, 1947, pp. 111-148.   Descriptive and critical
overview of Schubert's total piano output.   Musical examples.
Brown, Maurice J. E.   Schubert's Variations.   London:
Macmillan, 1954, 104p.   Critical remarks, focusing on
Schubert's use of variations.   The Impromptu in B♭,
op. 142, no. 3, Variations on a theme by Anselm Hütten-
brenner and others are chosen for discussion.   Musical
examples.
Dale, Kathleen.   Nineteenth-Century Piano Music: A Handbook for Pianists.   London: Oxford University Press,
1954, 320p.   Highlights stylistic traits and unique contribution to the literature of the piano.   Form, harmony
and other musical aspects discussed in relation to style.
Locate discussion of individual works through index.
Duncan, Edmondstoune.   Schubert.   London: Dent, 1934,
pp. 147-156.   Critical and analytic discussion.   Musical
examples.
Einstein, Alfred.   Schubert.   New York: Oxford University
Press, 1951, 343p.   Brief critical observations.   Musical
examples.   Use index to locate specific pieces.
Ferguson, Donald N.   Piano Music of Six Great Composers.
Plainview, N. Y. : Books for Libraries, 1947, pp. 125-
145.   Descriptive and critical commentary with some
analytic insights.   Musical examples.
Gal, Hans.   Franz Schubert and the Essence of Melody.

London: Gollancz, 1974, 205p. Descriptive and critical
remarks with emphasis on the lyrical aspects. Musical
examples.
Hutchings, Arthur. Schubert. London: Dent, 1964,
pp. 141-150. Critical remarks on Schubert's sonatas and
the Wanderer Fantasy. Musical examples.
Matthews, Denis, ed. Keyboard Music. New York:
Praeger, 1972, pp. 185-198. Background, critical evaluation, historical perspective, stylistic traits and mention
of specific works. Musical examples.
Whaples, M. K. "Style in Schubert's piano music from
1817-1818," Music Review 35:3-4 (1974), 260-280. Overview with comments on style and influences. Musical
examples.

Piano Sonatas--General

Brown, M. J. "Schubert's piano sonatas," Musical Times
116 (Oct. 1975), 873-875. Brief, general remarks of a
critical nature. No musical examples.
Cone, Edward T. "Schubert's Beethoven," Musical Quarterly 56:4 (Oct. 1970), 779-793. Shows influence of
Beethoven on Schubert. Musical examples.
Elder, D. "Paul Badura-Skoda on the Schubert sonatas,"
Clavier 12:3 (1973), 7-24. Remarks on style and interpretation from the performer's point of view. Musical
examples.
Radcliffe, Philip. Schubert Piano Sonatas. Seattle: University of Washington Press, 1971, 56p. Well-written
background, description and analytical insights. Intended
for the serious student. Musical examples.

Piano Sonata D. 894, G major

Payne, D. "Achieving the effect of freedom in musical
composition," Piano Quarterly 20:78 (1971-1972), 12-14+.
Analytic remarks with musical examples.

Piano Sonata D. 960, B♭ major

Sutton, W. "Schubert: Piano sonata in B flat (D. 960),"
Music Teacher 51 (Nov. 1972), 11-12. Brief analytic insights. No musical examples.
Wolff, K. "Observations on the scherzo of Schubert's B-flat
sonata op. posth (D. 960)," Piano Quarterly 24:92 (1975-
1976), 28-29. Brief analytic remarks. Musical examples.
Scherzo only.

SCHUMANN, ROBERT, 1810-1856

Piano Music--General

Abraham, Gerald, ed. Schumann: A Symposium. London:
Oxford University Press, 1952, pp. 12-97. Thorough
summary of Schumann's piano works with many analytic
insights. Musical examples.
Chissell, Joan. Schumann. London: Dent, 1967, pp. 100-
121. Excellent summary of Schumann's piano output.
Good, objective musical criticism intended for student.
Musical examples.
Dale, Kathleen. Nineteenth-Century Piano Music: A Hand-
book for Pianists. London: Oxford University Press,
1954, 320p. Highlights stylistic traits. Form, harmony
and other musical aspects discussed in relation to style.
Locate discussion of individual works through index.
Einstein, Alfred. Music in the Romantic Era. New York:
Norton, 1947, pp. 205-209. No specific analyses, but an
excellent description of Schumann's art. No musical ex-
amples.
Elder, D. "Cortot on Schumann," Clavier 3:5 (1964), 14-18.
Remarks on style with a view towards performance.
Music for entire piece given.
Ferguson, Donald N. Piano Music of Six Great Composers.
Plainview, N. Y. : Books for Libraries, 1947, pp. 147-
181. Descriptive and critical commentary showing Schu-
mann's stylistic traits. Musical examples.
Longyear, Rey M. Nineteenth Century Romanticism in Music.
Englewood Cliffs, N. J. : Prentice-Hall, 1969, pp. 66-71.
Intended for student. Overview with descriptive and crit-
ical remarks. Musical examples.
Matthews, Denis, ed. Keyboard Music. New York:
Praeger, 1972, pp. 230-242. Background, historical
perspective, forms, stylistic traits with discussion of
specific pieces. Musical examples.
Patterson, Annie. Schumann. London: Dent, 1934,
pp. 150-163. Overview of Schumann's piano output.
Critical remarks with musical examples.
Siegel, L. "The piano cycles of Schumann and the novels
of Jean Richter," Piano Quarterly 18:69 (1969), 16-22.
Scholarly examination of Schumann's unique fusion of
literature and music. Musical examples.
Walker, Alan, ed. Robert Schumann: The Man and His
Music. London: Barrie & Jenkins, 1972, pp. 41-108.
The most thorough summary of Schumann's piano works
listed here. Critical and analytic commentary. Musical
examples.

Carnaval, op. 9

Elder, D. "Master lesson; seven pieces from Schumann's
'Carnaval,'" Clavier 7:2 (1968), 21-28. Performance-
oriented remarks, useful here for their characterization
of the pieces under discussion. Musical examples.
Leichtentritt, Hugo. Musical Form. Cambridge, Mass. :
Harvard University Press, 1959, pp. 323-325. Condensed
analysis, focusing on variation techniques. Musical examples.
Tischler, Hans. The Perceptive Music Listener. Englewood Cliffs, N.J. : Prentice-Hall, 1955, pp. 150-155.
Brief analysis. Each section discussed with musical examples.

Fantasy for Piano, op. 17, C major

Rosen, Charles. The Classical Style: Haydn, Mozart,
Beethoven. New York: Viking Press, 1971, pp. 451-453.
Analytic observations on the essence of Romanticism in
this work. Musical examples.

Nachtstück, op. 23, no. 4, F major

Walton, Charles W. Basic Forms in Music. Port Washington, N. Y. : Alfred Publishing Co. , 1974, pp. 37-40.
Condensed analysis with full musical quotation. No score
needed.

Novellette no. 8, op. 21, F♯ minor

Tovey, Donald Francis. Essays in Musical Analysis:
chamber music. London: Oxford University Press, 1956,
pp. 142-149. Critical observations and analyses with
musical examples.

Piano Sonata, op. 22, G minor

Sutton, W. "Schumann: Piano sonata in G minor, op. 22,"
Music Teacher 52 (April 1973), 14-15. Brief analytic remarks. No musical examples.

SCRIABIN, ALEXANDER, 1872-1915

Piano Music--General

Bowers, Faubion. "How to play Scriabin," Piano Quarterly

19:74 (1970-1971), 12-18.   Stylistic traits and technical
  problems discussed.   Musical examples.
Bowers, Faubion.   The New Scriabin: Enigma and Answers.
  New York: St. Martin's Press, 1973, 210p.   Discusses
  the 10 sonatas at length and Scriabin's style and harmonic
  system.   Musical examples.
Hull, A. Eaglefield.   A Great Russian Tone-Poet: Scriabin.
  New York: AMS Press, 1970, 304p.   Thorough summation of Scriabin's piano output.   Critical and analytic remarks.   Musical examples.
Randlett, S.   "Elements of Scriabin's keyboard style,"
  Piano Quarterly 20:78 (1971-1972), 26-30 (also nos. 74-
  77 of vol. 20).   Stylistic traits and technical problems
  discussed.   Mainly for the pianist.   Musical examples.

Fantastic Poem for Piano, op. 45, no. 2, C major

Talley, H.   "Scriabine the inscrutable; or, Making the com-
  plicated simple-analysis of the Fantastic Poem in C,"
  Clavier 3:5 (1964), 28-31.   Harmonic analysis.   Complete
  musical example.

Piano Sonata no. 3, op. 23, F♯ minor

William, Sister M.   "Scriabin-the mystic," Clavier 4:6
  (1965), 35-37.   Descriptive and analytic remarks.   Complete musical example.

SHOSTAKOVICH, DMITRI, 1906-1975

Piano Music--General

Kay, Norman.   Shostakovich.   London: Oxford University
  Press, 1971, 80p.   Critical and analytic remarks with
  musical examples.   Hard to locate specific works because
  of lack of index.   Musical examples.

24 Preludes

Martynov, Ivan.   Dmitri Shostakovich: The Man and His
  Work.   New York: Greenwood Press, 1969, pp. 53-55.
  Very brief evaluation of the 24 preludes.   Mainly de-
  scriptive commentary.   No musical examples.
Matthews, Denis, ed.   Keyboard Music.   New York:
  Praeger, 1972, pp. 313-314.   Brief critical remarks.
  Musical examples.

SIBELIUS, JEAN, 1865-1957

Piano Music--General

Abraham, Gerald, ed. The Music of Sibelius. N. Y. :
Norton, 1947, pp. 97-107. Thorough summary and appraisal of all Sibelius' piano works. Musical examples.
Layton, Robert. Sibelius. London: Dent, 1965, pp. 143-
149. Brief, but sound critical appraisal of Sibelius'
piano efforts. Musical examples.

SMETANA, BEDRICH, 1824-1884

Piano Music--General

Clapham, John. Smetana. London: Dent, 1972, pp. 57-64.
Descriptive and critical overview with musical examples.
Large, Brian. Smetana. London: Duckworth, 1970, 473p.
Brief critical observations with musical examples. Com-
ments on individual pieces located through index.

SWEELINCK, JAN PIETERSZOON, 1562-1621

Koyboard Music--General

Curtis, Alan. Sweelinck's Keyboard Music. London: Oxford University Press, 1969, 243p. Background, historical significance of Sweelinck's music, style and other relevant information. Full discussion with musical examples.

TCHAIKOVSKY, PETER ILITCH, 1840-1893

Piano Music--General

Abraham, Gerald, ed. The Music of Tchaikovsky. New
York: Norton, 1946, pp. 114-123. Descriptive and critical commentary. Musical examples.
Evans, Edwin. Tchaikovsky. London: Dent, 1966, pp. 169-
178. Descriptive overview of Tchaikovsky's piano works
and critical appraisals of them.

WEBER, CARL MARIA VON, 1786-1826

Piano Music--General

Dale, Kathleen. Nineteenth-Century Piano Music: A Handbook for Pianists. London: Oxford University Press,
1954, 320p. Highlights stylistic traits and unique contribution to the literature of the piano. Form, harmony
and other musical aspects discussed in relation to style.
Locate discussion of individual works through index.
Saunders, William. Weber. New York: Da Capo, 1970,
pp. 221-227. Background and critical remarks. ·No
musical examples.
Warrack, John. Carl Maria von Weber. London: Hamish
Hamilton, 1968, 377p. Background and critical commentary. Musical examples. Use index to locate commentary on specific works.

WEBERN, ANTON, 1883-1945

Piano Variations, op. 27

Fiore, Mary E. "Webern's use of motive," in Lincoln,
Harry, ed. The Computer and Music. Ithaca, N. Y. :
Cornell University Press, 1970, pp. 115-122. Computer
analysis showing the first 12 measures of the third move-
ment as the theme. For the advanced student.
Jones, James Rives. "Some aspects of rhythm and meter in
Webern's opus 27," Perspectives of New Music 7:1 (Fall-
Winter 1968), 103-109. Rhythmic analysis of the first 14
measures of the third movement. For the advanced stu-
dent.
Kolneder, Walter. Anton Webern: An Introduction to His
Works. Translated by Humphrey Searle. Berkeley:
University of California Press, 1968, pp. 140-144.
Analysis with musical examples.
Lewin, D. "A metrical problem in Webern's op. 27,"
Journal of Music Theory 6:1 (1962), 124-132. Detailed
analysis for the advanced student.
Ogdon, W. "A Webern Analysis," Journal of Music Theory
6:1 (1962), 133-138. Detailed analysis for the advanced
student.
Riley, H. "A study in constructivist procedures: Webern's
Variations for piano, op. 27, first movement," Music Re-
view 27:3 (1966), 207-210. Analysis with musical exam-
ples. First movement only.

Travis, R. "Directed motion in Schoenberg and Webern,"
Perspectives of New Music 4:2 (1966), 87-88. Analysis
for the advanced student.
Westergaard, P. "Webern and 'total organization': an analy-
sis of the second movement of piano variations, op. 27,"
Perspectives of New Music 1:2 (1963), 107-120. Detailed,
intense analysis of second movement. For the advanced.
Musical examples.

3 Little Pieces, op. 11

Wintle, C. "An early version of derivation: Webern's
op. 11/3," Perspectives of New Music 13:2 (1975), 166-
177. Analysis for the advanced student. Musical examples.

CHAPTER II: OPERAS

BARTOK, BELA, 1881-1945

Bluebeard's Castle

Jellinek, George. "First and only," Opera News 39:16 (Feb.
22, 1975), 11-13. Background, composition history,
musical characteristics and structure discussed. Musical
examples.
Stevens, Halsey. The Life and Music of Béla Bartók. New
York: Oxford University Press, 1953, pp. 285-294.
Well-rounded discussion of linguistic, plot, and musical
features. Mentions some affective devices. Musical examples.
Veress, Sandor. "Bluebeard's Castle," in Béla Bartók: A
Memorial Review. Oceanside, N.Y.: Boosey & Hawkes,
1950, pp. 36-53. Thorough analysis. Treats plot, form,
motifs, tonalities and style. Musical examples.

BEETHOVEN, LUDWIG VAN, 1770-1827

Fidelio

Burk, John N. The Life and Works of Beethoven. New
York: Modern Library, 1953, pp. 313-319. Short, basic
commentary with no musical examples.
Carner, Mosco. "Simone Mayr and his 'L'amor coniugale,'"
Music & Letters 52:3 (July 1971), 239-258. A study in
detail of Mayr's work as one of the three forerunners of
Beethoven's Fidelio. Advanced.
Dean, Winton. "Beethoven and Opera," in Arnold, Denis
and Nigel Fortune. The Beethoven Companion. London:
Faber and Faber, 1971, pp. 331-381. Complete background, with discussion of the many sketches and versions
leading to the completed Fidelio. Also, influences found
in Fidelio are traced. Not an analysis.

56

Dent, Edward J. The Rise of Romantic Opera. Cambridge: Cambridge University Press, 1976, pp. 125-134. Examination of romantic traits and tendencies. Critical remarks on music and observations on style. No musical examples.

Dickinson, Alan Edgar Frederic. Beethoven. London: Nelson, 1941, pp. 140-151. Background and critical remarks. No musical examples.

Harrison, John. "A perilous quest," Opera News 36:16 (March 11, 1972), 24-25. Critical remarks, mentioning musical devices used to portray moods and events. Musical examples.

Kolodin, Irving. The Interior Beethoven. New York: Knopf, 1975, pp. 188-199. Traces the many changes leading to the finished Fidelio. Not an analysis, but a detailed commentary on Beethoven's creative process.

Misch, Ludwig. Beethoven Studies. Norman: University of Oklahoma Press, 1953, pp. 139-152. The background of the four overtures to Fidelio. Not an analytic discussion of the music.

Sadie, Stanley. Beethoven. London: Faber & Faber, 1967, pp. 38-43. Simplified remarks on plot and music. Musical examples.

Scherman, Thomas K. and Louis Biancolli, eds. The Beethoven Companion. New York: Doubleday, 1972, pp. 654-669. Background, plot summary and analytic remarks by various writers on music.

BELLINI, VINCENZO, 1801-1835

General

Dent, Edward J. The Rise of Romantic Opera. Cambridge: Cambridge University Press, 1976, pp. 162-175. Examination of romantic traits and tendencies. Critical remarks on music and observations on style. No musical examples.

Oliver, A. Richard. "Romanticism and Opera," Symposium 23:3-4 (Fall-Winter 1969), 325-332. Shows relationship of French melodrama at the beginning of the 19th century to the beginning of Romantic opera in western Europe with special reference to Bellini.

Orrey, Leslie. Bellini. New York: Farrar, Straus and Giroux, 1969, 176p. Bellini's works from a musical point of view rather than an historical one. Discusses melodic style, influences, method of composition, and compares the melodic writing of Bellini and Chopin.

Weinstock, Herbert. Vincenzo Bellini: His Life and His
Operas. New York: Knopf, 1971, 554p. Background
and descriptive commentary with some musical examples.
Not analytic.

Beatrice di Tenda

Borome, J. A. "Bellini and Beatrice di Tenda," Music &
Letters 42:4 (1961), 319-335. Background, story synopsis
and act-by-act commentary with musical examples.

Norma

Freeman, John W. "The long line," Opera News 34:23
(April 4, 1970), 24-25. Musical forms and melodic line
are examined. Musical examples.

Il Pirata

Commons, J. "Bellini and the 'Pirates,'" Music and Musicians 14 (May 1966), 18-19. Background, compositional
history and critical remarks. No musical examples.

I Puritani

Porter, Andrew. "Bellini's last opera," Opera 11 (May
1960), 315-321. Circumstances surrounding the composition of I Puritani. Not much discussion of the music itself.

BERG, ALBAN, 1885-1935

General

Leibowitz, Rene. Schoenberg and His School. Translated
from the French by Dika Newlin. New York: Da Capo
Press, 1970, pp. 171-182. Thorough discussion of formal structure, relationship of musical form to plot and
overall unity. Musical examples.

Lulu

Carner, Mosco. Alban Berg. New York: Holmes &
Meier, 1975, pp. 195-242. Thorough discussion and
analysis with musical examples.
Jarman, D. "Berg's surrealist opera," Music Review 31:3

(1970), 232-240. Background, analytic remarks with musical examples and comparison of Berg's sources with the libretto.

Jarman, D. "Dr. Schön's five-strophe aria: some notes on tonality and pitch association in Berg's Lulu, " Perspectives of New Music 8:2 (Spring-Summer 1970), 23-48. Advanced analysis.

Jarman, D. "Rhythmic and metric techniques in Alban Berg's Lulu, " Musical Quarterly 56:3 (July 1970), 349-366. Advanced analytic commentary. Berg's use of rhythm as a structural element.

Krenek, Ernst. Exploring Music. Translated by Margaret Shenfield & Geoffrey Skelton. New York: October House, 1966, pp. 113-122. General discussion, mentioning Berg's treatment of Wedekind's original text, his tonal language and orchestration. Some comparison with Wozzeck. Not an analysis.

Perle, George. "The character of Lulu: a sequel, " Music Review 25:4 (1964), 311-319. Comparison of Berg's own final version with the usually performed earlier version. No musical analyses or musical examples.

Perle, George. "Lulu: the formal design, " Journal of the American Musicological Society 17:2 (1964), 179-192. Formidable analysis for the advanced student.

Perle, George. "Lulu: thematic material and pitch organization, " Music Review 26:4 (1965), 264-302. Thorough analysis with musical examples. Not for the amateur.

Redlich, H. F. Alban Berg. London: John Calder, 1957, pp. 163-202. Exhaustive analysis. Musical examples.

Reich, Willi. Alban Berg. Translated by Cornelius Cardew. New York: Harcourt, Brace & World, 1965, pp. 156-177. Exhaustive analysis, taken scene by scene.

Wozzeck

Carner, Mosco. Alban Berg. New York: Holmes & Meier, 1975, pp. 145-194. Thorough discussion and analysis with musical examples.

Chittum, Donald. "The triple fugue in Berg's Wozzeck, " Music Review 28:1 (Feb. 1970), 52-62. Detailed musical analysis with musical examples of Act II, Scene II. Not for the amateur.

Davies, Lawrence. Paths to Modern Music: Aspects of Music From Wagner to the Present Day. London: Barrie & Jenkins, 1971, pp. 87-99. Discussion centers on the literary aspects and musical devices used to enhance drama.

Deri, Otto. Exploring Twentieth-Century Music. New York:
   Holt, Rinehart and Winston, 1968, pp. 331-343. Analysis with musical examples. For the intermediate student.
Freeman, John W. "The man who feels," Opera News 33:24
   (April 12, 1969), 24-25. Background, musical structure,
   musical devices and characterization examined. Musical
   examples.
Hansen, Peter S. An Introduction to Twentieth Century
   Music. second edition. Boston: Allyn and Bacon, 1967,
   pp. 207-210. Plot description accompanied by condensed
   musical analysis. Mentions Berg's use of instruments
   and musical devices to achieve drama and unity.
Klein, J. W. "Wozzeck--a summing up," Music & Letters
   44:2 (1963), 132-139. A critical evaluation. Not an
   analysis. No musical examples.
Machlis, Joseph. Introduction to Contemporary Music.
   New York: Norton, 1961, pp. 371-382. Descriptive
   commentary with analytic insights. Written in easy to
   read style for student and amateur.
Perle, George. "The Musical Language of Wozzeck," in
   Mitchell, William J. and Felix Salzer, eds. The Music
   Forum. New York: Columbia University Press, 1967,
   pp. 204-259. Technical discussion on organizational elements used in lieu of tonality and how a tonal center may
   be achieved by atonal means. Shows that whole-tone patterns and scale segments are other units of Berg's musical vocabulary.
Perle, George. "Representation and symbol in the music of
   Wozzeck," Music Review 32:4 (1971), 281-308. Thorough
   analysis, examining the leitmotifs and their role. Quite
   detailed, with musical examples.
Perle, George. "Woyzeck and Wozzeck," Musical Quarterly
   53:2 (1967), 206-216. Detailed recounting of Berg's adaptation of Büchner's original text Woyzeck for his libretto
   Wozzeck. Not a discussion of the music.
Redlich, H. F. Alban Berg. London: John Calder, 1957,
   pp. 74-111. Full treatment. Influences, form, characterization, tonality and place Wozzeck occupies in Berg's
   stylistic development. Musical examples. Berg's own
   lecture on Wozzeck is on pp. 261-285.
Reich, Willi. Alban Berg. Translated by Cornelius Cardew.
   New York: Harcourt, Brace & World, 1965, pp. 117-142.
   Exhaustive analysis, taken scene by scene.
Reich, Willi. "Wozzeck, a guide to the words and music,"
   Musical Quarterly 38:1 (Jan. 1952), 1-21. Step-by-step
   analysis with musical examples.

BERLIOZ, HECTOR, 1803-1869

General

Barzun, Jacques. Berlioz and the Romantic Century. Boston: Little, Brown & Co., 1950. Vol. I, pp. 298-308;
Vol. II, pp. 132-153; 203-227. Background and critical
remarks on all three of Berlioz's operas. No musical
examples.
Dickinson, A. E. "Berlioz's stage works," Music Review
31:2 (1970), 136-157. An overview of Berlioz's stage
works with musical examples. Particularly useful for
discussion of Berlioz's lesser known works.
Dickinson, A. E. The Music of Berlioz. London: Faber
& Faber, 1972, 280p. Full treatment of Berlioz's
operas. More descriptive than analytic.
Elliot, J. H. Berlioz. revised edition. London: Dent,
1967, pp. 196-204. Critical commentary with musical
examples.

Benvenuto Cellini

Cairns, D. "Benvenuto Cellini," Music and Musicians 15
(Jan. 1967), 18-20. Background, performance history
and critical remarks. No musical examples.
Macdonald, Hugh. "The original Benvenuto Cellini," Musical Times 107 (Dec. 1966), 1042-1045. Traces the many
versions and reasons for variant versions. Musical examples.

Les Troyens (The Trojans)

Cairns, David. "Berlioz and Virgil: a consideration of Les
Troyens as a Virgilian opera," Proceedings of the Royal
Music Association XCV (1968-69), 97-110. Derivation of
Berlioz's opera from the Aeneid and consideration of debt
to Virgil.
Dickinson, A. E. "Berlioz and The Trojans," Tempo 48
(Summer 1958), 24-28. Shows Les Troyens to be the cli-
max of Berlioz's steady pursuit of music-drama. Discus-
sion of works leading to Les Troyens. Musical examples.
Fogel, Susan Lee. "An unusual sound," Opera News 34:2
(Sept. 20, 1969), 14-16. Berlioz's unique treatment of
the orchestra in relation to voice. Musical characteriza-
tion illustrated.
Heyworth, Peter, ed. Berlioz, Romantic and Classic:
Writings by Ernest Newman. London: Gollancz, 1972,

pp. 197-233. Critical commentary by a renowned writer
on music. Not an analysis.

BIZET, GEORGES, 1838-1875

General

Cooper, Martin. Georges Bizet. London: Oxford University Press, 1938, 136p. Descriptive and critical remarks with mention of background and influences in Bizet's
music. Musical examples.
Dean, Winton. Bizet. London: Dent, 1948, 262p. Good
musical discussion of Bizet's operas. Easy to read, intelligent writing for the amateur.

Carmen

Machlis, Joseph. The Enjoyment of Music. third edition.
New York: Norton, 1970, pp. 195-201. Analytic overview with musical examples.

Djamileh

Klein, J. W. "Reflections on Bizet's Djamileh," Music Review 35:3-4 (1974), 293-300. Background and critical remarks on this little known opera. No musical examples.

Les Pêcheurs de Perles (Pearl Fishers)

Klein, J. W. "The centenary of Bizet's The Pearl Fishers,"
Music Review 25:4 (1964), 302-310. Performance history,
place in Bizet's output and critical commentary on the
work itself. No musical examples.

BORODIN, ALEXANDER, 1833-1887

General

Abraham, Gerald. Borodin: The Composer and His Music.
London: Reeves, n. d. pp. 64-118. Descriptive commentary with musical examples.

Prince Igor

Dianin, Serge. Borodin. Translated from the Russian by

Robert Lord. London: Oxford University Press, 1963, pp. 271-326. Full description of background leading to completed version with many analytic comments. Motifs traced thoroughly. Musical examples.

BRITTEN, BENJAMIN, 1913-1976

General

Howard, Patricia. The Operas of Benjamin Britten: An Introduction. New York: Praeger, 1969, 236p. Full treatment of the operas with short synopses and analytic commentary. Musical examples.

Martin, George. "Benjamin Britten: twenty five years of opera," Yale Review 60:1 (Oct. 1970), 24-44. General discussion of Britten's operas and reasons for successes and failures. Mentions recurrent themes in his work.

White, Eric Walter. Benjamin Britten: His Life and Operas. Berkeley: University of California Press, 1970, 256p. Good overview of Britten's operas, with analytic remarks. Musical examples.

Billy Budd

Whittall, A. "A war and a wedding: two modern British operas," Music & Letters 55:3 (1974), 299-306. A critical evaluation, mainly concerned with dramatic action. A few outstanding musical devices are mentioned in relation to the action they help portray. No musical examples.

Curlew River

Evans, P. "England," Musical Quarterly 52:4 (1966), 503-507. Descriptive remarks supported with musical examples. Highlights of outstanding musical features.

Death in Venice

Dickinson, A. E. "Britten's new opera," Musical Quarterly 60:3 (1974), 470-478. Analytic commentary with musical examples.

White, Eric Walter. "The voyage to Venice," Opera News 39:7 (Dec. 14, 1974), 15-19. Resumé of Britten's output with descriptive remarks on Death in Venice. Musical examples.

Owen Redgrave

Evan, Peter. "Britten's television opera," Musical Times
112:1539 (May 1971), 425-428. Synopsis, musical procedures, analytical comments and story sources.
Raynor, H. "Opera: Owen Redgrave," Music Review
32:3 (1971), 271-273. Brief critical remarks with no
musical examples.

Peter Grimes

Garbutt, J. W. "Music and Motive in Peter Grimes,"
Music & Letters 44:4 (1963), 334-342. A critical assessment of the dramatic integrity of Peter Grimes. Some
mention made of the music, but not an analysis. No
musical examples.
McDonald, Katherine. "At home with the sea," Opera News
31:16 (Feb. 11, 1967), 24-25. Analytic and critical commentary with musical examples.

CHERUBINI, LUIGI, 1760-1842

General

Deane, Basil. Cherubini. London: Oxford University
Press, 1965, 53p. Guide book for musical amateur.
Overview with analytic remarks.

DEBUSSY, CLAUDE, 1862-1918

Pelléas et Mélisande

Cooper, Martin. French Music: From the Death of Berlioz
to the Death of Fauré. London: Oxford University Press,
1951, pp. 114-118. Compact treatment dealing with influences leading to Pelléas; the relationship of text and
music, harmony, orchestral color and characterization.
Gilman, Lawrence. Debussy's Pelléas et Mélisande. N.Y.:
G. Schirmer, 1907, 84p. Written during Debussy's life-
time, but still useful for its tracing of leitmotifs and story
synopsis.
Liebich, Louise. Claude Achille Debussy. London: John
Lane, 1918, pp. 64-80. Contemporary description with
analytic remarks. Musical examples.
Lockspeiser, Edward. Debussy. London: Dent, 1951,

pp. 209-228.   Concise summary of outstanding features.
Recitative, leitmotifs and musical influences are discussed.
Lockspeiser, Edward.   Debussy: His Life and Mind.   New
York: Macmillan, 1962, Vol. I, pp. 189-202.   Influences,
both literary and musical, that helped shape Pelléas.
Some analytic commentary on the music.   No musical
examples.
Luten, C. J.   "Emerging from a shadow," Opera News
36:10 (Jan. 29, 1972), 24-25.   Brief critical remarks
focusing on the atmosphere generated by the orchestral
part and drama of the vocal line.   Musical examples.
Nichols, Roger.   Debussy.   London: Oxford University
Press, 1973, pp. 33-45.   Clear discussion of Debussy's
aims and method.   Specific musical effects are analyzed.
Musical examples.
Thompson, Oscar.   Debussy.   New York: Dover, 1967,
pp. 343-352.   Background, plot and discussion of the
music.   No musical examples.
Thompson, Oscar.   Debussy: Man and Artist.   New York:
Dover, 1965, pp. 122-142.   Traces development of
Pelléas and its reception.   Historic, not analytic.

DELIUS, FREDERICK, 1862-1934

General

Heseltine, Philip.   Frederick Delius.   New York: Oxford
University Press, 1952, pp. 74-98.   Critical commentary.
No musical examples.
Hutchings, Arthur.   Delius.   London: Macmillan, 1949,
pp. 119-134.   Overview.   Discusses choice of libretto,
public reception, musical characteristics.
Redwood, Christopher, ed.   A Delius Companion.   London:
John Calder, 1976, pp. 217-238.   Extensive overview
with descriptive and critical commentary.

A Village Romeo and Juliet

Jefferson, Alan.   Delius.   New York: Octagon Books, 1972,
pp. 47-49.   Brief, but informative remarks on influences
and characters in opera.

DONIZETTI, GAETANO, 1797-1848

General

Dean, Winton. "Donizetti's serious operas," Proceedings of
the Royal Music Association 100 (1973-1974), 123-141.
Full discussion of style, influence, and some comparison
with Verdi. Musical examples.

Don Pasquale

Ashbrook, William. "Eleven-day wonder," Opera News 35:6
(Dec. 5, 1970), 24-25. Discusses speed of composition,
Donizetti's self-borrowings and other anecdotes relating
to Don Pasquale's compositional history. Musical examples.
Lelash, Marjorie. "Triumph of incongruity," Opera News
29:9 (Jan. 9, 1965), 24-25. Element of surprise in
music examined. Musical examples.

Emilia di Liverpool

Commons, J. "Emilia di Liverpool," Music & Letters 40
(July 1959), 207-228. Full discussion of stage history,
sources libretto and music.

Lucia di Lammermoor

McDonald, Katherine. "Fatal Meeting," Opera News 30:16
(Feb. 19, 1966), 24-25. Musical characterization and
critical commentary with musical examples.

DVORAK, ANTONIN, 1841-1904

General

Colles, H. C. "The Operas," in Fischl, Viktor, ed.,
Antonin Dvořák: His Achievement. Westport, Conn.:
Greenwood, 1970, pp. 134-165. Summarizes Dvořák's
operatic achievement. Some critical commentary. No
musical examples.
Robertson, Alec. Dvořák. London: Dent, 1945, pp. 127-
143. Overview with critical commentary. Musical examples.

FALLA, MANUEL DE, 1876-1946

La Vida Breve

Demarquez, Suzanne. Manuel de Falla. Translated from
the French by Salvatore Attanasio. New York: Chilton
Book Co., 1968, pp. 55-66. Descriptive commentary.
No musical examples.

GERSHWIN, GEORGE, 1898-1937

Porgy and Bess

Ewen, David. A Journey to Greatness: The Life and Music
of George Gershwin. London: Allen, 1956, pp. 184-211.
Background and descriptive remarks with some commentary on the music beginning on page 200. No musical
examples.
Grunfeld, F. "The great American opera," Opera News 24
(March 19, 1960), 6-9. Background and critical commentary.
Mellers, Wilfrid. Music in a New Found Land. New York:
Knopf, 1965, pp. 392-413. Background, descriptive and
analytic commentary with musical examples. Shows relationship of Gershwin's opera to jazz and pop.

GLINKA, MIKHAIL, 1804-1857

General

Brown, David. Mikhail Glinka: A Biographical and Critical
Study. London: Oxford University Press, 1974, 340p.
Thorough treatment. Includes background, brief plot sum-
mary, creative process and many analytic remarks.
Musical examples.

GLUCK, CHRISTOPH WILLIBALD, 1714-1787

General

Cooper, Martin, H. C. "Opera in France," in New Oxford
History of Music, Vol. VII (The Age of Enlightenment,
1745-1790). London: Oxford University Press, 1973,
pp. 226-239. Traces Gluck's operas, mentioning salient
musical characteristics.

Einstein, Alfred. Gluck. Translated by Eric Blom. London: Dent, 1936, 238p. Good summary of Gluck's
achievement with critical remarks on individual works.
Garlington, A. S. "'Le merveilleux' and operatic reform in
18th-century French opera," Musical Quarterly 49:4 (1963),
484-497. Gluck's treatment of "the marvelous," or scenes
depicting heaven, hell, magic and other extra-human
phenomena.
Howard, Patricia. Gluck and the Birth of Modern Opera.
London: Barrie and Rockliff, 1963, 118p. Gluck's innovations in the development of the aria, recitative,
overture and other crucial aspects of opera. Musical
examples.
Newman, Ernest. Gluck and the Opera: A Study in Musical History. London: Gollancz, 1964, 300p. Summary
of Gluck's achievement. No musical examples.
Rushton, J. "Iphigénie en Tauride: the operas of Gluck
and Piccini," Music & Letters 53:4 (1972), 411-430. A
comparison of the settings of Iphigénie by Gluck and
Piccini. Background and critical remarks on the drama
and music. Musical examples.

GOUNOD, CHARLES, 1818-1893

General

Harding, James. Gounod. New York: Stein and Day,
1973, 251p. Critical commentary. No analyses or
musical examples.

Faust

Fogel, Susan Lee. "The uses of simplicity," Opera News
36:14 (Feb. 26, 1972), 24-25. Musical devices used to
strengthen characterization. Musical examples.

Romeo and Juliet

McDonald, Katherine Griffith. "The variety of the heart,"
Opera News 32:24 (April 13, 1968), 24-25. Remarks on
musical style and musical depiction. Comparison of the
three love scenes. Musical examples.

HANDEL, GEORGE FRIDERIC, 1685-1759

General

Bukofzer, Manfred F. Music in the Baroque Era: From Monteverdi to Bach. New York: Norton, 1947, pp. 322-332. Overview of Handel's operas, mentioning characteristic forms, aria types and dance rhythms used.

Dean, Winton. Handel and the Opera Seria. London: Oxford University Press, 1970, 220p. Excellent study. Focus on Handel's theatrical craftsmanship and distinguishes several different types of opera.

Dent, Edward J. "The Operas," in Abraham, Gerald, ed. Handel: A Symposium. New York: Oxford University Press, 1954, pp. 12-65. Thorough musical discussion of Handel's operas. Many analytic comments and observations on style.

Lang, Paul Henry. George Frideric Handel. New York: Norton, 1966, 731p. Overview of Handel's works, commenting on formal and other musical characteristics. No analyses.

Rolland, Romain. Handel. Translated by A. Eaglefield Hull. New York: Holt, 1916, pp. 122-134. General discussion of the operas. Formal characteristics, melody and recitative are noted, as well as Keiser's influence on Handel.

Streatfield, R. A. Handel. New York: Da Capo Press, 1964, pp. 221-255. Survey of all Handel's operas with light critical commentary.

Wolff, Hellmuth Christian. "Italian Opera," in New Oxford History of Music, Vol. V (Opera and Church Music, 1630-1750). London: Oxford University Press, 1975, pp. 138-151. Discusses librettos, musical characteristics, performance practice and prior influences. A survey.

Tamerlano

Knapp, J. M. "Handel's Tamerlano: the creation of an opera," Musical Quarterly 56:3 (1970), 405-430. Examines sources for libretto and how Handel adapted them. Also looks at Handel's compositional process.

Teseo

Kimbell, D. "The libretto of Handel's Teseo," Music & Letters 44:4 (1963), 371-379. Story synopsis and comparison of libretto to source, Quinault's Thésée.

HAYDN, (FRANZ) JOSEPH, 1732-1809

General

Brenet, Michael. Haydn. Translated by C. Leonard Leese.
London: Oxford University Press, 1926, pp. 61-69.
Light overview, mainly of a descriptive nature. Some
critical remarks.
Geiringer, Karl. Haydn: A Creative Life in Music.
Berkeley: University of California Press, 1968, pp. 286-
296. Brief, but solid resumé of Haydn's operatic output.
Places his operas in context, showing influences.
Hughes, Rosemary. Haydn. London: Dent, 1962, pp. 194-
201. Concise overview of Haydn's operatic achievement.
No musical examples.
Landon, H. C. Robbins. "Haydn's Marionette Operas," in
The Haydn Yearbook, Vol. I. Bryn Mawr, Pa. : Presser,
1962, pp. 111-199. Scholarly report. Thematic indexes
to operas provided.
Landon, H. C. Robbins. "The Operas of Haydn," in New
Oxford History of Music. Vol. VII (The Age of Enlight-
enment, 1745-1790). London: Oxford University Press,
1973, pp. 172-199. Survey of Haydn's operas. Traces
Gluck's influence and Haydn's stylistic growth.

HOFFMANN, E. T. A. , 1776-1822

Undine

Garlington, Aubrey S. Jr. "Notes on dramatic motives in
opera: Hoffmann's 'Undine,'" Music Review 32:2 (May
1971), 136-145. Remarks on Hoffmann's use of leitmotiv
and his influence on Weber. Musical examples.

JANACEK, LEOS, 1854-1928

General

Hollander, Hans. Leos Janáček: His Life and Work.
Translated by Paul Hamburger. London: John Calder,
1963, pp. 124-153. General discussion of musical and
dramatic elements as well as Janáček's choice of
libretti. An overview of all his operas.

Jenufa

Freeman, John. "Born of suffering," Opera News 39:8 (Dec.
21, 1974), 20-21. Brief descriptive remarks with musical examples.

LALO, EDOUARD, 1823-1892

Le Roi d'Ys

Cooper, Martin. French Music: From the Death of Berlioz
to the Death of Fauré. London: Oxford University Press,
1951, pp. 36-37. Short, critical remarks on Wagner's
influence and Lalo's distinct musical contribution to French
opera.

MASSENET, JULES, 1842-1912

General

Finck, Henry T. Massenet and His Operas. New York:
   John Love, 1910, 245p. Old, but still useful for its full
   discussion of the operas. Mentions leading singers of the
   time.
Harding, James. Massenet. London: Dent, 1970, 229p.
   Book-length discussion of life of Massenet, background of
   operas, characterization, staging, musical characteristics.

Esclarmonde

Davis, Peter G. "In San Francisco: a major Massenet
   revival," Opera News 39:3 (Sept. 1974), 41-44. Background, history and descriptive remarks on this seldom
   performed work.

Werther

Stocker, L. "Werther; the novel and the opera," Opera
   Journal 6:4 (1973), 23-30. Background, tracing the story
   from Goethe's novel to Massenet. Not a discussion of
   the music.

MONTEVERDI, CLAUDIO, 1567-1643

General

Arnold, Denis. Monteverdi. New York: Farrar, Straus,
Cudahy, 1963, pp. 103-130. Clear discussion of
Monteverdi's achievement, highlighting specific musical
features.
Hoover, Kathleen. "Prophet of Music," Opera News 26:17
(March 10, 1962), 9-13. Overview of Monteverdi's
achievement and innovation in dramatic music.
Prunières, Henry. Monteverdi: His Life and Work. Translated from the French by Marie D. Mackie. New York:
Dover, 1972. 293p. Excellent survey of Monteverdi's
music for the student. Musical and dramatic features
are singled out and Monteverdi's innovations seen in historical context.
Redlich, Hans Ferdinand. Claudio Monteverdi: Life and
Works. London: Oxford University Press, 1952, pp. 94-
116. The place of Monteverdi's innovations in music history is stressed along with specific comments on affective
devices. Musical examples.
Schrade, Leo. Monteverdi: Creator of Modern Music. New
York: Norton, 1950, 384p. Background, descriptive and
critical commentary on all Monteverdi's operas. Special
mention of the forms and innovations. Musical examples.

MOZART, WOLFGANG AMADEUS, 1756-1791

General

Abert, A. A. "The Operas of Mozart," in New Oxford History of Music. Vol. VII (The Age of Enlightenment,
1745-1790). London: Oxford University Press, 1973.
pp. 97-172. Survey of Mozart's operas, showing stylistic
growth both musically and dramatically. Musical examples.
Abraham, Gerald. "The Operas," in Landon, H. C. Robbins. The Mozart Companion. New York: Norton, 1969,
pp. 283-323. Excellent overview with many critical remarks on specific operas. Assesses Mozart's unique contribution to opera.
Blom, Eric. Mozart. London: Dent, 1935, pp. 275-300.
Brief overview of the operas with critical commentary.
Musical examples.
Dent, Edward J. Mozart's Operas: A Critical Study.

second edition. London: Oxford University Press, 1947,
276p. Extremely detailed treatment of the dramatic aspects. The music is lightly treated, and then only as an
adjunct to the drama. Influences are mentioned.
Einstein, Alfred. Mozart: His Character, His Work.
Translated by Arthur Mendel and Nathan Broder. New
York: Oxford University Press, 1945, pp. 383-471.
General, learned discussion covering diverse aspects
such as Mozart's attitude towards libretti, artistic growth
and Masonic elements, to name a few. No real analytic
commentary on the music.
Hughes, Spike. Famous Mozart Operas. 2nd revised edi-
tion. New York: Dover, 1972, 238p. Abduction from the
Seraglio, Figaro, Don Giovanni, Così fan Tutte, and
Magic Flute discussed analytically with musical examples.
Landon, H. C. Robbins. "Mozart on the eighteenth century
stage: how did Mozart's contemporaries view the operas
which we now consider immortal?" Hi Fi/Musical America 15:62-64+, Nov. 1965. Brief survey of the contemporary response to Mozart's operas.
Liebner, Janos. Mozart on the Stage. New York:
Praeger, 1972, 254p. Excellent treatment of Mozart as
dramatist. Specific musical elements are highlighted. A
total view.
Mann, William. The Operas of Mozart. New York: Ox
ford University Press, 1977, 656p. Thorough discussion
of all the operas. Musical examples.
Moberly, R. B. Three Mozart Operas: Figaro, Don Giovanni, The Magic Flute. New York: Dodd, Mead, 1968,
303p. Running commentary of the blow-by-blow variety.
Little analytic commentary, but useful for dramatic
sources and background. No musical examples.
Rosen, Charles. The Classical Style: Haydn, Mozart,
Beethoven. New York: Viking Press, 1971, pp. 288-
325. Mozart's comic operas explored for underlying
sonata form principles. Demonstrates techniques of classical balance even in highly dramatic moments. Musical
examples.
Sadie, Stanley. Mozart. New York: Grossman Publishers,
1970, pp. 145-164. Brief overview of the operas with
critical commentary. No musical examples.
Sitwell, Sacheverell. Mozart. New York: Appleton, 1932,
pp. 103-117. Concise summary of Mozart's operatic
achievement, spotlighting important characteristics.

Abduction from the Seraglio (Entführung aus dem Serail)

Abert, A. A. "The Operas of Mozart," in New Oxford His-

tory of Music, Vol. VII (The Age of Enlightenment, 1745-
1790). London: Oxford University Press, 1973, pp. 141-
147. Focuses on Mozart's characterization and growth as
a dramatist.

La Clemenza di Tito

Sadie, Stanley. "Mozart's last opera," Opera 20 (Oct.
1969), 837-843. Circumstances under which Clemenza
was written and a critical discussion of the opera.

Così fan Tutte

Hughes, Spike. "Così is like that," Opera News 29:15 (Feb.
20, 1965), 24-25. Brief remarks on Mozart's ability to
portray the characters through the music.
Keahey, Delores Jerde. "Così fan Tutte: Parody or
Irony?" in Glowacki, John. Paul A. Piske: Essays in
His Honor. Austin: University of Texas, 1966, pp. 116-
130. Detailed discussion on dramatic intentions of Così.
Wadsworth, Stephen. "The course of love," Opera News
40:8 (Dec. 20/27 1975), 14-16. Critical commentary on
structure and characterization. Musical examples.
Williams, B. "Passion and cynicism; remarks on Così fan
Tutte," Musical Times 114 (April 1973), 361+. General
discussion with critical remarks. No musical examples.

Don Giovanni

Einstein, Alfred. "Concerning some recitatives in Don Giovanni," Music & Letters 19 (1938), 417-425. Warns a-
gainst feeling that Mozart's last version is the most au-
thentic. Describes the many changes Mozart made mere-
ly to accommodate singers or the public. Also two
recitatives not written by Mozart are uncovered in a
later version.
Gounod, Charles. Mozart's Don Giovanni: A Commentary.
Translated from the third French edition by Windeyer
Clark and J. T. Hutchinson. New York: Da Capo Press,
1970, 144p. Of interest because of its author and detailed treatment.
Henning, C. "Thematic metamorphosis in Don Giovanni,"
Music Review 30:1 (1969), 22-26. Analysis of motives
and their transformations to depict characterization.
Shows how Mozart began with motives and arrived at
themes--the reverse of the symphonic process.

Jefferson, Alan. "Don Giovanni, James Bond & Co."
    Opera 16 (Dec. 1965), 864-867. The concept of "hero"
    as seen in Don Giovanni.
Jenkins, Speight, Jr. "The unrelated," Opera News 33:10
    (Jan. 4, 1969), 24-25. Brief remarks on characteriza-
    tion and how the music helps to depict personality.
Rosen, Charles. The Classical Style: Haydn, Mozart,
    Beethoven. New York: Viking Press, 1971, pp. 296-
    302. Formal analysis demonstrating underlying sonata
    form principle in the sextet of Act II. Musical ex-
    amples.
Warburton, Annie O. Analyses of Musical Classics: Book
    4. London: Longman, 1974, pp. 103-107. Descriptive
    remarks on Act I, scene 5. No musical examples.
Wellesz, E. "Don Giovanni and the drama giocoso," Music
    Review 4 (1943), 121-126. Builds case for considering
    Don Giovanni to be a basically tragic opera with comic
    elements, rather than the reverse.

Idomeneo

Abert, A. A. "The Operas of Mozart," in New Oxford His-
    tory of Music, Vol. VII (The Age of Enlightenment, 1745-
    1790). London: Oxford University Press, 1973, pp. 135-
    140. Idomeneo's place in Mozart's stylistic growth.
    Mentions influences of Gluck on this early opera of
    Mozart. Musical examples.
Heartz, D. "The genesis of Mozart's Idomeneo," Musical
    Quarterly 55:1 (1969), 1-19. A detailed history of
    Idomeneo. States Mozart's source for the libretto and
    how it was adapted. No musical examples.

Magic Flute (Die Zauberflöte)

Batley, E. M. "Textual unity in Die Zauberflöte," Music
    Review 27:2 (1966), 81-02. A detailed study to disprove
    theories that the libretto we are accustomed to is an al-
    teration of the original plot.
Faust, Carl R. "Seven keys to the Flute," Opera News
    34:12 (Jan. 17, 1970), 22-23. A brief study on Mozart's
    use of key in Magic Flute. Musical examples.
Haldeman, L. W. "The triumph of Papageno," Opera
    Journal 1:1 (1968), 11-15. Analysis of plot and charac-
    ters. Not a discussion of the music.
Hughes, Spike. "Gift of surprise," Opera News 31:19
    (March 4, 1967), 24-25. Musical characterization and

element of freshness and surprise examined.   Musical
examples.

King, A. Hyatt.   Mozart in Retrospect: Studies in Criticism
and Bibliography.   London: Oxford University Press,
1955, pp. 141-163.   Traces Mozart's borrowing of melodies from himself and other composers in the composition of
Magic Flute.   Thesis in not Mozart's poverty of invention,
but rather the importance of association that the melodies
had for Mozart.

Lee, M. Owen.   "A delicate balance," Opera News 38:7
(Dec. 15, 1973), 28-29.   Critical remarks on characterization and meaning of plot.

Marriage of Figaro (Le nozze di Figaro)

Abert, A. A.   "The operas of Mozart," in New Oxford History of Music, Vol. VII (The Age of Enlightenment, 1745-
1790).   London: Oxford University Press, 1973, pp. 149-
154.   Characterization, musical features and the models
Mozart drew upon are the main focus.

Blom, Eric.   "The literary ancestry of Figaro," Musical
Quarterly 13:4 (1927), 528-539.   Traces sources for
libretto of Figaro in detail.   Not a discussion of the
music.

Mackerras, Charles.   "What Mozart really meant," Opera
16 (April 1965), 240-246.   Delves into the differences
between Mozart's first version of Nozze and the many
later versions designed to suit a singer or public taste.
Musical examples.

Noske, F. R.   "Musical quotation as a dramatic device:
the fourth act of Le nozze di Figaro," Musical Quarterly
54:2 (1968), 185-198.   Mozart's parodies and alterations
of tunes in Figaro as a means of heightening dramatic
effect.   Elevated discussion with musical examples.

Noske, F.   "Social tensions in Le nozze di Figaro," Music
& Letters 50:1 (1969), 45-62.   Examination of Nozze's
dramatic forces from a sociological point of view.
Mozart was keenly aware of social customs and exploited
their full dramatic potential.   Musical examples.

Rosen, Charles.   The Classical Style.   New York: Viking
Press, 1971, pp. 290-295.   Formal analysis of sextet,
showing use of sonata form in Act III.   Musical examples.

Warburton, Annie O.   Analyses of Musical Classics: Book
4.   London: Longman, 1974, pp. 96-103.   Compact
analysis of Act III with no musical examples.

MUSSORGSKY, MODEST, 1839-1881

General

Calvocoressi, M. D. Modest Mussorgsky: His Life and
Works. London: Rockliff, 1956. 322p. Traces full
history of the development of Boris. Other operas discussed with characteristic musical devices indicated.
Riesemann, Oskar von. Moussorgsky. Translated from the
German by Paul England. New York: Knopf, 1929,
pp. 181-273. Full historical account of the development
of Boris and Khovanstchina. Story adaptations, revisions,
etc. Very little musical commentary.

Boris Godunov

Abraham, Gerald. Slavonic and Romantic Music: Essays
and Studies. New York: St. Martin's Press, 1968,
pp. 178-194. Comparison of Mussorgsky's Boris with
Pushkin's original text. Also traces Mussorgsky's re-
working of material from Salammbo into Boris. Shows
how music intended for a completely different opera was
adapted to suit Boris.
Jacobs, Arthur. "Will the real Boris Godunov please stand
up?" Opera 22:5 (May 1971), 388-396. Rimsky-Korsakov's
version of Boris against Mussorgsky's original is examined. Also discusses the many options among Mussorgsky's
revisions.
Kerman, Joseph. "The puzzle of Boris: what makes
Mussorgsky's original the strongest?" Opera News 39:12
(Jan. 25, 1975), 9-12. Untangles the history of the different versions of Boris.
Machlis, Joseph. The Enjoyment of Music. third edition.
New York: Norton, 1970, pp. 203-207. Analytic overview with musical examples.

ORFF, CARL, 1895-

General

Liess, Andreas. Carl Orff. Translated by Adelheid and
Herbert Parkin. London: Calder and Boyars, 1966,
pp. 77-157. Detailed coverage with many analytic remarks.

PERGOLESI, GIOVANNI BATTISTA, 1710-1736

La Serva Padrona

Henning, Cosmo. "Where comic opera was born," Opera
20 (April 1969), 294-301. Examines Pergolesi's role in
the establishment of comic opera (opera buffa). Some
standard comic effects mentioned. Musical examples.

PICCINI, NICCOLO, 1728-1800

General

Rushton, J. "Iphigénie en Tauride: the operas of Gluck
and Piccini," Music & Letters 53:4 (1972), 411-430.
A comparison of the settings of Iphigénie by Gluck and
Piccini. Background and critical remarks on the drama
and music. Musical examples.

POULENC, FRANCIS, 1899-1963

Dialogues of the Carmelites

Freeman, John W. "Song of the scaffold," Opera News
30:18 (March 5, 1966), 14-15. Critical commentary
supported by musical examples.

PROKOFIEV, SERGEI, 1891-1953

General

Lloyd-Jones, David. "Prokofiev and the opera," Opera 13
(August 1962), 513-517. Concise overview of Prokofiev's
operatic achievement. Some remarks on specific works.
Nestyev, Israel V. Prokofiev. Translated from the Russian by Florence Jonas. Stanford, Calif.: Stanford
University Press, 1960, 528p. Brief commentaries on
all the operas reviewing prominent features. Some critical commentary.
Porter, Andrew. "Prokofiev's late operas," Musical Times
108 (April 1967), 312-314. An overview of Prokofiev's
later operatic achievement. Some critical commentary on
the music and stylistic character. No musical examples.

Flaming Angel

Jefferson, A. "The Angel of Fire," Music and Musicians
13 (August 1965), 32-35. Descriptive and analytic remarks with musical examples.
Payne, A. "Prokofiev's The Fiery Angel," Tempo 74
(Autumn 1965), 21-23. A review with critical commentary. No musical examples.

War and Peace

Brown, D. "Prokofiev's War & Peace," Music and Musicians 21 (October 1972), 24-26. Compositional history
and critical commentary. No musical examples.
McAllister, R. "Prokofiev's Tolstoy epic," Musical Times
113 (Sept. 1972), 851-855. Composition history of War
and Peace. No discussion of the music.
Yarustovsky, B. "Prokofiev's War and Peace," Music
Journal 18 (April-May 1960), 32+. Brief critical remarks. No musical examples.

PUCCINI, GIACOMO, 1858-1924

General

Ashbrook, William. The Operas of Puccini. New York:
Oxford University Press, 1968, 269p. All the operas
with plot summaries and analytic commentary on the
music. Musical examples.
Carner, Mosco. Puccini: A Critical Biography. New
York: Knopf, 1959, 500p. Descriptive and critical commentary on all Puccini's operas. Musical examples.
Macdonald, Ray S. Puccini: King of Verismo. New York:
Vantage Press, 1973, 211p. An unusual book, discussing
all the operas from the point of view of realistic dramatic treatment (Verismo) and the use of leitmotiv. Musical
examples.

La Bohème

Downes, Edward. "The feel of reality," Opera News 30:24
(April 16, 1966), 24-25. Critical and analytic commen-
tary supported by musical examples.
Machlis, Joseph. The Enjoyment of Music. third edition.
New York: Norton, 1970, pp. 208-212. Analytic over-
view with musical examples.

Girl of the Golden West (La fanciulla del West)

Carner, Mosco. "How Puccini won the West," Music &
Musicians 11 (Dec. 1962), 10-12. Background, critical
commentary on the music and discussion of special effects. No musical examples.

Madama Butterfly

Ashbrook, William. "The real hero," Opera News 29:20
(March 27, 1965), 24-25. Musical characterization
demonstrated. Musical examples.
Freeman, John W. "A wisp on the horizon," Opera News
32:22 (March 30, 1968), 24-25. Focuses on Puccini's
musical characterization.

Turandot

McDonald, Katherine Griffith. "The Sun and the Moon,"
Opera News 25:27 (March 4, 1961), 21-23. Analytic remarks and comments on influences in Turandot. Musical
examples.

PURCELL, HENRY, c. 1659-1695

General

Holland, Arthur Keith. Henry Purcell: The English Musical Tradition. Plainview, N. Y.: Books for Libraries,
1970, 248p. Survey of Purcell's output focusing on historical context, elements of musical style and use of
poetry.
Moore, Robert Etheridge. Henry Purcell and the Restora-
tion Theatre. Westport, Conn.: Greenwood Press, 1974,
223p. Full treatment of all Purcell's dramatic works.
Westrup, J. A. Purcell. London: Dent, 1937, pp. 115-
125. Concise critical commentary, highlighting historical
context, libretto origins and musical characteristics. Includes similar information on Purcell's other dramatic
works.

Dido and Aeneas

Arundell, Dennis Drew. Henry Purcell. Plainview, N. Y.:
Books for Libraries, 1970, pp. 67-71. Brief, but effec-
tive resumé of important features of Dido. Musical ex-

amples. Includes similar information on Purcell's other dramatic works.

Arundell, Dennis. "New light on Dido and Aeneas," Opera 13 (July 1962), 445-448. Discussion of manuscript versions and where first performed. Interesting background remarks.

Kushner, David Z. "Henry Purcell's Dido and Aeneas: an analytic discussion," Radford Review 23:2 (Spring 1969), 43-58. May be difficult to locate this periodical, but included here because it is an analysis. Also can be found in American Music Teacher 21:1 (Sept.-Oct. '71), 25-28.

RAVEL, MAURICE, 1875-1937

General

Demuth, Norman. Ravel. London: Dent, 1947, pp. 158-165. Concise review of Ravel's two operas. For the musical amateur.

Myers, Rollo H. Ravel: Life and Works. New York: Thomas Yoseloff, 1960, pp. 202-210. Brief review of important characteristics of the operas. Orchestration, musical depiction, form and plot are discussed.

Stuckenschmidt, H. H. Maurice Ravel: Variations on His Life and Work. Translated from the German by Samuel R. Rosenbaum. New York: Chilton, 1968, pp. 103-107. Commentary on music and plot with some psychological observations on the character of the works.

L'Enfant et les sortileges

Orenstein, Arbie. Ravel: Man and Musician. New York: Columbia University Press, 1975, pp. 193-195. Condensed summary of the musical and plot characteristics.

RIMSKY-KORSAKOV, NIKOLAI, 1844-1908

General

Montagu-Nathan, M. Rimsky-Korsakof. New York: Duffield and Co., 1917, pp. 69-95. Antiquated, but useful review of all the operas showing influences and musical characteristics.

ROSSINI, GIOACCHINO, 1792-1868

General

Dent, Edward J. The Rise of Romantic Opera. Cambridge:
Cambridge University Press, 1976, pp. 110-124. Examination of romantic traits and tendencies. Critical remarks on music and observations on style. No musical
examples.
Edward, H. Sutherland. Rossini and His School. London:
Sampson, Low, Marston & Co. , n. d. 114p. Thorough
discussion of Rossini's operatic achievement, showing
influences on him as well as his influence on other opera
composers.
Gossett, P. "Gioacchino Rossini and the convention of
composition," Acta Musicologica 42:1-2 (1970), 48-58.
A scholarly discussion of Rossini's compositional habits.
Some clues to his creative process.
Harding, James. Rossini. London: Faber & Faber, 1971,
92p. Simplified treatment, but discussion of musical
highlights with examples.
Meyerowitz, Jan. "How seriously can we take Rossini's
operas?" High Fidelity 18:11 (Nov. 1968), 61-65. Virtues
and shortcomings of the serious operas examined. Reasons for their lack of popularity compared to the success
of the comic operas.
Payne, Nicolas. "Rossini as dramatist," Opera 20 (March
1969), 186-193. Critical remarks on the music as well
as the drama. Shows stylistic growth of Rossini. Musical examples.
Toye, Francis. Rossini: A Study in Tragi-Comedy. New
York: Norton, 1963, 269p. Mainly a biography, but includes background and critical commentary on the operas.
Not analytic and no musical examples.

Le Comte Ory

Hammond, Tom. "Rossini and Le Comte Ory," Opera 14
(Feb. 1963), 76-79. Background, plot and place of Comte
Ory in Rossini's stylistic growth.

La Gazza Ladra (Thieving Magpie)

Hammond, Tom. "Rossini's real-life opera," Opera 17
(Jan. 1966), 6-10. Critical remarks.

Italiana in Algieri

Freeman, John W.   "Fit for a Sultan," Opera News 38:6
(Dec. 8, 1973), 36-37.   Critical observations on Rossini's
craft.   Musical observations.

Otello

Klein, J. W.   "Verdi's Otello and Rossini's," Music & Letters 45:2 (1964), 130-140.   A comparison of plot treatment by Rossini and Verdi of Shakespeare's Othello.

Siege of Corinth

Mastroianni, J. F.   "The long and thorny saga of L'Assedio
di Corinto," Opera News 39:21 (April 19, 1975), 12-16.
Background and place of Siege in Rossini's output.   Brief
compositional history.   Musical examples.

SAINT-SAËNS, CAMILLE, 1835-1921

General

Hervey, Arthur   Saint-Saëns.   Plainview, N.Y.;   Books
for Libraries Press, 1969, pp. 43-81.   Descriptive commentary and background on all the operas.
Lyle, Watson.   Camille Saint-Saëns: His Life and Art.
Westport, Conn. :   Greenwood Press, 1970, pp. 146-170.
A bit old, but useful for its descriptive commentary and
background on all the operas.

Samson et Dalila

McDonald, Katherine.   "What makes Samson run," Opera
News 29:7 (Dec. 26, 1964), 24-25.   Background and
musical characterization.   Musical examples.

SCHOENBERG, ARNOLD, 1874-1951

General

Jacobson, Robert.   "Eternal Revolutionary," Opera News
39:5 (November 1974), 38-42.   Good layman's overview
of Schoenberg's technique in vocal writing (Sprechgesang).
Reich, Willi.   Schoenberg: A Critical Biography.   Trans-

lated by Leo Black. London: Longman, 1968. 268p.
Background, plot and formal scheme are discussed.
Wellesz, Egon. Arnold Schönberg. Translated by W. H.
Kerridge. New York: Da Capo Press, 1969, pp. 126-
138. Condensed analyses of Erwartung and Glückliche
Hand with musical examples.
Wörner, Karl Heinrich. "Arnold Schoenberg and the
Theater," Musical Quarterly 48:4 (October 1962), 444-
460. A general discussion of Schoenberg's dramatic ideas
as seen in his works. Moses and Aaron studied in some
detail from a dramatic point of view. No musical examples.

Erwartung

Buchanan, Herbert H. "A key to Schoenberg's Erwartung
(Op. 17)," Journal of the American Musicological Society
20:3 (Fall 1967), 434-449. How Schoenberg retains a link
with the tonal world in this piece by deliberate reference
to his earlier work Am Wegrand.
Rosen, Charles. Arnold Schoenberg. New York: Viking
Press, 1975, pp. 39-49. Good analyses dealing with
complex musical elements.
Wellesz, Egon. Arnold Schönberg. New York: Da Capo
Press, 1969, pp. 126-131. Descriptive and critical commentary with musical examples.

Moses and Aaron

Babbitt, Milton. "Three essays on Schoenberg," in Boretz,
Benjamin and Edward T. Cone. Perspectives on Schoen-
berg and Stravinsky. Princeton, N. J. : Princeton Uni-
versity Press, 1968, pp. 53-60. By nature of its sub-
ject, a complex discussion. However, for those studying
Moses and Aaron, a useful descriptive guide. A detailed
analysis of Act I, Scene I appears on pages 61-67. For
the advanced student.
Boretz, Benjamin, comp. Perspectives on Schoenberg and
Stravinsky. Princeton, N. J. : Princeton University
Press, 1968, pp. 61-77. Detailed analysis of Act I,
Scene I. For the advanced student.
Freeman, John W. "Voice in the wilderness," Opera News
30:25 (May 7, 1966), 14-15. Analytic remarks supported
by musical examples.
Stuckenschmidt, H. H. "An introduction to Schönberg's
opera Moses and Aaron," in Glowacki, John. Paul A.
Piske: Essays in His Honor. Austin: University of

Texas Press, 1966, pp. 243-256. Background and artistic development leading to Moses with an analysis.
Wörner, Karl H. Schoenberg's 'Moses and Aaron.' Translated by Paul Hamburger. London: Faber & Faber, 1963, 208p. Exhaustive treatment of the opera from many points of view. Musical analysis, religious elements, philosophic concepts and a bibliography of related materials are included. Musical examples.

SCHUBERT, FRANZ, 1797-1828

General

Bie, Oscar. Schubert: The Man. New York: Dodd, Mead, 1928, pp. 194-215. Overview of Schubert's operas with reasons for lack of success. Descriptive commentary on Rosamunde.
Brown, Maurice J. E. Schubert: A Critical Biography. London: Macmillan, 1961, 414p. Overview with brief critical and descriptive remarks. No musical examples or analyses.
Brown, Maurice J. E. "Schubert's two major operas: a consideration of actual stage production," Music Review 20:2 (Feb. 1959), 104-118. Detailed plot summary with musical examples. Critical commentary and reasons for lack of popularity given.
Dent, Edward J. The Rise of Romantic Opera. Cambridge: Cambridge University Press, 1976, pp. 135-144. Examination of romantic traits and tendencies. Critical remarks on music and observations on style. No musical examples.
Einstein, Alfred. Schubert. Translated by David Ascoli. London: Cassel, 1951, 391p. Comments on style, forms and orchestration in the operas, supported by musical examples.

SCHUMANN, ROBERT, 1810-1856

General

Abraham, Gerald. "The Dramatic Music," in Abraham, Gerald, ed. Schumann: A Symposium. London: Oxford University Press, 1952, pp. 260-282. Summarizes Schumann's dramatic output, with special emphasis on Genoveva.

Chissell, Joan. Schumann. London: Dent, 1967, pp. 169-
186. Summary of Schumann's dramatic works with critical commentary.
Cooper, Frank. "Operatic and Dramatic Music," in Walker,
Alan. Robert Schumann: The Man and His Music. London: Barrie & Jenkins, 1972, pp. 324-349. Good critical overview of Schumann's dramatic output. Musical examples.

Genoveva

Siegal, Linda. "A Second look at Schumann's Genoveva,"
Music Review 36:1 (Feb. 1975), 17-41. Detailed critical
commentary with musical examples.

SMETANA, BEDRICH, 1824-1884

General

Clapham, John. Smetana. New York: Octagon Books,
1972, pp. 90-115. Good analytic survey of Smetana's
considerable operatic output.
Large, Brian. Smetana. London: Duckworth, 1970,
pp. 160-369. Full treatment of Smetana's operas.
Musical techniques, plots and background are provided.

Bartered Bride

Abraham, Gerald. Slavonic and Romantic Music: Essays
and Studies. New York: St. Martin's Press, 1968,
pp. 28-39. Discusses sketches and ideas that preceded
the finished work. Not an analysis.

The Secret

Clapham, John. "Smetana's Romeo and Juliet," Music and
Musicians 20:237 (May 1972), 24-25. Background, descriptive and critical commentary. No musical examples.

SPONTINI, GASPARO, 1774-1851

General

Dent, Edward J. The Rise of Romantic Opera. Cambridge:
Cambridge University Press, 1976, pp. 95-109. Exam-

ination of romantic traits and tendencies. Critical remarks on music and observations on style. No musical
examples.

STRAUSS, RICHARD, 1864-1949

General

Del Mar, Norman. Richard Strauss: A Critical Commentary on His Life and Works. New York: Free Press of
Glencoe, 1962; 1972, 3v. Extremely comprehensive with
much analytic commentary.
Kennedy, Michael. Richard Strauss. London: Dent, 1976,
pp. 141-194. Full coverage of Strauss' entire operatic
output, written in an easy to read style. Critical com-
mentary on orchestration, plot, symbolism and form.
Musical examples.
Krause, Ernst. Richard Strauss: The Man and His Work.
London: Collet's, 1964, pp. 277-475. Lengthy treatment
of all Strauss' operas with some critical commentary.
Very strong on background and aesthetics.
Mann, William. Richard Strauss: A Critical Study of the
Operas. London: Cassell & Co., Ltd. 1964, 402p.
All the operas, done in the manner of a running commen-
tary with musical examples.
Marek, George R. Richard Strauss: The Life of a Non-
Hero. New York: Simon & Schuster, 1967, 350p. All
the operas discussed focusing on background and political
influences. Very little musical criticism.
Newman, Ernest. Richard Strauss. Plainview, N.Y.: Books
for Libraries, 1969, pp. 104-137. Brief overview with
critical remarks.

Arabella

Jefferson, Alan. "An introduction to Arabella," Opera 16
(Jan. 1965), 9-12. Background and critical remarks.

Ariadne auf Naxos

Lee, M. Owen. "Death and Transfiguration," Opera News
34:22 (March 28, 1970), 24-25. Brief remarks on a
central idea in Ariadne--transformation. Musical examples illustrate word painting.

Elektra

Breuer, Robert. "Of timeless passions," Opera News 31:7
(Dec. 10, 1966), 24-25. Elektra as an expression of its
time. Brief look at some leitmotifs with musical examples.
Carner, Mosco. "Witches' cauldron," Opera News 35:18
(Feb. 27, 1971), 24-26. Place of Elektra in Strauss'
output, characterization, motifs and musical devices.

Die Frau ohne Schatten (Woman Without a Shadow)

Jenkins, Speight, Jr. "Kaleidoscope," Opera News 31:8
(Dec. 17, 1966), 25-27. An examination of the leitmotif.
Musical examples.
Snook, Lynn. "The myth and the 'Shadow,'" Opera 18 (June
1967), 454-459. Explores plot for psychological-mythical
meaning.

Der Rosenkavalier

Rockwell, John. "Something old, something new," Opera
News 33:15 (Feb. 8, 1969), 24-25. Strauss' style and
musical depiction. Musical examples.

Salome

McDonald, Katherine Griffith. "Daughter of desperation,"
Opera News 26:14 (Feb. 17, 1962), 23-25. Examples of
Strauss' tone painting techniques. Musical examples.

Die schweigsame Frau (The Silent Woman)

Feasey, Norman. "The Silent Woman--an introduction (historical note included)," Opera 12 (Nov. 1961), 692-697.
Background, synposis and some critical remarks on the
music.

STRAVINSKY, IGOR, 1882-1971

General

Vlad, Roman. Stravinsky. Translated by Frederick and
Ann Fuller. London: Oxford University Press, 1960.
232p. Brief, but ample commentaries on background, influences and musical details.

White, Eric Walter. Stravinsky: The Composer and His
Works. Berkeley: University of California Press, 1966,
608p. Complete treatment of all the operas. Background,
plot and musical details are explored.

The Rake's Progress

Cooke, D. "The Rake and the 18th century," Musical Times
103 (Jan. 1962), 20-23. Analytical remarks with musical
examples. Also, critical appraisal of Stravinsky's imita-
tion of 18th-century musical style.

TCHAIKOVSKY, PETER ILITCH, 1840-1893

General

Abraham, Gerald. The Music of Tchaikovsky. New York:
Dutton, 1946, pp. 124-182. Overview of all ten operas.
Largely descriptive and nonanalytic. Some critical commentary.
Abraham, Gerald. Slavonic and Romantic Music: Essays
and Studies. New York: St. Martin's Press, 1968,
pp. 116-177. Survey of all ten Tchaikovsky operas, including plot action and description of musical characteristics. Other musical influences on Tchaikovsky are
mentioned.

Iolanthe

Lloyd-Jones, D. "A background to Iolanthe," Musical Times
109 (March 1968), 225-226. Background and performance
history. A few critical remarks on the music. No
musical examples.

Piquo Damo (Queen of Spades)

Jefferson, A. "Tchaikovsky's card-sharp Countess," Music
and Musicians 15 (Oct. 1966), 16-17. Background and
critical commentary with musical examples.

THOMSON, VIRGIL, 1896-

General

Hoover, Kathleen and John Cage. Virgil Thomson: His

Life and Music. Plainview, N. Y. : Books for Libraries,
1970, 288p. Discussion of all Thomson's operas with
some commentary on the music, style and influences.

VAUGHAN WILLIAMS, RALPH, 1872-1958

Hugh the Drover

Kennedy, Michael. The Works of Ralph Vaughan Williams.
London: Oxford University Press, 1964, pp. 179-184.
Descriptive commentary with observations on style.
Musical examples.

VERDI, GIUSEPPE, 1813-1901

General

Aycock, R. E. "Shakespeare, Boito, and Verdi," Musical
   Quarterly 58:4 (1972), 588-604. Traces adaptation of
   plots, mainly Otello and Falstaff, from the original
   Shakespeare to Boito and finally, Verdi. No discussion
   of music.
Bonavia, F. Verdi. London: Oxford University Press,
   1930, 161p. History of the writing of the operas. Some
   remarks on Verdi's style and influences.
Budden, Julian. The Operas of Verdi. New York:
   Praeger, 1973, 524p. All the operas, studied in detail.
   Mostly descriptive commentary with musical examples,
   but some observations on Verdi's style.
Gatti, Carlo. Verdi: The Man and His Music. Translated
   from the Italian by Elisabeth Abbott. New York: Putnam's Sons, 1955, 371p. Provides full history of the
   writing of the operas, but no real musical analysis. No
   musical examples.
Hussey, Dynely. Verdi. London: Dent, 1948, 355p.
   Thorough treatment of style, drama and characterization
   in an easy to read manner. Musical examples.
Kerman, Joseph. "Verdi's use of recurring themes," in
   Strunk Festschrift, 495-510. Verdi's use of leitmotif and
   their role in the structure of the operas.
Martin, George Whitney. Verdi: His Music, Life and
   Times. New York: Dodd, Mead, 1963, 633p. Mainly
   background of the composition of the operas and Verdi's
   life, but some discussion of the music throughout.
Noske, F. "Ritual scenes in Verdi's operas," Music &

Letters 54:4 (1973), 415-439.   Traces Verdi's use of
ritual to heighten dramatic effect.   Musical devices used
in connection with ritualistic scenes are mentioned.
Musical examples.
Osborne, Charles.   The Complete Operas of Verdi.   New
York: Knopf, 1970, 472p.   Thorough discussion of all
the operas, with plot synopsis, musical commentary and
influences in Verdi's writing.
Toye, Francis.   Giuseppe Verdi: His Life and Works.
New York: Knopf, 1931, 495p.   Background, influences
and appraisal of Verdi's music.   Musical examples.

Aida

Downes, Edward.   "The kindling word," Opera News 29:19
(March 20, 1965), 24-25.   Musical characterization and
mood painting in Aida.   Musical examples.
Machlis, Joseph.   The Enjoyment of Music.   third edition.
New York: Norton, 1970, pp. 179-182.   Overview with
analytic remarks.   Musical examples.
Osborne, Charles.   "The plot of Aida," Musical Times
110:1520 (Oct. 1969), 1034-1036.   Discussion on sources
for the libretto.

Attila

Matheson, Johann.   "Attila and Verdi's dramatic form," Opera
14 (Nov. 1963), 737-740.   Good discussion of formal
scheme of the drama and some critical remarks on the
music.

Don Carlos

McDonald, Katherine.   "Dark brilliance," Opera News
28:17 (March 7, 1964), 24-25.   Descriptive commentary
with musical examples.   Special remarks on the atmosphere of Don Carlos.
Porter, Andrew.   "A sketch for Don Carlos," Musical
Times 111:1531 (Sept. 1970), 882-885.   A study of the
sketches of the libretto.

Ernani

Weaver, William.   "The irresistible Ernani," Opera 18
(March 1967), 184-191.   Background, performance history
and critical remarks on style and form.

Falstaff

Alderson, R. "Is music really comic?" Opera Journal 6:1 (1973), 13-22. Detailed comparison of musical figures in Falstaff and Otello to show their similarity. Author feels music is not inherently comic, but depends on plot for humor. Musical examples.

Lelash, Marjorie. "He who laughs last," Opera News 28:19 (March 21, 1964), 24-26. Descriptive and critical commentary with musical examples. Special mention of Verdi's use of leitmotif.

Potter, John and Richard Brett. "Verdi's comic vision," Opera News 39:19 (April 5, 1975), 13-14. Brief descriptive remarks supported by musical examples. Highlights musical devices that enhance comic element.

La Forza del Destino (The Force of Destiny)

McDonald, Katherine. "Three under stress," Opera News 29:13 (Feb. 6, 1965), 24-25. Brief remarks on musical characterization and depiction. Musical examples.

Luisa Miller

Larkey, Lionel. "Love and intrigue," Opera News 32:16 (Feb. 17, 1968), 22-23. Place of Luisa in Verdi's output, remarks on musical form and characterization. Musical examples.

Tuggle, Robert A. "Why Luisa Miller," Opera News 36:4 (Dec. 11, 1971), 21-24. Descriptive overview, highlighting musical features of special interest. Musical examples.

Macbeth

Alper, C. D. "Verdi's use of the minor second interval in Macbeth," Opera Journal 4:4 (1971), 10-14. As the title implies, Verdi's use of the minor second for a particular dramatic effect is the subject of study.

McDonald, Katherine Griffith. "In tune with Shakespeare," Opera News 26:19 (March 24, 1962), 24-27. Verdi's methods of characterization through music. Musical examples.

Otello

Archibald, B. "Tonality in Otello," Music Review 35:1

(1974), 23-28.   Advanced, quite technical discussion of
Verdi's tonal language.   Not for the amateur.   Musical
examples.
Harrison, J.   "The beast in the mud: Otello from Othello,"
Opera Journal 5:4 (1972), 26-28.   A comparison of
Shakespeare's character, Othello, with Verdi's Otello.
Some mention of musical devices in characterization.
Hauger, George.   "Othello and Otello," Music & Letters
50:1 (Jan. 1969), 76-85.   A comparison of Shakespeare's
Othello with Verdi's.   Shows a considerable difference
between the two.

Rigoletto

Downes, Edward.   "His hand on his heart," Opera News
28:15 (Feb. 22, 1964), 24-26.   Special focus on the
dramatic quality of the music.   Musical examples.

Simon Boccanegra

Klein, J. W.   "Some reflections on Verdi's Simon Boccanegra," Music & Letters 43:2 (1962), 115-122.   Traces
the revisions of Simon from its early form to the finished
product.   Musical examples.

La Traviata

Machlis, Joseph.   The Enjoyment of Music.   third edition.
New York: Norton, 1970, pp. 175-179.   Brief overview
with analytic remarks.   Musical examples.

Il Trovatore

Klein, Howard.   "At white heat," Opera News 30:5 (Dec. 4,
1965), 24-25.   Explores Verdi's use of tonality in
Trovatore.   Musical examples.

I Vespri Siciliani (Sicilian Vespers)

Freeman, John W.   "Things to come," Opera News 38:18
(March 8, 1974), 20-21.   Vespri's place in Verdi's output and descriptive commentary.   Musical examples.

WAGNER, RICHARD, 1813-1883

General

Bekker, Paul. Richard Wagner: His Life in His Work.
Translated by M. M. Bozman. Plainview, N. Y.: Books
for Libraries Press, 1970, 522p. All the operas, with
analytic remarks. No musical examples, but some discussion of the music.
Donington, Robert. Wagner's "Ring" and Its Symbols. London: Faber & Faber, 1974, 342p. The story of the
Ring perceived on a symbolic level. Psychological forces
and ancient myths based on these forces are called into
play in Wagner's story. A chart of leitmotifs is provided.
Henderson, W. J. Richard Wagner: His Life and His
Dramas. second edition, revised, New York: Putnam's,
1923, 504p. Orderly overview of the operas, giving background, plot and all the leitmotifs. Handy guide.
Jacobs, Robert L. Wagner. London: Dent, 1965, 278p.
Extremely brief treatment of the operas, but Wagner's
musical characteristics and stylistic growth are treated
in an easy to read manner.
Newman, Ernest. A Study of Wagner. New York: Putnam's, 1899, 401p. An earlier version of Newman's
Wagner: Man and Artist cited below. Explores Wagner's
theories as they apply to his music.
Newman, Ernest. Wagner as Man and Artist. London:
Dent, 1914, 386p. Ample discussion of Wagner's theories,
philosophies and style as they apply to his operas. Leitmotifs are covered.
Raphael, Robert. Richard Wagner. New York: Twayne,
1969, 153p. Interesting focus on Wagner's achievement
from a literary and philosophical viewpoint. Discussion
of the music as well from this angle. No musical examples.

The Flying Dutchman (Der fliegende Holländer)

Downes, Edward. "Wings of the storm," Opera News 29:14
(Feb. 13, 1965), 24-26. Musical depiction and leitmotifs
briefly discussed. Musical examples.

Götterdämmerung (Twilight of the Gods)

Ryde, Peter John. "Götterdämmerung--possible solutions to
some Wagner problems," Opera 22:1 (Jan. 1971), 26-31.
A new interpretation of the Ring cycle story. Explains
basic story inconsistency.

Das Liebesverbot

Badacsonyi, George. "Wagner's Shakespearian opera," Opera 16 (Feb. 1965), 89-92. Critical evaluation of this little performed early opera of Wagner's.

Lohengrin

McDonald, Katherine Griffith. "Study in black and white," Opera News 32:15 (Feb. 10, 1068), 24-25. Analytic commentary with musical examples.

Die Meistersinger (The Mastersingers)

Kerman, Joseph. "Night Music," Opera News 31:12 (Jan. 14, 1967), 24-25. Discusses some of the many special and ingenious effects of the opera. The Nightwatchman scene is the focus. Musical examples.

Raynor, Robert M. Wagner and 'Die Meistersinger'. London: Oxford University Press, 1940, 263p. Thorough treatment, showing sources, creative development and a descriptive commentary with musical examples of leitmotifs.

Parsifal

Beckett, L. "Parsifal as drama," Music & Letters 52:3 (1971), 259-271. Discussion in depth of the symbolism in the story and the story's relationship to religion. No discussion of the music.

Honig, Joel. "Transfigured Knight," Opera News 30:22 (April 2, 1966), 26-27. Analytic remarks on the prelude to Parsifal.

Das Rheingold

Downes, Edward. "Bridge to a new world," Opera News 33:17 (Feb. 22, 1969), 25-26. Mini-synopsis of Rheingold with special focus on use of motifs.

Rienzi

Scherman, Thomas. "The riddle of Rienzi," Music Journal 21 (Nov. 1963), 26-28+. Background, brief descriptive and critical remarks. No musical examples.

The Ring

Hamilton, David. "How Wagner forged his Ring," Opera
News 39:15 (Feb. 15/March 1975), 21-26. General remarks on Wagner's grand time scale, sense of structure
and genius for transition. Motifs mentioned. Musical
examples.
Jacobs, R. L. "A Freudian view of The Ring," Music Review 26:3 (1965), 201-219. A psychoanalytic view of the
dramatic forces of the Ring story. Scant mention of the
music itself.
Smith, Patrick J. "Wotan's tragic stature," Opera News
39:15 (Feb. 15/March 1975), 54-56. The role of Wotan
in the Ring.
Wagner, Wieland. "Thoughts on The Ring," Opera 15
(Autumn 1964), 8-13. Wagner's grandson on the psychological forces and symbolism of the Ring.

Tristan and Isolde

Machlis, Joseph. The Enjoyment of Music. third edition.
New York: Norton, 1970, pp. 192-194. Brief analytic
overview with musical examples.

Die Walküre (The Valkyrie)

Abraham, Gerald. A Hundred Years of Music. London:
Duckworth, 1949, pp. 122-129. Detailed analysis of
entire Act I. Mainly from a formal point of view, rather
than harmonic or rhythmic. Motifs identified.
Downes, Edward. "The subject is love," Opera News 33:18
(March 1, 1969), 24-25. Remarks on central theme of
Walküre and ingenious use of leitmotiv.
Machlis, Joseph. The Enjoyment of Music. third edition.
New York: Norton, 1970, pp. 187-192. Brief overview
with analytic remarks. Musical examples.
Sutcliff, James Helme. "Mortal Coils," Opera News 32:17
(Feb. 24, 1968), 24-25. Brief remarks on Walküre's
place in the Ring cycle and the stage of artistic develop-
ment it represents.

WEBER, CARL MARIA VON, 1786-1826

General

Dent, Edward J. The Rise of Romantic Opera. Cambridge:

Cambridge University Press, 1976, pp. 145-161. Examination of romantic traits and tendencies. Critical remarks on music and observations on style. No musical examples.

Einstein, Alfred. Music in the Romantic Era. New York: Norton, 1947, pp. 111-116. Brief overview of Weber's historic position in Romantic opera. Mention made of his musical characteristics and influence on Wagner.

Saunders, William. Weber. New York: Da Capo, 1970, 348p. All Weber's operas with focus on musical technique and characteristics.

Warrack, John. Carl Maria von Weber. London: Hamish Hamilton, 1968, 377p. Full discussion of all Weber's operas with musical characteristics and influences highlighted. Musical examples.

Der Freischütz

McDonald, Katherine Griffith. "Fresh from the forest," Opera News 36:21 (April 15, 1972), 24-25. Brief descriptive remarks with musical examples. Discusses characterization and the early romantic atmosphere of the opera.

CHAPTER III: VOCAL MUSIC

BACH, JOHANN SEBASTIAN, 1685-1750

General

Bukofzer, Manfred F. Music in the Baroque Era. New
York: Norton, 1947, pp. 291-297. Brief summation of
Bach's achievement in the Cantatas, Masses and Passions.
Useful for placing Bach's output in perspective. No
musical examples.
Forkel, Johann Nikolaus. Johann Sebastian Bach. London:
Constable & Co., 1920, 321p. Background and descriptive commentary. Not strong on analytic or critical in-
sights. No musical examples. Beware actual age of
this book (1820).
Geiringer, Karl. Johann Sebastian Bach. New York: Oxford University Press, 1966, 382p. Solid discussion on
specific works. Descriptive, critical and analytic with
musical examples.
Pirro, André. J. S. Bach. Translated from the French
by Mervyn Savill. New York: Orion Press, 1957, 269p.
Descriptive commentary with background. Some critical
remarks. Musical examples.
Schweitzer, Albert. J. S. Bach. English translation by
Ernest Newman. London: Breitkopf & Hartel, 1911,
2 Vols. In spite of the age of this famous work, still
useful for its observations on Bach's word-painting and
its other analytic insights. Musical examples.
Spitta, Philipp. Johann Sebastian Bach. Translated from
the German by Clara Bell and J. A. Fuller-Maitland.
New York: Dover, 1951, 3 vols. Background with critical and descriptive remarks. Quite thorough and a
standard work. However, very old (1880). Musical examples.
Terry, Charles Sanford. Bach: An Introduction. New
York: Dover, 1963, pp. 62-104. As title indicates, an
introduction. Background and critical commentary with
some analytic insights in easy-to-read style.

Watt, R. K. "On the origins of Bach's chorale texts,"
American Choral Review 16:1 (1974), 15-20. No discussion of the music, but a study of the sources of Bach's
texts.
Williams, C. F. Abdy. Bach. London: Dent, 1934,
pp. 105-146. Descriptive and critical commentary intended for student or musical amateur. Musical examples.

Cantatas

Hirsch, A. "Number symbolism in Bach's first cantata
cycle: 1723-1724," Bach 6:3 (1965), 11-19; 6:4 (1974),
14-19; 7:1 (1976), 27-32. Detailed commentary on Bach's
use of an extra-musical device; namely, number symbol-
ism.
Hudson, F. "Bach's wedding music," Current Musicology 7
(1968), 111-120. Background and descriptive commentary.
Musical examples.
Marshall, R. L. "Bach the progressive; observations on
his later works," Musical Quarterly 62:3 (1976), 313-357.
Background and stylistic traits employed in the cantatas.
Shows musical influences.
Palisca, Claude V. Baroque Music. Englewood Cliffs,
N. J. : Prentice-Hall, 1968, pp. 202-215. Concise sum-
mation with remarks on specific musical features.
Musical examples.
Robertson, Alec. The Church Cantatas. New York:
Praeger, 1972, 356p. A guide to all the church cantatas.
Many entries have some descriptive commentary along
with information on instrumentation, composition date and
other relevant facts. No musical examples.
Robertson, Alec. Requiem: Music of Mourning and Consola-
tion. New York: Praeger, 1968, pp. 183-201. Six
cantatas, nos. 32, 106, 262, 82, 95 and 27 described and
commented upon. Analytic insights with musical examples.
Steinitz, Paul. "German church music" in The New Oxford
History of Music. Vol. 5 (Opera and Church Music).
London: Oxford University Press, 1975, pp. 741-764.
Excellent overview of the highpoints with closer examination of specific stylistic traits and formal principles common to the cantatas. Musical examples.
Westrup, J. A. Bach Cantatas. London: British Broadcasting Corp., 1966, 60p. A general discussion of Bach's
technique and style in the cantatas. Many specific works
used as examples. Influences, symbolism, use of choral
melodies are some aspects mentioned. Musical examples.

Whittaker, W. Gillies. The Cantatas of Johann Sebastian
   Bach: Sacred and Secular. London: Oxford University
   Press, 1959, 2 vols. Exhaustive treatment of all the
   cantatas. Musical examples.

Chorales (4-part)

Marshall, R. L. "How Bach composed four-part chorales,"
   Musical Quarterly 56:2 (1970), 198-220. Bach's techniques of composition. Musical examples.

Motets

Pisano, R. C. "On Bach's motets: analysis of compositional technique used for double choir," Choral Journal
   9:3 (1968), 21-23. Analytic commentary focusing on
   Bach's technique of writing for double choir. Musical
   examples.
Pisano, R. C. "On Bach's motets: introductory notes,"
   American Choral Review 5:3 (1963), 1+. Descriptive
   commentary. No musical examples.

Oratorios

Geiringer, Karl. "Bach's oratorios," American Choral Review 9:3 (1967), 22-25. Brief comments with musical
   examples.

Passions

Steinitz, Paul. "German church music," in The New Oxford
   History of Music. Vol. 5 (Opera and Church Music).
   London: Oxford University Press, 1975, pp. 653-658.
   Good capsule overview of Bach's achievement in this
   form. Stylistic highpoints are illustrated with musical
   examples.
Young, Percy M. The Choral Tradition. New York:
   Norton, 1971, pp. 130-136. Both the St. John Passion
   and St. Matthew Passion discussed briefly. Musical ex-
   amples.

Cantata no. 79

Leaver, R. A. "The libretto of Bach's 'Cantata no. 79': a
   conjecture," Bach 6:1 (1975), 3-11. Not a discussion of
   the music, but some thoughts on the possible librettist
   for this cantata.

Cantata no. 131, "Aus der Tiefe rufe ich, Herr, zu dir"

Herz, Gerhard. "BWV 131: Bach's first cantata," in Landon, H. C. Robbins, ed. Studies in Eighteenth-Century
Music. London: Allen & Unwin, 1970, pp. 272-291.
Thorough discussion for the advanced student on background and analysis of this cantata. Musical examples.

Cantata no. 140: Wachet auf, ruft uns die Stimme

Kerman, Joseph. Listen. second edition. New York:
Worth Publishers, 1976, pp. 132-137. Background and
analysis with musical examples. For the student.

Christmas Oratorio

Young, Percy M. The Choral Tradition. New York: Norton, 1971, pp. 112-116. Brief descriptive and critical
remarks. Musical examples.

"Jesu, Meine Freude," Motet

Tovey, Donald Francis. Essays in Musical Analysis. London: Oxford University Press, 1937, Vol. V, pp. 73-82.
Critical commentary for the informed student. Musical
examples.

Magnificat

Tovey, Donald Francis. Essays in Musical Analysis. London: Oxford University Press, 1937, Vol. V, pp. 50-60.
Thorough analysis and critical commentary for the informed student. Musical examples.
Young, Percy M. The Choral Tradition. New York: Norton, 1971, pp. 149-151. Brief descriptive remarks with
musical examples.

Mass in B minor

David, Hans T. "Johann Sebastian Bach's great Mass,"
Bach 2:1 (1971), 29-32. Brief explanatory remarks on
plan of work. Detailed chart showing plan and tonality
appended.
Leaver, R. A. "Number associations in the structure of
Bach's Credo, BWV 232," Bach 7:3 (1976), 17-24.
Number symbolism in the "Credo" traced in detail.
Tovey, Donald Francis. Essays in Musical Analysis. Lon-

don: Oxford University Press, 1937, Vol. V, pp. 20-49.
Thorough analysis and critical commentary for the informed student. Musical examples.
Young, Percy M. The Choral Tradition. New York: Norton, 1971, pp. 140-149. Discussion with concise analysis. Musical examples.

Musical Offering

Wolff, C. "New research on Bach's 'Musical Offering,'"
Musical Quarterly 57:3 (1971), 379-408. Scholarly research to shed light on long-standing mysteries on the
order of the pieces, instrumentation and conception.
Musical examples.

St. Matthew Passion

Brainard, P. "Bach's parody procedure and the 'St.
Matthew Passion,'" Journal of the American Musicological
Society 22:2 (1969), 241-260. Bach's use of pre-existing
material in the St. Matthew Passion examined.

BARBER, SAMUEL, 1910-

General

Broder, Nathan. Samuel Barber. New York: G. Schirmer,
1954, pp. 60-67. Descriptive and critical commentary.
Musical examples.

BARTOK, BELA, 1881-1945

Cantata Profana

Stevens, Halsey. The Life and Music of Béla Bartók.
revised edition. New York: Oxford University Press,
1964, pp. 164-169. Analytic and critical commentary
with musical examples.

BEETHOVEN, LUDWIG VAN, 1770-1827

General

McCaldin, Denis. "The choral music," in Arnold, Denis &

Nigel Fortune. The Beethoven Companion. London:
Faber & Faber, 1971, pp. 387-439. Descriptive, criti-
cal and analytic overview with musical examples.
Scherman, Thomas K. and Louis Biancolli. The Beethoven
Companion. New York: Doubleday, 1972, 1230p.
Program-note style commentary on all Beethoven's works.
No musical examples. See table of contents for discus-
sion of specific works.

Masses

Robertson, A. "Beethoven and the liturgy," Musical Times
111 (Dec. 1970), 1260-1262. Beethoven's view of the
liturgy as an explanation for some musical ideas.
Musical examples.

Christus am Oelberge

Tyson, A. "Beethoven's oratorio," Musical Times 111
(April 1970), 372-375. Descriptive and critical commentary with Beethoven's deafness and stylistic development
considered. Musical examples.
Tyson, A. "The 1803 version of Beethoven's 'Christus am
Oelberge,'" Musical Quarterly 56:4 (1970), 551-584. A
discussion of versions. Musical examples.

Mass in C major

Young, Percy M. The Choral Tradition. New York: Norton, 1971, pp. 205-213. Descriptive and critical remarks. Musical examples.

Missa Solemnis

Cooper, Martin. Beethoven: The Last Decade, 1817-1827.
London: Oxford University Press, 1970, pp. 221-275.
Thorough discussion with analytic insights. Musical
examples.
Hutchings, A. "Beethoven: Mass in D," Music & Musicians
19 (Dec. 1970), 30-36. Thorough background and analysis. Musical examples.
Kirkendale, W. "New roads to old ideas in Beethoven's
'Missa Solemnis,'" Musical Quarterly 56:4 (1970), 665-
701. A variety of insights in Beethoven's conception of
this work by examination of the setting and musical effects. Musical examples.
Tovey, Donald Francis. Essays in Musical Analysis. Lon-

104　　　　　　　　　　　　　　　　　　　　　VOCAL MUSIC

don:　Oxford University Press, 1937, Vol. V, pp. 161-
184.　Thorough analytic and critical commentary for the
informed student.　Musical examples.

BERG, ALBAN, 1885-1935

Songs

Carner, Mosco.　Alban Berg:　The Man and the Work.
New York:　Holmes & Meier, 1977, pp. 79-98.　Thor-
ough discussion with musical examples.
Redlich, H. F.　Alban Berg:　The Man and His Music.
London:　John Calder, 1957, pp. 35-73.　Influences,
methods and style examined.　Musical examples.

Four Songs:　Op. 2, no. 4

Stuckenschmidt, H. H.　"Debussy or Berg?　the mystery of
chord progression, " Musical Quarterly 51:3 (1965), 453-
459.　Analytic discussion on influence of Debussy on Berg.
Musical examples.

5 Songs, Op. 4

Chadwick, N.　"Thematic integration in Berg's Altenberg
songs, " Music Review 29:4 (1968), 300-304.　The theme
as a unifying device.　Musical examples.

BERLIOZ, HECTOR, 1803-1869

General

Dickinson, A. E. F.　The Music of Berlioz.　London:
Faber & Faber, 1972, pp. 39-124.　Thorough treatment
of the music with many examples.
Elliot, J. H.　Berlioz.　London:　Dent, 1967, 234p.　Critical remarks with musical examples.　Intended for student
or musical amateur.
Primmer, Brian.　The Berlioz Style.　London:　Oxford
University Press, 1973, 202p.　Discussion of Berlioz's
treatment of melody, tonality, harmony and style.　Musical examples.

Songs

Dickinson, A. E.　"Berlioz's songs, " Musical Quarterly

55:33 (1969), 329-343.   Thorough descriptive and critical
overview.   Musical examples.

Requiem

Robertson, Alec.   Requiem: Music of Mourning and Consolation.   New York: Praeger, 1968, 85-95.   Background,
influences and extensive discussion of the music.   Musical examples.

BORODIN, ALEXANDER, 1833-1887

Songs

Dianin, Serge.   Borodin.   Translated from the Russian by
Robert Lord.   London: Oxford University Press, 1963,
pp. 257-266.   Critical and analytic remarks with musical
examples.

BRAHMS, JOHANNES, 1833-1897

General

Evans, Edwin.   Historical, Descriptive and Analytic Account
of the Entire Works of Johannes Brahms.   Vol. I: The
Vocal Music.   London: William Reeves, 1912, 599p.
Descriptive commentary on all the vocal works.   No musical examples.
Geiringer, Karl.   Brahms: His Life and Work.   second
edition.   New York: Oxford University Press, 1947,
pp. 266-323.   Solid discussion of the songs and choral
works.   No musical examples.
Niemann, Walter.   Brahms.   Translated from the German
by Catherine Alison Phillips.   New York: Knopf, 1929,
pp. 349-443.   Descriptive and critical discussion.   No
musical examples.
Specht, Richard.   Johannes Brahms.   Translated by Eric
Blom.   London: Dent, 1930, pp. 201-215.   Descriptive
and critical comments.   Antiquated style, but still useful
for its objective observations.   No musical examples.

Songs

Friedlaender, Max.   Brahms' Lieder.   Translated by C.
Leonard Leese.   London: Oxford University Press, 1928,

263p.   Brief remarks on all the songs.   Musical examples.
Harrison, Max.   The Lieder of Brahms.   London: Cassell,
1972, 152p.   Many faceted discussion on the influences,
style and formal design of all Brahms' lieder.   Musical
examples.
Sams, Eric.   Brahms Songs.   Seattle: University of Washington Press, 1972, 68p.   Thorough discussion of all the
songs with musical examples.

German Requiem

Boyd, M.   "Brahms Requiem: A note on thematic integra-
tion," Musical Times 113 (Feb. 1972), 140-141.   Themat-
ic unity in the Requiem outlined.   Musical examples.
Musgrave, M.   "Historical influences in the growth of
Brahms' Requiem," Music & Letters 53:1 (1972), 3-17.
Influences on the Requiem and certain individual stylistic
traits examined.   Musical examples.
Newman, W. S.   "A 'basic motive' in Brahms' 'German
Requiem,'" Music Review 24:3 (1963), 190-194.   Analytic
commentary on unifying melodic concepts in the Requiem.
Musical examples.
Robertson, Alec.   Requiem: Music of Mourning and Consola-
tion.   New York: Praeger, 1968, pp. 175-182.   Background, descriptive and critical commentary.   Musical
examples.
Tovey, Donald Francis.   Essays in Musical Analysis.   London: Oxford University Press, 1937, Vol. V, pp. 211-
225.   Thorough analytic and critical commentary for the
informed student.   Musical examples.
Young, Percy M.   The Choral Tradition.   New York: Norton, 1971, pp. 243-246.   Brief remarks with analysis.
No musical examples.

Der Tod, das ist die kühle Nacht, op. 96, no. 1

Kielian, M.   & others, "Analysis symposium," In Theory
Only 2 (Sept. 1976), 16-29+.   Advanced analysis with
musical examples.

Vier ernste Gesänge (Four Serious Songs)

Boyd, M.   "Brahms and the 'Four Serious Songs,'" Musical
Times 108 (July 1967), 593-595.   Background and analytic
commentary.   Musical examples.

BRITTEN, BENJAMIN, 1913-1976

War Requiem

Robertson, Alec. Requiem: Music of Mourning and Consolation. New York: Praeger, 1968, pp. 265-285. Extensive commentary with background and critical assessment. Musical examples.

BRUCKNER, ANTON, 1824-1896

General

Watson, Derek. Bruckner. London: Dent, 1975, 174p. Critical and analytic remarks for student or musical amateur. Musical examples.

BYRD, WILLIAM, 1543-1623

General

Fellowes, Edmund H. William Byrd. second edition. London: Oxford University Press, 1948, 271p. Thorough study of all Byrd's works. Musical examples.

CACCINI, GIULIO, d. 1618?

Le Nuove Musiche

Baron, J. H. "Monody: A study in terminology," Musical Quarterly 54:4 (1968), 462-474. An examination of monodic style and the Nuove Musiche. Musical examples.
Fortune, Nigel. "Solo song and cantata," in The New Oxford History of Music. Vol. 4 (The Age of Humanism). London: Oxford University Press, 1968, pp. 154-159. The significance of the Nuove Musiche as well as a discussion of the music itself. Musical examples.

CHERUBINI, LUIGI, 1760-1842

Requiem

Robertson, Alec. Requiem: Music of Mourning and Consola-

tion. New York: Praeger, 1968, pp. 75-85. Solid discussion of the music. Musical examples.

CHOPIN, FREDERIC, 1810-1849

Songs

Walker, Alan. Frederic Chopin. New York: Taplinger,
1967, pp. 187-211. Thorough discussion of the songs
with critical evaluations. Musical examples.

COPLAND, AARON, 1900-

12 Poems of Emily Dickinson

Smith, Julian. Aaron Copland. New York: Dutton, 1955,
pp. 253-257. Critical discussion with musical examples.
Young, Douglas.   "Copland's Dickinson songs," Tempo 103
(1972), 33-37. Critical and analytic remarks. Musical
examples.

DEBUSSY, CLAUDE, 1862-1918

General

Lockspeiser, Edward. Debussy. London: Dent, 1951,
pp. 117-142; 204-231. Thorough critical overview with
musical examples.
Thompson, Oscar. Debussy: Man and Artist. New York:
Dover, 1965, pp. 276-306; 359-363. Descriptive commentary. No musical examples.

DELIUS, FREDERICK, 1862-1934

General

Beecham, Sir Thomas. Frederick Delius. New York:
Knopf, 1960, 228p. Thorough treatment of Delius' life
and influences as they affected the music. Less specific
discussion of the music itself than the other works cited
here. Provides good picture of the composer. No
musical examples.
Hutchings, Arthur. Delius. London: Macmillan, 1949,

pp. 97-118; 155-165.   Discussion of all the music with
musical examples.
Jefferson, Alan. Delius. London: Dent, 1972, 179p.
Excellent discussion of all the music and Delius' unique
idiom in an easy-to-read style. Musical examples.
Palmer, Christopher. Delius: Portrait of a Cosmopolitan.
New York: Holmes & Meier, 1976, 199p. Thorough
critical review showing influence and style. Musical
examples.
Warlock, Peter. Frederick Delius. New York: Oxford
University Press, 1952, pp. 99-119. Not as objective as
the other works on Delius, but a useful discussion of the
music. Written by a friend and admirer of Delius.

Mass of Life

Payne, A. "Also sprach Delius," Music & Musicians 13
(Nov. 1964), 20-21. Program-note style commentary.
Brief, no musical examples.

Requiem

Payne, A. "Delius' Requiem," Tempo 76 (Spring 1966),
12-17. Critical and analytic commentary with musical
examples.
Rippin, J. "Delius' Requiem," Musical Opinion 89 (May
1966), 465-467. Background and descriptive commentary.
No musical examples.
Robertson, Alec. Requiem: Music of Mourning and Consolation. New York: Praeger, 1968, pp. 262-264. Critical
assessment. Musical examples.

DES PREZ, JOSQUIN, c. 1450-1521

General

Bridgman, Nanie. "The Age of Ockeghem and Josquin," in
The New Oxford History of Music. Vol. 3 (Ars Nova and
the Renaissance). London: Oxford University Press,
1960, pp. 262-272. Critical overview of the masses,
motets and secular music. Musical examples.
Novack, Saul. "Fusion of design and tonal order in Mass
and Motet," in The Music Forum. Vol. II, pp. 187-263.
Formal design in various works analyzed. For the advanced. Musical examples.
Reese, Gustave. Music in the Renaissance. revised edition.

New York: Norton, 1959, pp. 228-260. Detailed descriptive overview with musical examples.

Motets

Ruff, L. M. "Some formal devices in Josquin's motets," Consort 25 (1968-1969), 362-372. Good review of formal schemes and stylistic traits. Many specific works discussed briefly. Musical examples.

Missa Pange Lingua

Kerman, Joseph. Listen. second edition. New York: Worth Publishers, 1976, pp. 64-66. Brief analysis for the student. Musical examples.

Plus nulz regretz

Aldrich, P. "An approach to the analysis of Renaissance music," Music Review 30:1 (1969), 2+. Thorough analysis. Somewhat advanced. Musical examples.

DUFAY, GUILLAUME, c. 1400-1474

General

Reese, Gustave. Music in the Renaissance. revised edition. New York: Norton, 1959, pp. 48-86. Detailed descriptive overview with musical examples.

Van den Borren, Charles. "Dufay and his school," in The New Oxford History of Music. Vol. 3 (Ars Nova and the Renaissance). London: Oxford University Press, 1960, pp. 214-231. Thorough overview of Dufay's place and style. The motets, Masses, songs and dance forms covered. Musical examples.

Le serviteur hault guerdonne

Kottick, E. L. "Flats, modality, and musica ficta in some early Renaissance chansons," Journal of Music Theory 12:2 (1968), 271-273. Advanced analyses. Musical examples.

DVORAK, ANTONIN, 1841-1904

General

Fishl, Viktor, ed. Antonin Dvořák: His Achievement.
Westport, Conn. : Greenwood Press, 1970, pp. 166-191.
Critical discussion of specific works. Musical examples.
Robertson, Alec. Dvořák. London: Dent, 1947, pp. 94-103;
117-126. Critical discussion of specific works. Musical
examples.

Requiem

Robertson, Alec. Requiem: Music of Mourning and Consolation. New York: Praeger, 1968, pp. 110-116. Critical
evaluation with musical examples.

ELGAR, EDWARD, 1857-1934

General

Parrott, Ian. Elgar. London: Dent, 1971, 143p. Brief
critical remarks. Musical examples.
Young, Percy M. Elgar, O. M.. A Study of a Musician.
London: Collins, 1955, pp. 294-325. Descriptive and
critical commentary with musical examples. Lengthy remarks on Gerontius.

Dream of Gerontius

Kennedy, Michael. Portrait of Elgar. London: Oxford
University Press, 1968, pp. 76-108. Full background
and description. No musical examples.
Robertson, Alec. Requiem: Music of Mourning and Consolation. New York: Praeger, 1968, pp. 239-251. Background and descriptive commentary. Musical examples.
Young, Percy M. The Choral Tradition. New York: Norton, 1971, pp. 256-260. Critical remarks with musical
examples.

FAURE, GABRIEL, 1845-1924

General

Suckling, Norman. Fauré. London: Dent, 1946, pp. 56-89;

153-180.   Handy guide for the student.   Critical and
analytic with musical examples.
Vuillermoz, Emile.   Gabriel Fauré.   Translated by Kenneth
Schapiro.   Philadelphia: Chilton Book Co., 1960, 265p.
Mainly descriptive commentary.   No musical examples.

Requiem

Boyd, M.   "Fauré's 'Requiem':   a reappraisal," Musical
Times 104 (June 1963), 408-409.   Brief critical and
analytic remarks.   Musical examples.
Robertson, Alec.   Requiem: Music of Mourning and Consolation.   New York: Praeger, 1968, pp. 117-122.   Critical
discussion of the music.   Musical examples.

FRANCK, CESAR, 1822-1890

General

Davies, Laurence.   Franck.   London: Dent, 1973, pp. 105-
114.   Brief critical and descriptive overview for the student.   Musical examples.
Demuth, Norman.   César Franck.   London: Dennis Dobson,
n.d., 228p.   Full discussion with musical examples.

Oratorios

Vallas, Leon.   César Franck.   Translated by Hubert Foss.
N.Y.:   Oxford University Press, 1951, 283p.   Full discussion and criticism.   No musical examples.

GABRIELI, GIOVANNI, 1551-1612

Madrigals

Arnold, Denis.   Giovanni Gabrieli.   London: Oxford University Press, 1974, pp. 21-47.   Solid discussion on
style with comments on many specific works.   Written
for the student.   Musical examples.

GESUALDO, DON CARLO, c. 1560-1613

General

Heseltine, Philip & Cecil Gray.   Carlo Gesualdo, Prince of

Venosa. Westport, Conn.: Greenwood, 1971, 145p.
Thorough discussion of the music, though not as substan-
tial as the Watkins book listed here.   Musical examples.
Watkins, Glenn.   Gesualdo: The Man and His Music.
Chapel Hill: University of North Carolina, 1973, 334p.
Thorough, analytic discussion of the music.   Musical ex-
amples.

Madrigals

Dent, E. J.   "The sixteenth century madrigal," in The New
Oxford History of Music.   Vol. 4 (The Age of Humanism).
London: Oxford University Press, 1968, pp. 67-69.
Brief examination of Gesualdo's unique style.   Musical
examples.
Einstein, Alfred.   The Italian Madrigal.   Translated by
Alexander H. Krappe, Roger H. Sessions and Oliver
Strunk.   Princeton, N. J.:   Princeton University Press,
1949, Vol. II, pp. 688-717.   Excellent discourse for the
more advanced student.   Musical examples.

GRIEG, EDVARD, 1843-1907

General

Abraham, Gerald, ed.   Grieg: A Symposium.   Norman:
University of Oklahoma Press, 1950, pp. 71-92; 106-110.
Thorough overview and critical assessment with musical
examples.
Finck, Henry T.   Grieg and His Music.   New York: Dodd,
Mead, 1922, pp. 246-270.   Critical overview.   No musi-
cal examples.

Songs

Horton, John.   Grieg.   London: Dent, 1974, pp. 165-195.
Thorough critical review with musical examples.

HANDEL, GEORGE FRIDERIC, 1685-1759

General

Abraham, Gerald.   Handel: A Symposium.   London: Oxford University Press, 1954, pp. 66-199.   Thorough overview including the oratorios, cantatas and church music.

Dean, Winton. Handel's Dramatic Oratorios and Masques.
    London: Oxford University Press, 1959, 694p. Thor-
    ough, scholarly treatment. Musical examples.
Lang, Paul Henry. George Frideric Handel. New York:
    Norton, 1966, 731p. Solid treatment of all the works.
    Special chapters on oratorios and, in particular, the
    Messiah. Musical examples.
Streatfield, R. A. Handel. New York: Da Capo, 1964,
    pp. 256-325. Old (written 1910) but useful for critical
    comments on the oratorios and choral works. Special
    chapter on Messiah. No musical examples.

Oratorios

Bukofzer, Manfred F. Music in the Baroque Era. New
    York: Norton, 1947, pp. 333-341. Excellent descriptive
    overview with comments on his musical style. No musi-
    cal examples.
Rolland, Romain. Handel. New York: Johnson Reprint,
    1969, pp. 134-143. Very brief overview. No musical
    examples. A 1916 reprint.
Young, Percy M. Handel. London: Dent, 1947, pp. 151-
    167. Brief critical overview. Written for the student.
    Musical examples.
Young, Percy M. The Oratorios of Handel. London:
    Dennis Dobson, 1949, 244p. Thorough treatment, includ-
    ing background of the oratorio and the music itself.
    Musical examples.

Israel in Egypt

Tovey, Donald Francis. Essays in Musical Analysis.
    London: Oxford University Press, 1937, Vol. V, pp. 82-
    113. Thorough analysis and critical commentary for the
    informed student. Musical examples.

Messiah

Gelles, G. "Mozart's version of 'Messiah,'" American
    Choral Review 10:2 (1968), 55-65. A close examination
    of Mozart's orchestration of the Messiah. Musical exam-
    ples.
Larsen, Jens Peter. Handel's Messiah. New York: Nor-
    ton, 1957, 336p. Thorough treatment of many aspects of
    Messiah. The development of the Handelian oratorio, the
    text, versions, sources and the music examined. Musi-
    cal examples.

Tobin, John. Handel's Messiah. London: Cassel, 1969,
279p. Scholarly, in-depth treatment of many aspects of
Messiah. Editions, sources, orchestra, performance
style, harmonic structure and a critical evaluation are
included. Musical examples.
Young, Percy M. The Choral Tradition. New York: Norton, 1971, pp. 16-124. Descriptive, critical and analytic
remarks. No musical examples.

HAYDN, FRANZ JOSEPH, 1732-1809

General

Geiringer, Karl. Haydn: A Creative Life in Music.
Berkeley: University of California Press, 1968, pp. 373-
396. Brief overview of the masses, choruses and
oratorios. Background and critical comments. For the
student. No musical examples.
Hughes, Rosemary. Haydn. London: Dent, 1962, pp. 121-
138. Critical and analytic commentary for the student.
Musical examples.
Landon, H. C. Robbins. Haydn: Chronicle and Works.
Vol. III (Haydn in England, 1791-1795). Bloomington:
Indiana University Press, 1976, pp. 323-404. Thorough
discourse on background, style and influences. Critical
and analytic with musical examples.
Landon, H. C. Robbins. Haydn: Chronicle and Works.
Vol. IV (Haydn: The Years of "The Creation," 1796-
1800). Bloomington: Indiana University Press, 1977,
656p. Thorough discourse with analytic insights and
critical remarks. Musical examples. Use index to locate discussion of specific works. Strong discussion on
"The Creation. "

Masses

Olleson, Edward. "Church music and oratorio, " in New
Oxford History of Music. Vol. 7 (The Age of Enlightenment). London: Oxford University Press, 1973, pp. 319-
327. Overview of Haydn's masses, highlighting musical
style and period influences. Musical examples.

Oratorios

Hadden, J. Cuthbert. Haydn. London: Dent, 1934, pp.
116-127. Brief summary and critical discussion of the

"Creation" and "Seasons." For the student. No musical
examples.
Olleson, Edward. "Church music and oratorio," in The New
Oxford History of Music. Vol. 7 (The Age of Enlightenment). London: Oxford University Press, 1973, pp. 332-
335. Brief descriptive commentary. No musical examples.

The Creation

Levarie, Siegmund. "The closing numbers of 'Die Schöp-
fung,'" in Landon, H. C. Robbins, ed. Studies in
Eighteenth-Century Music. London: Allen & Unwin,
1970, pp. 315-322. Advanced discussion on structural
balance of this work. Musical examples.
Olleson, Edward. "The origin and libretto of Haydn's 'Creation,'" in The Haydn Yearbook, Vol. IV. Bryn Mawr,
Pa. : Theodore Presser Co. , n. d. , pp. 148-168. Background. No discussion of the music.
Tovey, Donald Francis. Essays in Musical Analysis. London: Oxford University Press, 1937, Vol. V, pp. 114-
146. Thorough analysis and critical commentary for the
informed student. Musical examples.
Young, Percy M. The Choral Tradition. New York: Norton, 1971, pp. 182-190. Highlights significant musical
elements. Background and descriptive remarks on both
the Creation and the Seasons. Musical examples.

The Seasons

Tovey, Donald Francis. Essays in Musical Analysis. London: Oxford University Press, 1937, Vol. V, pp. 146-
161. Thorough analytic and critical commentary for the
informed student. Musical examples.

HINDEMITH, PAUL, 1895-1963

When Lilacs Last in the Dooryard Bloomed

Robertson, Alec. Requiem: Music of Mourning and Consolation. New York: Praeger, 1968, pp. 252-259. Background, descriptive and critical commentary. Musical
examples.

HOLST, GUSTAV, 1874-1934

General

Holst, Imogen. Gustav Holst: A Biography. second edition. London: Oxford University Press, 1969, 210p. Biography with discussion of the music. No musical examples.
Holst, Imogen. The Music of Gustav Holst. London: Oxford University Press, 1968, 169p. Entire volume devoted to the music. Musical examples.

ISAAC, HEINRICH, c. 1450-1517

General

Novack, Saul. "Fusion of design and tonal order in Mass and Motet," in The Music Forum. Vol. II, pp. 187-263. Formal design in various works analyzed. For the advanced. Musical examples.

IVES, CHARLES EDWARD, 1874-1954

General

Cowell, Henry & Sidney. Charles Ives and His Music. New York: Oxford University Press, 1955, 245p. Biographical and critical. Use index to locate discussion of individual works. Musical examples.
Hitchcock, H. Wiley. Ives. London: Oxford University Press, 1977, pp. 9-41. Solid discussion of the music of a complex composer. For the student. Musical examples.
Lamb, G. H. "Charles Ives 1874-1954," Choral Journal 15:2 (1974), 12-13. Brief critical remarks on the choral works. No musical examples.
Smith, G. "Charles Ives: the man and his music," Choral Journal 15:3 (1974), 17-20. Critical overview of Ives' choral works. No musical examples.
Tipton, J. R. "Some observations on the choral style of Charles Ives," American Choral Review 12:3 (1970), 99-105. Analytic remarks on Ives' musical techniques and style. Musical examples.

Songs

Boatwright, H. "The songs," Music Educators Journal 61
(Oct. 1974), 42-47. Background and general stylistic
traits examined. No musical examples.

The Celestial Country

Balshaw, P. A. "'The Celestial Country': an introduction,"
Choral Journal 15:7 (1975), 16-20. Analysis with musical examples.

JANACEK, LEOS, 1854-1928

General

Hollander, Hans. Leos Janáček: His Life and Work.
Translated by Paul Hamburger. London: John Calder,
1963, pp. 154-170. Descriptive commentary on specific
pieces. No musical examples.

JOSQUIN   see   DES PREZ, JOSQUIN

LASSUS, ORLANDUS, 1532-1594

General

Coates, Henry & Gerald Abraham. "The perfection of the
a capella style," in The New Oxford History of Music.
Vol. 4 (The Age of Humanism). London: Oxford University Press, 1968, pp. 333-350. Masses, motets, psalms
and magnificat of Lassus are discussed critically and
analytically. Musical examples.

Chansons

Van den Borren, Charles. "The French Chanson," in The
New Oxford History of Music. Vol. 4 (The Age of
Humanism). London: Oxford University Press, 1968,
pp. 21-25. Brief assessment of Lassus' unique contribution to the chanson. No musical examples.

Madrigals

Einstein, Alfred. The Italian Madrigal. Translated by

Alexander H. Krappe, Roger H. Sessions, and Oliver
Strunk. Princeton, N. J. : Princeton University Press,
1949, Vol. II, pp. 477-498. Excellent discourse for the
more advanced student. Musical examples.

LISZT, FRANZ, 1811-1886

General

Beckett, Walter. Liszt. London: Dent, 1963, pp. 120-130.
  Brief remarks with musical examples for the student.
Searle, Humphrey. The Music of Liszt. second revised
  edition. New York: Dover, 1966, 207p. Concentrates
  on the music with little biographical information. Use
  table of contents for discussion of specific works. Musical examples.
Walker, Alan, ed. Franz Liszt: The Man and His Music.
  New York: Taplinger, 1970, pp. 221-247; 318-345. The
  songs, oratorios and masses discussed at length. Musical examples.

Via Crucis

Hill, C. "Liszt's 'Via Crucis,'" Music Review 25:3 (1964),
  202-208. Description and analysis. Musical examples.
Robertson, Alec. Requiem: Music of Mourning and Consolation. New York: Praeger, 1968, pp. 154-158. Descriptive commentary with critical assessment. Musical examples.

MACHAUT, GUILLAUME DE, c. 1300-1377

General

Reaney, Gilbert. "Ars Nova in France," in The New Oxford
  History of Music. Vol. 3 (Ars Nova and the Renaissance).
  London: Oxford University Press, 1960, pp. 15-29.
  Masses, motets and secular polyphony of Machaut re-
  viewed. His harmony and stylistic traits examined.
  Musical examples.

MAHLER, GUSTAV, 1860-1911

General

Gartenberg, Egon. Mahler: The Man and His Music. New
    York: Schirmer Books, 1978, 406p. Brief historical and
    critical remarks on specific works. For the student.
    Use index to locate discussion of specific works.
Mitchell, Donald. Gustav Mahler: The Wunderhorn Years.
    Boulder, Colo.: Westview Press, 1975, 461p. Scholarly
    presentation. Full compositional background and discus-
    sion of the music. Musical examples.

Ballads

Kravitt, E. F. "The ballad as conceived by Germanic com-
    posers of the late romantic period," Studies in Romanti-
    cism 12:2 (1973), 499-515. The attraction of the roman-
    tic ballad to composers such as Mahler, Wolf and Strauss.
    Discusses their techniques of word-painting. Musical ex-
    amples.

Songs

Barford, Philip. Mahler Symphonies and Songs. Seattle:
    University of Washington Press, 1970, 64p. Brief criti-
    cal remarks with musical examples. Intended for student.
Kravitt, E. F. "The orchestral lied: an inquiry into its
    style and unexpected flowering around 1900," Music Re-
    view 37:3 (1976), 209-226. The need for greater subtlety
    and nuance of expression seen as a reason for the flower-
    ing of the orchestral lied. Some musical effects exam-
    ined. Musical examples.
Roman, Z. "Structure as a factor in the genesis of Mahler's
    songs," Music Review 35:2 (1974), 157-166. Structural
    points emphasized to show Mahler's approach to text.
    Musical examples.

Das Klagende Lied

Diether, J. "Mahler's 'Klagende Lied'--genesis and evolu-
    tion," Music Review 29:4 (1968), 268-287. Background
    and conception of the "Klagende Lied." Some discussion
    of the music. Musical examples.
La Grange, Henry-Louis de. Mahler. New York: Double-
    day, 1973, I, pp. 735-738. Background with descriptive
    and analytic remarks. No musical examples.

Des Knaben Wunderhorn

La Grange, Henry-Louis de. Mahler. New York: Doubleday, 1973, I, pp. 758-780. Thorough, methodical treatment. Background, form and other pertinent information
with musical examples.

Das Lied von der Erde

Gartenberg, Egon. Mahler: The Man and His Music. New
York: Schirmer Books, 1978, pp. 336-346. Descriptive
and critical discussion with musical examples.
Tischler, Hans. The Perceptive Music Listener. Englewood Cliffs, N. J. : Prentice-Hall, 1955, pp. 166-172.
Descriptive and analytic commentary with emphasis on
form. Musical examples.

Lieder eines fahrenden Gesellen

La Grange, Henry-Louis de. Mahler. New York: Doubleday, 1973, I, pp. 741-746. Full background with analytic
insights. No musical examples.

MARENZIO, LUCA, 1553-1599

Madrigals

Dent, E. J. "The sixteenth century madrigal," in The New
Oxford History of Music. Vol. 4, (The Age of Humanism). London: Oxford University Press, 1968, pp. 62-
67. Brief examination of Marenzio's place and stylistic
characteristics. Musical examples.
Einstein, Alfred. The Italian Madrigal. Translated by
Alexander H. Krappe, Roger H. Sessions, and Oliver
Strunk. Princeton, N. J. : Princeton University Press,
1949, Vol. II, pp. 608-688. Excellent discourse for the
more advanced student. Musical examples.

MENDELSSOHN, FELIX, 1809-1847

General

Radcliffe, Philip. Mendelssohn. London: Dent, 1954,
pp. 117-144. Critical overview for the student. Musical
examples.

Werner, Eric. Mendelssohn. Translated from the German
by Dika Newlin. London: Free Press of Glencoe, 1963,
545p. Thorough, analytic discussion of the music. Musical examples. Use index to locate discussion of specific works.

Choral Music

Werner, E. "Mendelssohn's choral music," American Choral Review 7:2 (1964), 1-4. Descriptive and critical
commentary with musical examples.

Elijah

Mintz, D. "Mendelssohn's 'Elijah' reconsidered," Studies
in Romanticism 3:1 (1963), 1-9. Discussion centering on
text and musical style. No musical examples.
Werner, Jack. Mendelssohn's "Elijah." London: Chappell
& Co., 1965, 109p. Background, performance history,
analyses of all the movements and revisions. Musical
examples.

MESSIAEN, OLIVIER, 1908-

General

Johnson, Robert Sherlaw. Messiaen. Berkeley: University
of California Press, 1975, 221p. Full-length book on all
of Messiaen's music. Very thorough with charts, diagrams and musical examples.
Nichols, Roger. Messiaen. London: Oxford University
Press, 1975, 79p. Critical commentary intended for the
student. Musical examples.

MONTEVERDI, CLAUDIO, 1567-1643

General

Arnold, Denis. Monteverdi. London: Dent, 1963, 212p.
Descriptive and critical commentary with historical perspective. For the student. Musical examples.
Fortune, N. "Duet and trio in Monteverdi," Musical Times
108 (May 1967), 417-419+. An examination of Monteverdi's
writing in polyphonic textures as opposed to the fashion-
able monodic style of the time. Musical examples.

Prunières, Henry. Monteverdi: His Life and Work. Translated from the French by Marie D. Mackie. New York: Dover, 1972, 293p. Easy-to-read discussion of the music and musical examples.

Stevens, D. "Monteverdi's Venetian church music," Musical Times 108 (May 1967), 414+. An overview with remarks on style. Musical examples.

Young, Percy M. The Choral Tradition. New York: Norton, 1971, pp. 61-68. Brief overview of the madrigals, masses and vespers. Musical examples.

Madrigals

Arnold, Denis. Monteverdi Madrigals. Seattle: University of Washington Press, 1967, 61p. Thorough critical and analytic discussion for the student. Musical examples.

Bukofzer, Manfred F. Music in the Baroque Era. New York: Norton, 1947, pp. 33-38. Brief commentary focusing on the changes that Monteverdi wrought on the madrigal form. Musical examples.

Dent, E. J. "The sixteenth century madrigal," in The New Oxford History of Music. Vol. 4 (The Age of Humanism). London: Oxford University Press, 1968, pp. 69-73. Brief overview focusing on stylistic characteristics. Musical examples.

Einstein, Alfred. The Italian Madrigal. Translated by Alexander H. Krappe, Roger H. Sessions, and Oliver Strunk. Princeton, N. J.: Princeton University Press, 1949, Vol. II, pp. 717-728; 850-872. Excellent discourse for the more advanced student. Musical examples.

Reese, Gustave. Music in the Renaissance. revised edition. New York: Norton, 1959, pp. 437-443. Detailed descriptive overview with musical examples.

Messa a 4 voci da capella

Brindle, R. S. "Monteverdi's G minor mass: an experiment in construction," Musical Quarterly 54:3 (1968), 352-360. Criticism and analysis with musical examples.

Messe et Salmi

Roche, H. "Monteverdi--an interesting example of second thoughts," Music Review 32:3 (1971), 193-204. Background, descriptive and critical commentary. Musical examples.

Vespro della Beata Vergine

Bonta, S. "Liturgical problems in Monteverdi's 'Marian
Vespers,'" Journal of the American Musicological Society
20:1 (1967), 87-106. Advanced discussion. Musical examples.

MOZART, WOLFGANG AMADEUS, 1756-1791

General

Blom, Eric. Mozart. London: Dent, 1935, pp. 167-188.
Critical overview for student or musical amateur. Musi-
cal examples.
Einstein, Alfred. Mozart: His Character, His Work.
Translated by Arthur Mendel and Nathan Broder. London:
Oxford University Press, 1945, pp. 319-380. Survey,
descriptive commentary and observations on style. Mu-
sical examples.
Landon, H. C. Robbins and Donald Mitchell. The Mozart
Companion. New York: Norton, 1956, pp. 324-376.
Concise analytic survey of the concert arias and church
music. Musical examples.
Olleson, Edward. "Church music and oratorio," in The
New Oxford History of Music, Vol. 7 (The Age of En-
lightenment). London: Oxford University Press, 1973,
pp. 359-363. Brief remarks on Mozart's lieder and
concert arias. Musical examples.

Coronation Mass K. 317

Young, Percy M. The Choral Tradition. New York: Norton, 1971, pp. 168-170. Brief descriptive remarks.
Musical examples.

Requiem

Blume, F. "Requiem but no peace," Musical Quarterly
47:2 (1961), 147-169. Scholarly discourse on authenticity.
Not an analytic discussion.
Robertson, Alec. Requiem: Music of Mourning and Consolation. New York: Praeger, 1968, pp. 64-74. Thorough
background and extensive discussion of the music. Musical examples.
Vanson, F. "Mozart's final masterpiece: the Requiem in
D minor, K. 626," Choir 55 (Aug. 1964), 146-147.

Background and brief critical commentary. No musical
examples.
Young, Percy M. The Choral Tradition. New York: Norton, 1971, pp. 178-182. Brief background and descriptive
commentary. No musical examples.

MUSSORGSKY, MODEST, 1839-1881

General

Calvocoressi, M. D. Modest Mussorgsky. London:
Rockliff, 1956, 322p. Mussorgsky's technique, influences
and musical style discussed. Musical examples.
Calvocoressi, M. D. Musorgsky. Translated by A. Eaglefield Hull. London: Kegan Paul, n. d. , pp. 91-133. An
earlier work by the same author listed here. Musical
examples.
Calvocoressi, M. D. Mussorgsky. London: Dent, 1946,
pp. 62-94; 181-183. Critical discussion intended for student. Musical examples.

Songs and Dances of Death

Midlaugh, B. "Modeste Mussorgsky's 'Songs and Dances of
Death, '" NATS 26:2 (1969), 2+. Critical and analytic
commentary. Musical examples.

OCKEGHEM, JOHANNES, c. 1425-1495

General

Bridgman, Nanie. "The Age of Ockeghem and Josquin," in
The New Oxford History of Music Vol. 3 (Ars Nova and
the Renaissance). London: Oxford University Press,
1960, pp. 239-260. Overview of Ockeghem's place,
forms used, musical style and influence. Musical examples.

PALESTRINA, GIOVANNI, 1526-1594

General

Coates, Henry. Palestrina. London: Dent, 1948, 243p.
Critical guide for the student or musical amateur. Musical examples.

Coates, Henry and Gerald Abraham. "The perfection of the
a capella style," in The New Oxford History of Music.
Vol. 4 (The Age of Humanism). London: Oxford University Press, 1968, pp. 312-333. Palestrina's style,
masses and motets examined. Musical examples.
Reese, Gustave. Music in the Renaissance. revised edition.
New York: Norton, 1959, 455-481. Detailed descriptive
overview with musical examples.

Masses

Marshall, R. L. "The paraphrase technique of Palestrina
in his Masses based on hymns," Journal of the American
Musicological Society 16:3 (1963), 347-372. Learned discussion on the use of borrowed themes. Musical examples.

POULENC, FRANCIS, 1899-1963

Songs

Bernac, Pierre. Francis Poulenc: The Man and His Songs.
Translated by Winifred Radford. New York: Norton,
1977, 233p. Descriptive and analytic commentary on all
the songs. No musical examples.
Bernac, P. "The songs of Francis Poulenc," NATS 21:3
(1965), 2-6. Extensive critical commentary with catalog
of songs of Poulenc. No musical examples.

PURCELL, HENRY, c. 1659-1695

General

Arundell, Dennis Drew. Henry Purcell. Plainview, N. Y. :
Books for Libraries, 1970, 135p. Descriptive and criti-
cal commentary with musical examples.
Holland, Arthur Keith. Henry Purcell. Plainview, N. Y. :
Books for Libraries, 1970, pp. 107-191. General dis-
cussion focusing on style and poetic materials used as
text. Musical examples.
Westrup, J. A. Purcell. London: Dent, 1960, 323p.
Descriptive, critical and analytic remarks for the student.
Musical examples.

RACHMANINOFF, SERGEI, 1873-1943

Songs

Culshaw, John. Rachmaninov. New York: Oxford University Press, 1950, pp. 120-137. Full discussion of the songs with numerous musical examples.

RAVEL, MAURICE, 1875-1937

General

Myers, Rollo H. Ravel: Life and Works. New York: Thomas Yoseloff, 1960, pp. 116-152. Background and descriptive commentary with musical examples.
Nichols, Roger. Ravel. London: Dent, 1977, 199p. Descriptive and critical commentary for the student. Musical examples.
Orenstein, Arbie. Ravel: Man and Musician. New York: Columbia University Press, 1975, 291p. Brief, program-note commentaries. No musical examples.

Songs

Demuth, Norman. Ravel. London: Dent, 1947, pp. 93-104. Descriptive and critical commentary for the student. Musical examples.
Stuckenschmidt, H. H. Maurice Ravel. Translated from the German by Samuel R. Rosenbaum. Philadelphia: Chilton, 1968, 271p. Mainly background and description, but some critical observations. No musical examples.

ROUSSEL, ALBERT, 1869-1937

General

Deane, Basil. Albert Roussel. London: Barrie and Rockliff, 1961, pp. 132-149. Overview with musical examples.

SAINT-SAËNS, CAMILLE, 1835-1921

General

Hervey, Arthur. Saint-Saëns. Plainview, N.Y.: Books

for Libraries, 1969, pp. 115-124. A brief overview of
the Masses, Oratorios and Cantatas. No musical examples.
Lyle, Watson. Camille Saint-Saëns. Westport, Conn.:
Greenwood, 1970, pp. 171-176. Brief remarks. No
musical examples.

SCHOENBERG, ARNOLD, 1874-1951

General

MacDonald, Malcolm. Schoenberg. London: Dent, 1976,
pp. 95-110; 167-181. The choral music and songs discussed. Written for the student. Musical examples.
Reich, Willi. Schoenberg: A Critical Biography. Translated by Leo Black. London: Longman, 1968, 268p.
Descriptive and critical. No musical examples.
Wellesz, Egon. Arnold Schoenberg. Translated by W. H.
Kerridge. New York: Da Capo Press, 1969, pp. 59-
154. An overview of Schoenberg's music, including vocal
works. Written in an easy to read style. Musical examples.

Choral Music

Newlin, D. "Arnold Schoenberg as a choral composer,"
American Choral Review 6:4 (1964), 1+. Descriptive
and critical overview. No musical examples.

Songs

Bunting, R. L. "Arnold Schoenberg's songs with piano accompaniment," NATS 27:1 (1970), 26-31. Compact analytic discussion with musical examples. Advanced.

Pierrot Lunaire

Ferguson, Donald N. Image and Structure in Chamber
Music. Minneapolis: University of Minnesota Press,
1964, pp. 309-320. Brief analysis with text translated
into English. No musical examples.
Keller, H. "Whose fault is the speaking voice," Tempo 75
(Winter 1965-1966), 12-17. The relationship of atonality
to the speaking voice part in Pierrot. No musical examples.
Klein, L. "Twentieth-century analysis: essays in minia-

ture, " Music Educators Journal 53 (Feb. 1967), 115-116.
Analytic commentary for the beginning student. No musical examples.
Whittall, Arnold. Schoenberg Chamber Music. Seattle:
University of Washington Press, 1972, pp. 27-31. Descriptive and analytic commentary for the student. Musical examples.

SCHUBERT, FRANZ, 1797-1828

General

Abraham, Gerald, ed. The Music of Schubert. New York:
Norton, 1947, pp. 149-197; 217-233. Thorough critical
discussion with musical examples.
Bie, Oscar. Schubert: The Man. New York: Dodd, Mead,
1928, pp. 80-122; 176-215. Somewhat subjective descriptive commentary. Musical examples.
Brown, Maurice J. E. Schubert: A Critical Biography.
London: Macmillan, 1961, 414p. Descriptive and critical
commentary with musical examples. Use index to locate
discussion of specific works.
Duncan, Edmondstoune. Schubert. London: Dent, 1934,
pp 118-146. Critical commentary intended for student
or musical amateur. Concise and easy to read. Musical examples.
Einstein, Alfred. Schubert: A Musical Portrait. New
York: Oxford University Press, 1951, 343p. Thorough,
learned discourse with musical examples. Use index to
locate discussion of specific works.
Gal, Hans. Franz Schubert and the Essence of Melody.
London: Gollancz, 1974, 205p. Descriptive, critical and
analytic. A thorough discussion of Schubert's musical
process. Musical examples.
Hutchings, Arthur. Schubert. London: Dent, 1945,
pp. 129-138. Descriptive and critical with musical examples. For the student.

Songs

Brown, Maurice J. E. Essays on Schubert. New York:
St. Martin's, 1966, pp. 59-84. In-depth discussion with
musical examples. Deals with part-songs for male voices
only.
Capell, Richard. Schubert's Songs. New York: Macmillan,
1957, 292p. Thorough critical and analytic treatment
with musical examples.

Duschak, A. G. "The influence of the songs of Franz
  Schubert," NATS 29:2 (1972), 30-31+. Survey of Schubert's influence on Schumann, Wagner and others. Certain stylistic and musical techniques examined. Musical
  examples.
Fischer-Dieskau, Dietrich. Schubert's Songs. Translated
  from the German by Kenneth S. Shitton. New York:
  Knopf, 1977, 33p. A thorough overview of all the songs.
  Much background and description with some analytic remarks. No musical examples.
Gray, W. "The classical nature of Schubert's lieder,"
  Musical Quarterly 57:1 (1971), 62-72. Emphasis placed
  on classical traits of form and objectivity in the songs,
  rather than the customary emphasis on romantic traits.
Kinsey, B. "Schubert and the poems of Ossian," Music Review 34:1 (1973), 22-29. Descriptive and analytic commentary. Musical examples.
Newton, G. "The songs of Franz Schubert," NATS 22:1
  (1965), 4-7. Background and descriptive commentary
  with special mention of the appoggiaturas in Schubert's
  songs. Musical examples.
Stein, J. M. "Schubert's Heine songs," Journal of Aesthetics and Art Criticism, 24:4 (1966), 559-566. Advanced
  discussion of the relationship of text and music. Musical
  examples.
Thomas, J. H. "Schubert's modified strophic songs with
  particular reference to Schwanengesang," Music Review
  34:2 (1973), 83-99. Advanced discussion on form and
  tonality in the strophic songs. Musical examples.

Erlkönig

Chittum, D. "Music theory and interpretation," American
  Music Teacher 17:4 (1968), 31+. Brief analysis intended
  for student. No musical examples.

Die schöne Müllerin

Pazur, R. "An interpretation of the pitch-structure of 'Die
  schoene Muellerin,'" In Theory Only 1 (Sept. 1975), 9-13.
  Advanced analytic discussion. Musical examples.

Schwanengesang

Kerman, J. "A romantic detail in Schubert's 'Schwanengesang,'" Musical Quarterly 48:1 (1962), 36-49. Close
  analytic discussion on word-painting techniques and other
  musical traits. Musical examples.

Die Winterreise

Greene, D. B. "Schubert's 'Winterreise': a study in the
aesthetics of mixed media," Journal of Aesthetics and
Art Criticism 29:2 (1970), 181-193. Advanced discussion
of relationship of text and musical form. Word-painting
also examined. Musical examples.
Kerman, Joseph. Listen. second edition. New York:
Worth Publishers, 1976, pp. 211-213. Background and
analysis with musical examples. For the student.
Marshall, H. L. "Symbolism in Schubert's 'Winterreise,'"
Studies in Romanticism 12:3 (1973), 607-632. Thorough
accounting of word-painting effects and symbols used to
portray text. Musical examples.

SCHUMANN, ROBERT, 1810-1856

General

Abraham, Gerald, ed. Schumann: A Symposium. London:
Oxford University Press, 1952, pp. 98-137; 283-299.
Thorough discussions of the songs and choral works by
exponents in the field. Musical examples.
Chissell, Joan. Schumann. London: Dent, 1967, pp. 122
135; 169-189. Critical discussion with musical examples.
For the student.
Schauffler, Robert Haven. Florestan: The Life and Work
of Robert Schumann. New York: Dover, 1963, pp. 369-
388; 433-438. Easy-to-read critical remarks with musical examples.
Walker, Alan, ed. Robert Schumann: The Man and His
Music. London: Barrie & Jenkins, 1972, pp. 120-161;
350-389. Thorough discussions of the songs and choral
works by leading scholars. Musical examples.

Songs

Sams, Eric. The Songs of Robert Schumann. New York:
Norton, 1969, 293p. Descriptive and analytic commentary
on each song. Musical examples.
Walsh, Stephen. The Lieder of Schumann. London: Cassell, 1971, 128p. Thorough critical and analytic discussion. Musical examples.

Dichterliebe

Large, J. and K. Weissenberger. "The irony of the allu-

sions in 'Dichterliebe,'" NATS 27:1 (1970), 22-25. Clues
to the interpretation of Heine's lyrics found in his allusions to specific objects. Not a discussion of the music.

Frauenliebe und Leben

Tischler, Hans. The Perceptive Music Listener. Englewood Cliffs, N.J.: Prentice-Hall, 1955, pp. 157-166.
Analytic commentary with emphasis on form. Musical
examples.

SCHÜTZ, HEINRICH, 1585-1672

General

Bukofzer, Manfred F. Music in the Baroque Era. New
York: Norton, pp. 88-95. Brief overview focusing on
formal and stylistic characteristics as well as Schütz's
place in music history. Musical examples.
Gerold, Theodore. "Protestant music on the continent,"
The New Oxford History of Music. Vol. 4 (The Age of
Humanism). London: Oxford University Press, 1968,
pp. 461-464. Brief assessment of Schütz's place in
musical history and his unique contribution. Musical
examples.
Moser, Hans Joachim. Heinrich Schütz: A Short Account
of His Life and Works. Translated and edited by Derek
McCulloch. New York: St. Martin's, 1967, 120p.
Same author cited here, but much briefer treatment.
Musical examples.
Moser, Hans Joachim. Heinrich Schütz: His Life and
Work. Translated from the second revised edition by
Carl F. Pfatteicher. St. Louis: Concordia, 1959, 740p.
Extensive commentary with musical examples.
Palisca, Glaude V. Baroque Music. Englewood Cliffs,
N.J.: Prentice-Hall, 1968, pp. 93-102. Concise sum-
mation with remarks on specific musical features. Musi-
cal examples.
Young, Percy M. The Choral Tradition. New York: Nor-
ton, 1971, pp. 68-74. Brief overview of the Psalms,
Seven Last Words and Passions. Musical examples.

Motets

Steinitz, Paul. "German Church Music," in The New Oxford History of Music. Vol. 5 (Opera and Church Music).

London: Oxford University Press, 1975, pp. 665-668.
Schütz's unique achievement in this form concisely described. Musical examples.

Passions

Steinitz, Paul. "German Church Music, " in The New Ox-
ford History of Music. Vol. 5 (Opera and Church Music).
London: Oxford University Press, 1975, pp. 625-628.
Brief critical evaluation with musical examples.

Cantiones Sacrae

Bray, R. "The 'Cantiones Sacrae' of Heinrich Schütz re-
examined, " Music & Letters 52:3 (1971), 299-305.
Stylistic traits examined. Musical examples.

Magnificat

Steinitz, Paul. "German Church Music, " in The New Ox-
ford History of Music. Vol. 5 (Opera and Church Music).
London: Oxford University Press, 1975, pp. 600-604.
Examination of Schütz's setting. Musical examples.

Musikalische Exequien

Robertson, Alec. Requiem: Music of Mourning and Consolation. New York: Praeger, 1968, pp. 171-175. Descriptive and critical commentary with musical examples.

Psalmen Davids, op. 2

Arnold, D. "Schütz's 'Venetian' psalms, " Musical Times
113 (Nov. 1972), 1071-1073. Descriptive and analytic
remarks. Musical examples.

                    SIBELIUS, JEAN, 1865-1957

General

Abraham, Gerald, ed. The Music of Sibelius. New York:
Norton, 1947, pp. 108-140. Thorough overview. Descriptive and critical with musical examples. Discussion
of Sibelius' musical style in another chapter.
Layton, Robert. Sibelius. London: Dent, 1965, pp. 107-
134. Overview with descriptive and critical commentary
intended for student. Musical examples.

STRAUSS, RICHARD, 1864-1949

General

Del Mar, Norman. Richard Strauss. New York: Free
Press of Glencoe, 1962, 3 vols. Exhaustive critical
commentary with musical examples. Use index to locate
discussion of specific works.
Kennedy, Michael. Richard Strauss. London: Dent, 1976,
pp. 206-218. Brief review of Strauss' output in this
medium. Musical examples.

Songs

Jefferson, Alan. The Lieder of Richard Strauss. London:
Cassell, 1971, 134p. Background and critical commentary
with musical examples.

STRAVINSKY, IGOR, 1882-1971

General

Friedberg, R. C. "The solo vocal works of Igor Stravinsky:
a review," NATS 23:1 (1966), 6-8+. An overview with
critical and analytic remarks. Musical examples. Cata-
log of solo works follows article.
Routh, Francis. Stravinsky. London: Dent, 1975, pp. 114-
129. Critical commentary with musical examples intended
for student.
Tansman, Alexandre. Igor Stravinsky: The Man and His
Music. Translated by Therese and Charles Bleefield.
New York: Putnam's, 1949, 295p. Easy-to-read de-
scriptive and critical summation with musical examples.
Use index to locate discussion of specific works.
Vlad, Roman. Stravinsky. Translated from the Italian by
Frederick and Ann Fuller. second edition. London:
Oxford University Press, 1967, 264p. Critical and
analytic overview with musical examples. Use index to
locate discussion of specific works.
White, Eric Walter. Stravinsky: The Composer and His
Works. Berkeley: University of California Press, 1966,
608p. Critical and analytic remarks with musical exam-
ples. Use index to locate discussion of specific works.

In Memoriam Dylan Thomas

Robertson, Alec. Requiem: Music of Mourning and Consola-

tion. New York: Praeger, 1968, pp. 220-225. Descriptive and analytic commentary. Musical examples.

Introitus

Spies, C. "Some notes on Stravinsky's Requiem settings,"
Perspectives of New Music 5:2 (1967), 98-123. Advanced
analysis with musical examples.
White, E. W. "Two new memorial works by Stravinsky,"
Tempo 74 (Autumn 1965), 20-21. Brief remarks with
musical examples.

Requiem Canticles

Salzman, E. "Stravinsky's 'Requiem Canticles,'" Musical
Quarterly 53:1 (1976), 80-86. Analytic commentary with
musical examples.
Souvtchinsky, P. "Thoughts on Stravinsky's 'Requiem
Canticles,'" Tempo 86 (Autumn 1968), 6-7. Brief critical remarks. No musical examples.
White, E. W. "Stravinsky's 'Requiem Canticles,'" Tempo
79 (Winter 1966-1967), 10-19. Thorough analysis with
musical examples. Advanced.

A Sermon, a Narrative and a Prayer

Boykan, M. "Neoclassicism and late Stravinsky," Perspectives of New Music 1:2 (1963), 166-169. Advanced analytic remarks. Musical examples.
Mason, C. "Stravinsky's new work," Tempo 59 (Autumn
1961), 5-14. Thorough analysis with musical examples.
Advanced.
Morton, L. "Ojai, California," Musical Quarterly 48:3
(1962), 392-396. Analytic remarks with musical examples.
Wilkey, J. W. "Igor Stravinsky's cantata, 'A Sermon, a
Narrative, and a Prayer,'" Choral Journal 10:2 (1969),
14-19. Analysis with musical examples.

T. S. Eliot: In Memoriam

White, E. W. "Two new memorial works by Stravinsky,"
Tempo 74 (Autumn 1965), 20-21. Brief remarks with
musical examples.

3 Songs from William Shakespeare

Hantz, Edwin. "Exempli gratia: What you hear is what you

get, " In Theory Only 2 (April-May 1976), 51-54.   Advanced analytic commentary.   Musical examples.

TCHAIKOVSKY, PETER ILITCH, 1840-1893

General

Abraham, Gerald, ed. The Music of Tchaikovsky.   New
York: Norton, 1946, pp. 197-235. Thorough discussion
with musical examples.

Songs

Garden, Edward. Tchaikovsky. London: Dent, 1973, 194p.
Brief critical remarks. No musical examples.

VAUGHAN WILLIAMS, RALPH, 1872-1958

General

Day, James. Vaughan Williams. London: Dent, 1961,
pp. 97-107. Brief review of Vaughan Williams' small
output in this medium. Musical examples.
Dickinson, A. E. F. Vaughan Williams. London: Faber &
Faber, 1963, 540p. Analytic commentary with musical
examples.
Howes, Frank. The Music of Ralph Vaughan Williams.
London: Oxford University Press, 1954, pp. 123-186.
Full discussion with musical examples.
Kennedy, Michael. The Works of Ralph Vaughan Williams.
London: Oxford University Press, 1964, 776p. Descrip-
tive commentary with observations on style. Musical ex-
amples.

VERDI, GIUSEPPE, 1813-1901

Requiem

Robertson, Alec. Requiem: Music of Mourning and Consola-
tion. New York: Praeger, 1968, pp. 96-110. Background
and extensive discussion of the music. Musical examples.
Rosen, D. "Verdi's 'Liber Scriptus' rewritten, " Musical
Quarterly 55:2 (1969), 151-169. The musical reasons for
Verdi's rewriting of the 'Liber Scriptus. '

Tovey, Donald Francis. Essays in Musical Analysis. London: Oxford University Press, 1937, Vol. II, pp. 195-209. Thorough analytic and critical commentary for the informed student. Musical examples.

Young, Percy M. The Choral Tradition. New York: Norton, 1971, 248-256. Background and full descriptive commentary with musical examples.

WEBERN, ANTON, 1883-1945

General

Kolneder, Walter. Anton Webern: An Introduction to His Works. Translated by Humphrey Searle. Berkeley: University of California Press, 1968, 232p. Clear analytic and critical discussions with musical examples. Use index to locate discussion of specific work.

Moldenhauer, Hans, comp. Anton von Webern: Perspectives. Seattle: University of Washington Press, 1966, pp. 53-77. Advanced discussion on the Dehmel Lieder of 1906-1908 and Webern's technique of choral composition. Musical examples.

Songs

Charles, H. "The posthumous songs of Anton Webern," NATS 28:1 (1971), 21-23+. Critical and analytic commentary with musical examples.

Canon for Voice and Clarinet, op. 16

Whittall, A. "A simple case of variation," Musical Times 108 (April 1967), 320-321. Analysis with musical examples.

Cantata no. 1, op. 29

Kramer, J. "The row as structural background and audible foreground; the first movement of Webern's First Cantata," Journal of Music Theory 15:1-2 (1971), 158-181. Highly advanced analysis.

Saturen, D. "Symmetrical relationships in Webern's First cantata," Perspectives of New Music 5:3 (1967), 142-143. Advanced analysis with musical examples.

Drei Lieder (Three Songs), op. 25

Chittum, D. "Some observations on the row technique in
   Webern's Opus 25," Current Musicology 12 (1971), 96-
   101. Analytic commentary. Advanced. Musical examples.
Lewin, D. "Some applications of communication theory to
   the study of twelve-tone music," Journal of Music Theory
   12:1 (1968), 76-80. Highly complex analysis of number
   one of this opus.
Sturhahn, G. E. "An aesthetic evaluation of Anton Webern's
   'Drei Lieder,' op. 25," NATS 25:4 (1969), 34-36. Critical and analytic commentary with musical examples.

Fünf Lieder (Five Songs), op. 3

Raney, C. "Atonality and serialism: a comparison of
   Webern's opus 2 and opus 23," NATS 25:1 (1968), 12+.
   Analytic commentary with musical examples.

WOLF, HUGO, 1860-1903

General

Newman, Ernest. Hugo Wolf. New York: Dover, 1966,
   pp. 153-225. Full critical discussion with musical examples.
Walker, Frank. Hugo Wolf: A Biography. New York:
   Knopf, 1968, 522p. Mainly a biography, but many critical observations interspersed. Musical examples. Use
   index to locate specific works.

Ballads

Kravitt, E. F. "The ballad as conceived by Germanic
   composers of the late romantic period," Studies in Romanticism 12:2 (1973), 499-515. The attraction of the romantic ballad to composers such as Mahler, Wolf and Strauss.
   Discusses their technique of word-painting.

Orchestra lied

Kravitt, E. F. "The orchestra lied: an inquiry into its
   style and unexpected flowering around 1900," Music Review 37:3 (1976), 209-226. The need for greater nuance
   of expression seen as a reason for the flowering of the

orchestral lied.   Some musical effects examined.   Musical examples.

Songs

Sams, Eric.   The Songs of Hugo Wolf.   London: Methuen
&   Co. ,   1961,   268p.   Descriptive and analytic commentary
on each song.   Musical examples.

Kennst du das Land?

Ivey, D.   "Comparative analysis--an approach to style,"
NATS 22:2 (1965),   18-21.   A stylistic comparison of
settings of Goethe's lyrics by Wolf, Schubert, Schumann
and Liszt.   No musical examples.

Mörike Lieder

Stein, J. M.   "Poem and music in Hugo Wolf's 'Mörike'
Songs," Musical Quarterly 53:1 (1967), 22-38.   Thorough critical treatment of the relationship of music and
text.   Musical examples.

CHAPTER IV: ORCHESTRAL MUSIC

BACH, JOHANN SEBASTIAN, 1685-1750

Suite for Orchestra no. 1, C major, S. 1066

Morehen, J. "J. S. Bach: Overture no. 1 in C major,"
  Music Teacher 54 (Aug. 1975), 13-14. Analysis. Intermediate level. No musical examples.
Schmidt, H. "Bach's C major orchestral suite: a new
  look at possible origins," Music & Letters 57:2 (1976),
  152-163. Some themes of the Suite traced to earlier
  works. Musical examples.
Tovey, Donald Francis. Essays in Musical Analysis. London: Oxford University Press, 1969, Vol. VI, pp. 1-7.
  Critical and analytic, with musical examples. For the
  student.

Suite for Orchestra no. 3, D major, S. 1068

Pilgrim, J. "J. S. Bach: Overture no. 3 in D major,"
  Music Teacher 53 (July 1974), 18-19. Analysis. Intermediate. No musical examples.

BALAKIREV, MILY, 1837-1910

Overtures

Garden, Edward. Balakirev. New York: St. Martin's,
  1967, pp. 159-175. Analyses of all Balakirev's overtures. Musical examples.

Symphonic Poems

Garden, Edward. Balakirev. New York: St. Martin's,
  1967, pp. 176-194. Analyses of all Balakirev's symphonic poems. Musical examples.

BARBER, SAMUEL, 1910-

General

Broder, Nathan. Samuel Barber. New York: G. Schirmer,
1954, pp. 88-97. Analytic remarks with musical examples.

BARTOK, BELA, 1881-1945

Concerto for Orchestra

French, G. G. "Continuity and Discontinuity in Bartók's
Concerto for Orchestra," Music Review 28:2 (1967), 122-
134. Thorough analysis focusing on psychological cohe-
sion of the work. No musical examples.
Machlis, Joseph. Introduction to Contemporary Music. New
York: Norton, 1961, pp. 191-194. Brief descriptive
commentary with musical examples. For the beginning
student.
Suchoff, Benjamin, ed. Béla Bartók Essays. New York:
St. Martin's, 1976, p. 431. Bartók's own brief analysis.
No musical examples.

Music for Strings, Percussion and Celesta

Chittum, D. "The synthesis of materials and devices in
non-serial counterpoint," Music Review 31:2 (1970), 130-
135. Analysis. Intermediate. Musical examples.
Deri, Otto. Exploring Twentieth-Century Music. New York:
Holt, Rinehart and Winston, 1968, pp. 251-256. Analysis
with musical examples. For the intermediate student.
Hansen. Peter S. An Introduction to Twentieth Century Music.
second edition. Boston: Allyn & Bacon, 1967, pp. 242-
245. Descriptive commentary with analytic insights. For
beginning student. Musical examples.
Machlis, Joseph. Introduction to Contemporary Music. New
York: Norton, 1961, pp. 194-196. Brief descriptive
commentary with musical examples. For the beginning
student.

BEETHOVEN, LUDWIG VAN, 1770-1827

General

Scherman, Thomas K. and Louis Biancolli, eds. The

Beethoven Companion. New York: Doubleday, 1972,
1230p. Program-note style commentary for the musical
amateur. An inclusive book dealing with (in this chapter)
overtures, ballet music, incidental music and other non-
symphonic orchestral music. No musical examples.

Overtures

Arnold, Denis and Nigel Fortune. The Beethoven Companion.
London: Faber & Faber, 1971, pp. 313-317. Brief over-
view, showing influence of Cherubini on Beethoven. Mu-
sical examples.
Fiske, Roger. Beethoven Concertos and Overtures. Seattle:
University of Washington Press, 1970, pp. 44-64.
Program-note style annotations giving background and
salient musical points. Musical examples.

Battle of Victoria

Misch, Ludwig. Beethoven Studies. Norman: University of
Oklahoma Press, 1953, pp. 153-166. A traditionally dis-
credited musical work placed in proper perspective. Musical examples.

Coriolan Overture, op. 62

Tovey, Donald Francis. Essays in Musical Analysis. London: Oxford University Press, 1969, Vol. IV, pp. 43-45.
Critical and analytic study with musical examples. For
the student.

Egmont Overture

Kerman, Joseph. Listen. second edition. New York:
Worth Publishers, 1976, pp. 198-199. Brief analysis
with musical examples. For the student.
Misch, Ludwig. Beethoven Studies. Norman: University
of Oklahoma Press, 1953, pp. 76-105. Survey of some
analytic views with emphasis on the thematic treatment.
Somewhat advanced. Musical examples.
Tovey, Donald Francis. Essays in Musical Analysis. Lon-
don: Oxford University Press, 1969, Vol. IV, pp. 45-47.
Critical and analytic commentary with musical examples.
For the student.

Fidelio Overture

Tovey, Donald Francis. Essays in Musical Analysis. Lon-

don: Oxford University Press, 1969, Vol. IV, pp. 41-43.
Brief critical and analytic remarks. Musical examples.
For the student.

Leonore Overtures

Misch, Ludwig. Beethoven Studies. Norman: University
of Oklahoma Press, 1953, pp. 139-152. Overview of
reasons for revisions and consequent four Leonore overtures. No musical examples.

Leonore Overture no. 1

Tovey, Donald Francis. Essays in Musical Analysis. Lon-
don: Oxford University Press, 1969, Vol. IV, pp. 40-41.
Brief critical and analytic remarks. Musical examples.
For the student.

Leonore Overtures 2 & 3

Tovey, Donald Francis. Essays in Musical Analysis. London: Oxford University Press, 1969, Vol. IV, pp. 28-40.
Critical and analytic study with musical examples. For
the student.

Overture in C major, "Zur Namensfeier," op. 115

Tovey, Donald Francis. Essays in Musical Analysis. London: Oxford University Press, 1969, Vol. IV, pp. 47-50.
Critical and analytic study with musical examples. For
the student. Beware of an error in Tovey, giving the
wrong opus number to this work.

BERG, ALBAN, 1885-1935

Three Orchestral Pieces, op. 6

Carner, Mosco. Alban Berg. New York: Holmes &
Meier, 1975, pp. 124-127. Background, description and
analytic remarks.
Redlich, H. F. Alban Berg: The Man and His Music.
London: John Calder; 1957, pp. 64-73. Background and
analytic remarks. Musical examples.
Reich, Willi. Alban Berg. Translated by Cornelius Cardew.
New York: Harcourt, Brace & World, 1965, pp. 114-115.
Brief analytic remarks on form. No musical examples.

BERLIOZ, HECTOR, 1803-1869

General

Primmer, Brian. The Berlioz Style. London: Oxford
University Press, 1973, 202p. Focuses on Berlioz's
style, as seen throughout his work. Melody, tonality,
harmony and influences are treated in separate chapters.
Musical examples.

Overtures

Dickinson, A. E. F. The Music of Berlioz. London:
Faber & Faber, 1972, pp. 159-175. Critical and analytic
remarks with musical examples.
MacDonald, Hugh. Berlioz Orchestra Music. London:
British Broadcasting Corp. , 1969, 64p. Analytic guide
for the student. Musical examples.

Beatrice et Benedict Overture

Tovey, Donald Francis. Essays in Musical Analysis. London: Oxford University Press, 1969, Vol. VI, pp. 53-54.
Critical and analytic with musical examples. For the
student.

Le Corsair Overture

Tovey, Donald Francis. Essays in Musical Analysis. London: Oxford University Press, 1969, Vol. VI, pp. 50-52.
Critical and analytic with musical examples. For the
student.

King Lear Overture

Tovey, Donald Francis. Essays in Musical Analysis. London: Oxford University Press, 1969, Vol. IV, pp. 82-86.
Critical and analytic study with musical examples. For
the student.

BIZET, GEORGES, 1838-1875

L'Arlésienne

Klein, J. W. "The centenary of Bizet's 'L'Arlésienne,'"
Music & Letters 53:4 (1972), 363-368. Background and
critical remarks. No musical examples.

BORODIN, ALEXANDER, 1833-1887

On the Steppes of Central Asia

Abraham, Gerald. Borodin: The Composer and His Music.
London: William Reeves, n. d. , pp. 56-62. Descriptive
commentary with musical examples.

BRAHMS, JOHANNES, 1833-1897

General

Horton, John. Brahms Orchestral Music. London: British
Broadcasting Corp. , 1968, 64p. Analytic guide for the
student. Musical examples.

Overtures

Niemann, Walter. Brahms. Translated from the German
by Catharine Alison Phillips. New York: Knopf,
pp. 307-310. Brief descriptive and critical commentary.
No musical examples.

Serenades

Niemann, Walter. Brahms. Translated from the German
by Catharine Alison Phillips. New York: Knopf,
pp. 302-306. Brief descriptive and critical commentary.
No musical examples.

Tragic Overture

Tovey, Donald Francis. Essays in Musical Analysis. London: Oxford University Press, 1969, Vol. VI, pp. 55-57.
Critical and analytic with musical examples. For the
student.

CARTER, ELLIOTT, 1908-

Variations for Orchestra

Machlis, Joseph. Introduction to Contemporary Music.
New York: Norton, 1961, pp. 592-594. Brief descrip-
tive and analytic commentary with musical examples.
For the beginning student.

COPLAND, AARON, 1900-

General

Smith, Julia. Aaron Copland. New York: Dutton, 1955,
   336p. Background, descriptive, critical and analytic
   commentary with musical examples. Easy to follow.
   See index for sections on specific works.

Appalachian Spring

Bruns, T. "An analysis of selected folk-style themes in
   the music of Bedrich Smetana and Aaron Copland," American Music Teacher 25:2 (1975), 8-10. Comparison of
   type and use of folk melody used in the Moldau and
   Appalachian Spring. Musical examples.
Machlis, Joseph. Introduction to Contemporary Music.
   New York: Norton, 1961, pp. 485-487. Brief descriptive remarks with musical examples. For the beginning
   student.

Connotations

Evans, P. "Copland's 'Connotations' for orchestra," Tempo
   64 (Spring 1963), 30-33. Analysis by same author cited
   elsewhere, but less complex and shorter. Musical examples.
Evans, P. "Copland on the serial road: an analysis of
   'Connotations,'" Perspectives of New Music 2:2 (1964),
   141-149. Analysis with musical examples. For the advanced student.

Inscape

Henderson, R. "Copland's 'Inscape,'" Tempo 87 (Winter
   1968-1969), 29-30. Brief, but solid analysis. No musical examples.

El salón México

Brown, A. "Copland: 'El salón México,'" Music Teacher
   55 (June 1976), 17-18. Analysis. No musical examples.
Cole, H. "Popular elements in Copland's music," Tempo
   95 (Winter 1970-1971), 6-10. Copland's sophisticated
   handling of popular music elements discussed. Musical
   examples.

DEBUSSY, CLAUDE, 1862-1918

General

Lockspeiser, Edward. Debussy. London: Dent, 1951,
pp. 182-203. Descriptive and critical commentary with
musical examples.

Nichols, Roger. Debussy. London: Oxford University
Press, 1973, 86p. A moderately technical discussion,
selecting works that best demonstrate Debussy's compositional techniques. Musical examples.

Thompson, Oscar. Debussy: Man and Artist. New York:
Dover, 1967, pp. 307-331. Background, critical and
analytic commentary. No musical examples.

Images for Orchestra: Ibéria

Machlis, Joseph. Introduction to Contemporary Music.
New York: Norton, 1961, pp. 129-130. Brief descriptive commentary with musical examples. For the beginning student.

Khamma

Orledge, R. "Debussy's orchestral collaborations," Musical
Times 116 (Jan. 1975), 30-31+. Debussy's collaboration
with Charles Koechlin on this tone poem. Musical examples.

Nocturnes

Kerman, Joseph. Listen. second edition. New York:
Worth Publishers, 1976, pp. 308-311. Background and
analysis with musical examples. For the student.

Prelude to the Afternoon of a Faun

Austin, William W. Debussy: Prelude to The Afternoon
of a Faun. (Norton Critical Scores). New York: Norton, 1971, 167p. Background, criticism and analysis
with actual score.

DELIUS, FREDERICK, 1862-1934

General

Hutchings, Arthur. Delius. London: Macmillan, 1949,

pp. 80-96. Excellent review of the orchestral works.
Mainly of a critical and descriptive nature. Musical
examples.
Jefferson, Alan. Delius. London: Dent, 1972, 179p.
Background, descriptive and critical commentary. Musical examples.
Palmer, Christopher. Delius: Portrait of a Cosmopolitan.
New York: Holmes & Meier, 1976, 199p. Music discussed from standpoint of influences that shaped Delius'
unique style. Discussion of individual works must be
found in index. Musical examples.
Warlock, Peter. Frederick Delius. New York: Oxford
University Press, 1952, pp. 99-119. General comments
of a descriptive and critical nature. Few musical examples.

DVORAK, ANTONIN, 1841-1904

General

Fischl, Viktor, ed. Antonin Dvořák: His Achievement.
Westport, Conn.: Greenwood, 1970, pp. 96-110. Overview with descriptive and critical remarks. No musical
examples.
Robertson, Alec. Dvořák. London: Dent, 1947, pp. 144-
156. Overview of the orchestral works with descriptive
and critical commentary. Musical examples.

ELGAR, EDWARD, 1857-1934

General

Parrot, Ian. Elgar. London: Dent, 1971, pp. 37-46; 56-
62. Much discussion of the Enigma Variations with speculation on the mysterious overall theme. Some remarks
on other orchestral works. Musical examples.
Young, Percy M. Elgar, O. M.: A Study of a Musician.
London: Collins, 1955, pp. 273-293. Review of Elgar's
orchestral works. Mainly descriptive with some critical
remarks. No musical examples.

Cockaigne Overture

Tovey, Donald Francis. Essays in Musical Analysis. London: Oxford University Press, 1969, Vol. IV, pp. 152-

154.   Critical and analytic study with musical examples.
For the student.

Concert Overture, "In the South"

Tovey, Donald Francis.   Essays in Musical Analysis.   London: Oxford University Press, 1969, Vol. VI, pp. 83-87.
Critical and analytic with musical examples.   For the
student.

Enigma Variations

Burley, Rosa and Frank C. Carruthers.   Edward Elgar:
The Record of a Friendship.   London: Barrie & Jenkins,
1972, pp. 116-129.   The circumstances of the composition of the 'Variations' with the commentary on each variation and the people represented.   No musical examples.
Kennedy, Michael.   Portrait of Elgar.   London: Oxford
University Press, 1968, pp. 55-75.   Thorough discussion
tracing the "friends" depicted in the variations.   Some
remarks on the music.   No musical examples.
Sams, Eric.   "Variations on an original theme (Enigma),"
Musical Times 111:1525 (March 1970), 258-262.   More
controversy over the key to Elgar's Enigma.   Possible
clues to mysterious overall theme.   Musical examples.
Tovey, Donald Francis.   Essays in Musical Analysis.   London: Oxford University Press, 1969, Vol. IV, pp. 149-
152.   Critical and analytic study with musical examples.
For the student.

Falstaff

Tovey, Donald Francis.   Essays in Musical Analysis.   London: Oxford University Press, 1969, Vol. IV, pp. 3-16.
Thorough critical and analytic study with musical exam-
ples.   For the student.

Introduction and Allegro for Strings

Tovey, Donald Francis.   Essays in Musical Analysis.   London: Oxford University Press, 1969, Vol. VI, pp. 87-89.
Critical and analytic with musical examples.   For the
student.

FALLA, MANUEL DE, 1876-1946

General

Demarquez, Suzanne. Manuel de Falla. Translated from
the French by Salvator Attanasio. Philadelphia: Chilton,
1968, 253p. Background, critical and analytic remarks.
Musical examples. See table of contents for discussion
of specific works.

FAURE, GABRIEL, 1845-1924

General

Suckling, Norman. Fauré. London: Dent, 1951, 229p.
Brief descriptive and critical remarks. Musical exam-
ples. See index for discussion of specific works.
Vuillermoz, Emile. Gabriel Fauré. Translated by Kenneth
Schapiro. Philadelphia: Chilton, 1969, 269p. Descrip-
tive and critical commentary. No musical examples.

FRANCK, CESAR, 1822-1890

General

Davies, Laurence. Franck. London: Dent, 1973, pp. 94-
104. Brief overview of the orchestral works with critical and analytic remarks. Musical examples.
Demuth, Norman. César Franck. London: Dennis Dobson,
n. d. , pp. 61-94. Descriptive, critical and analytic commentary. Musical examples.
Horton, John. César Franck. London: Oxford University
Press, 1948, pp. 28-41. Descriptive, critical and analytic commentary. Musical examples.
Vallas, Leon. César Franck. Translated by Hubert Foss.
New York: Oxford University Press, 1951, 283p. Descriptive, critical and analytic commentary. No musical
examples. See index for discussion of specific works.

GERSHWIN, GEORGE, 1898-1937

An American in Paris

Ewen, David. A Journey to Greatness: The Life and Music

of George Gershwin.   London: Allen, 1956, pp. 122-127.
Background and musical program.   No musical examples.
Goldberg, Isaac.   George Gershwin: A Study in American
    Music.   New York: Frederick Ungar, 1958, pp. 232-244.
    Background and descriptive commentary supported by
    musical examples.
Schwartz, Charles.   Gershwin: His Life and Music.   New
    York: Bobbs-Merrill, 1973, pp. 162-167.   Compositional
    history and analytic remarks.   No musical examples.

Rhapsody in Blue

Levine, H.   "Gershwin, Handy and the 'Blues,'" Clavier
    9:7 (1970), 10-20.   Specific examples of Handy's influence
    on Gershwin in the Rhapsody in Blue.   Musical examples.

GLUCK, CHRISTOPH WILLIBALD, 1714-1787

Iphigénie en Aulide Overture

Tovey, Donald Francis.   Essays in Musical Analysis.   Lon-
    don: Oxford University Press, 1969, Vol. VI, pp. 12-19.
    Critical and analytic remarks with musical examples.
    For the student.

Orpheus and Euridice Overture

Tovey, Donald Francis.   Essays in Musical Analysis.   Lon-
    don: Oxford University Press, 1969, Vol. VI, pp. 12-19.
    Critical and analytic remarks with musical examples.
    For the student.

GRIEG, EDVARD, 1843-1907

General

Abraham, Gerald, ed.   Grieg: A Symposium.   Norman:
    University of Oklahoma, 1950, pp. 16-25.   Descriptive
    and critical overview.
Finck, Henry T.   Grieg and His Music.   New York: Dodd,
    Mead, 1922, pp. 166-203.   Descriptive commentary.   No
    musical examples.
Horton, John.   Grieg.   London: Dent, 1974, pp. 149-164.
    Critical overview with musical examples.

HANDEL, GEORGE FRIDERIC, 1685-1759

General

Abraham, Gerald, ed. Handel: A Symposium. London:
Oxford University Press, 1954, pp. 200-232. Mainly a
discussion of concertos, but interspersed are comments
on Water Music and Fireworks. Musical examples.
Rolland, Romain. Handel. Translated by A. Eaglefield
Hull. New York: Henry Holt, 1916, pp. 181-202. Brief
overview focusing on stylistic characteristics and descriptive commentary. Musical examples.
Young, Percy M. Handel. London: Dent, 1961, pp. 104-
114. Not an in-depth discussion of specific works, but
more an examination of Handel's use of the orchestra.
Tone color, style, nuances, effects are commented upon.
Musical examples.

HINDEMITH, PAUL, 1895-1963

Mathis der Maler

Clendenin, W. R. "The spirit of Grünewald in Hindemith's
orchestral suite 'Mathis der Maler,'" American Music
Teacher 17:4 (1968), 16-18. Demonstrates how Hindemith
matches aspects of Grünewald's painting in his music.
No musical examples.
Hansen, Peter S. An Introduction to Twentieth Century
Music. second edition. Boston: Allyn & Bacon, 1967,
pp. 267-270. Descriptive commentary with analytic in-
sights. For the beginning student. Musical examples.
Machlis, Joseph. Introduction to Contemporary Music. New
York: Norton, 1961, pp. 204-208. Descriptive commen-
tary with musical examples. For the beginning student.

HOLST, GUSTAV, 1874-1934

General

Holst, Imogen. The Music of Gustav Holst. second edition.
London: Oxford University Press, 1968, 169p. Thorough discussion of all the music with a good section on
the Planets. Musical examples.

IVES, CHARLES EDWARD, 1874-1954

General

Cowell, Henry & Sidney. Charles Ives and His Music.
New York: Oxford University Press, 1955, 245p. Thorough discussion of Ives' music. See index for specific
works. Musical examples.
Echols, P. C. "The music for orchestra, " Music Educators
Journal 61 (Oct. 1974), 29-41. Overview with remarks
on style. Musical examples.
Perry, Rosalie Sandra. Charles Ives and the American
Mind. Kent, Ohio: Kent State University Press, 1974,
137p. Discussion of Ives' total output from standpoint of
its place in American culture. Musical examples.

Three Places in New England

Machlis, Joseph. Introduction to Contemporary Music. New
York: Norton, 1961, pp. 463-465. Brief descriptive
commentary with musical examples. For the beginning
student.

KODALY, ZOLTAN, 1882-1967

General

Eoszc, Laszlo. Zoltan Kodály: His Life and Works. London: Collet's, 1962, pp. 113-125. Critical and analytic.
Musical examples.

LISZT, FRANZ, 1811-1886

General

Beckett, Walter. Liszt. London: Dent, 1963, pp. 109-116.
Brief review, mainly of a descriptive nature. Musical
examples.
Searle, Humphrey. The Music of Liszt. second revised
edition. New York: Dover, 1966, 207p. Overview with
descriptive commentary. Musical examples.
Walker, Alan, ed. Franz Liszt: The Man and His Music.
New York: Taplinger, 1970, pp. 279-317. Thorough discussion. Descriptive, critical and analytic. Musical examples.

MENDELSSOHN, FELIX, 1809-1847

General

Jacob, Heinrich Eduard. Felix Mendelssohn and His Times.
Translated from the German by Richard and Clara Winston.
Westport, Conn.: Greenwood Press, 1973, 356p. Background, descriptive, critical and analytic commentary.
Musical examples. See index for discussion of specific
works.
Werner, Eric. Mendelssohn. Translated from the German
by Dika Newlin. New York: Free Press of Glencoe,
1963, 545p. Descriptive, critical, analytic. Musical examples. See index for discussion of specific works.

Hebrides Overture

Riedel, Johannes. Music of the Romantic Period. Dubuque,
Iowa: William C. Brown, 1969, pp. 43-44. Brief analytic description. No musical examples.
Tovey, Donald Francis. Essays in Musical Analysis. London: Oxford University Press, 1969, Vol. IV, pp. 90-93.
Critical and analytic study with musical examples. For
the student.

Melusine Overture

Tovey, Donald Francis. Essays in Musical Analysis. London: Oxford University Press, 1969, Vol. VI, pp. 37-40.
Critical and analytic with musical examples. For the
student.

Midsummer Night's Dream

Radcliffe, Philip. Mendelssohn. London: Dent, 1957,
pp. 148-149. Brief descriptive and critical remarks.
No musical examples.
Tovey, Donald Francis. Essays in Musical Analysis. London: Oxford University Press, 1969, Vol. IV, pp. 102-
109. Critical and analytic study with musical examples.
For the student.

Midsummer Night's Dream: Overture

Tovey, Donald Francis. Essays in Musical Analysis. London: Oxford University Press, 1969, Vol. IV, pp. 97-
102. Critical and analytic study with musical examples.
For the student.

Ruy Blas Overture

Laycock, R. "Score analysis--the Ruy Blas overture," The Instrumentalist 22 (May 1968), 96-99. Analysis with musical examples. Intended for the conductor, but useful for student.

Tovey, Donald Francis. Essays in Musical Analysis. London: Oxford University Press, 1969, Vol. IV, pp. 94-97. Critical and analytic study with musical examples. For the student.

MILHAUD, DARIUS, 1892-1974

Création du Monde

Hansen, Peter S. An Introduction to Twentieth Century Music. second edition. Boston: Allyn & Bacon, 1967, pp. 136-139. Descriptive commentary. For beginning student. Musical examples.

Machlis, Joseph. Introduction to Contemporary Music. New York: Norton, 1961, pp. 222-225. Descriptive commentary with musical examples. For the beginning student.

MOZART, WOLFGANG AMADEUS, 1756-1791

General

Blom, Eric. Mozart. London: Dent, 1956, pp. 210-214. Brief review of a descriptive and critical nature. Musical examples.

Einstein, Alfred. Mozart: His Character, His Work. Translated by Arthur Mendel and Nathan Broder. London: Oxford University Press, 1945, pp. 196-214. Review of the Divertimenti, Serenades and Cassations, showing their function, form and style. Musical examples.

Landon, H. C. Robbins. The Mozart Companion. New York: Norton, 1969, pp. 138-155. The dances and the Masonic funeral music discussed. Descriptive, critical and analytic. Musical examples.

Così fan Tutte Overture

Tovey, Donald Francis. Essays in Musical Analysis. London: Oxford University Press, 1969, Vol. VI, pp. 30-31. Brief remarks. For the student.

Divertimenti

Meyer, E. R. "The viennese divertimento," Music Review
  29:3 (1968), 166-170.   Basic stylistic characteristics examined.   No musical examples.

Impresario Overture

Tovey, Donald Francis.   Essays in Musical Analysis.   Lon-
  don: Oxford University Press, 1969, Vol. IV, pp. 21-23.
  Brief critical and analytic remarks.   Musical examples.
  For the student.

Magic Flute Overture

Tovey, Donald Francis.   Essays in Musical Analysis.   London: Oxford University Press, 1969, Vol. IV, pp. 23-25.
  Critical and analytic study with musical examples.   For
  the student.

MUSSORGSKY, MODEST, 1839-1881

General

Calvocoressi, M. D.   Mussorgsky.   London: Dent, 1946,
  pp. 175-180.   Very brief descriptive and critical review.
  Musical examples.
Calvocoressi, M. D.   Mussorgsky: The Russian Musical
  Nationalist.   second edition, revised.   London: Kegan,
  Paul, n. d., pp. 72-90.   Though antiquated in conception,
  useful for descriptive information.   Musical examples.

PROKOFIEV, SERGEI, 1891-1953

General

Nestyev, Israel V.   Prokofiev.   Translated from the Russian
  by Florence Jonas.   Stanford, Calif.: Stanford University
  Press, 1960, 528p.   Heavy on background with critical and
  descriptive remarks on the music interspersed.   Musical
  examples.   See index for discussion on individual works.

RACHMANINOFF, SERGEI, 1873-1943

General

Culshaw, John. Rachmaninov: The Man and His Music.
New York: Oxford University Press, 1950, pp. 72-74.
The Isle of the Dead and the Symphonic Dances discussed
briefly. No musical examples.
Piggott, Patrick. Rachmaninov Orchestral Music. London:
British Broadcasting Corp., 1974, 60p. Analytic guide
for the student. Musical examples.

Rhapsody on a Theme of Paganini

Sutton, W. "A theme of Paganini, " Musical Opinion 94
(March 1971), 287-288. Brief background and analysis.
No musical examples.

RAVEL, MAURICE, 1875-1937

General

Davies, Laurence. Ravel Orchestral Music. Seattle:
University of Washington Press, 1970, 64p. Analytic
guide for the student. Musical examples.
Demuth, Norman. Ravel. London: Dent, 1956, pp. 105-
122. Descriptive, critical and analytic commentary.
Musical examples.
Myers, Rollo H. Ravel: Life and Works. New York:
Thomas Yoseloff, 1960, 239p. Descriptive and critical.
Musical examples. See index for discussion of individual
works.
Nichols, Roger. Ravel. London: Dent, 1977, 199p.
Critical and analytic overview. Musical examples.
Orenstein, Arbio. Ravel: Man and Musician. New York·
Columbia University Press, 1975, 290p. Program-note
style commentary. Musical examples. See index for
discussion of individual works.
Stuckenschmidt, H. H. Maurice Ravel: Variations on His
Life and Work. Philadelphia: Chilton, 1968, 271p.
Program-note type commentary. No musical examples.

Daphnis et Chloe: Suite no. 2

Machlis, Joseph. Introduction to Contemporary Music. New
York: Norton, 1961, pp. 140-142. Descriptive commentary with musical examples. For the beginning student.

REGER, MAX, 1873-1916

Serenade in G major for Orchestra, op. 95

Tovey, Donald Francis. Essays in Musical Analysis. London: Oxford University Press, 1969, Vol. VI, pp. 65-73.
Thorough critical and analytic discussion with musical examples. For the student.

RIMSKY-KORSAKOV, NIKOLAI, 1844-1908

General

Nathan-Montagu, M. Rimsky-Korsakov. New York: Duffield, 1917, pp. 96-110. Descriptive commentary with musical examples.

Le Coq d'Or: Suite

Feinberg, S. "Rimsky-Korsakov's suite from 'Le Coq d'Or,'"
Music Review 30:1 (1964), 47-64. Thorough analytic commentary focusing on Rimsky-Korsakov's influence on Stravinsky. Musical examples.

ROUSSEL, ALBERT, 1869-1937

General

Deane, Basil. Albert Roussel. London: Barrie and Rockliff, 1961, pp. 60-99. Descriptive, critical and analytic discussion of the orchestral compositions and music for the theatre. Musical examples.

SAINT-SAËNS, CAMILLE, 1835-1921

General

Hervey, Arthur. Saint-Saëns. Plainview, N. Y.: Books for Libraries Press, 1969, pp. 85-94. Very light descriptive commentary. No musical examples.
Lyle, Watson. Camille Saint-Saëns: His Life and Art.
Westport, Conn.: Greenwood Press, 1970, pp. 114-124.
Descriptive commentary with musical examples.

Phaeton

Tovey, Donald Francis. Essays in Musical Analysis. London: Oxford University Press, 1969, Vol. IV, pp. 19-21.
Brief critical and analytic commentary with musical examples. For the student.

SATIE, ERIK, 1866-1925

General

Templier, Pierre-Daniel. Erik Satie. Translation by
Elena L. French and David S. French. Cambridge,
Mass. : The M. I. T. Press, c1969, 127p. Descriptive
and critical commentary. Few musical examples. No
index.

Parade

Machlis, Joseph. Introduction to Contemporary Music. New
York: Norton, 1961, pp. 213-216. Brief descriptive
commentary with musical examples. For the beginning
student.

SCHOENBERG, ARNOLD, 1874-1951

General

MacDonald, Malcolm. Schoenberg. London: Dent, 1976,
pp. 111-130. Full discussion with analytic commentary.
Musical examples.

Chamber Symphony, op. 9

Payne, Anthony. Schoenberg. London: Oxford University
Press, 1969, pp. 11-16. Analytic commentary with mu-
sical examples.
Wellesz, Egon. Arnold Schoenberg. Translated by W. H.
Kerridge. New York: Da Capo Press, 1969, pp. 104-
106. Analytic remarks. Musical examples.

Five Pieces for Orchestra, op. 16

Craft, Robert. "Schoenberg's Five Pieces for Orchestra, "
in Boretz, Benjamin and Edward T. Cone. Perspectives

on Schoenberg and Stravinsky.   Princeton, N. J. :   Prince-
ton University Press, 1968, pp. 3-24.   Thorough analysis
with musical examples.   For the advanced student.
Machlis, Joseph.   Introduction to Contemporary Music.
New York: Norton, 1961, pp. 354-357.   Brief descriptive
and analytic commentary with musical examples.   For the
beginning student.
Payne, Anthony.   Schoenberg.   London: Oxford University
Press, 1969, pp. 20-28.   Thorough analysis with musical
examples.
Wellesz, Egon.   Arnold Schoenberg.   Translated by W. H.
Kerridge.   New York: Da Capo Press, 1969, pp. 121-
125.   Analytic commentary with musical examples.

Pelleas und Melisande

Wellesz, Egon.   Arnold Schoenberg.   Translated by W. H.
Kerridge.   New York: Da Capo Press, 1969, pp. 88-103.
Descriptive, critical and analytic with musical examples.

Transfigured Night

Machlis, Joseph.   Introduction to Contemporary Music.   New
York: Norton, 1961, pp. 353-354.   Brief descriptive
commentary with remarks on the significance of this work.
Musical examples.   For the beginning student.

Variations for Orchestra, op. 31

Deri, Otto.   Exploring Twentieth-Century Music.   New York:
Holt, Rinehart and Winston, 1968, pp. 301-309.   Analysis
with musical examples.
Hansen, Peter S.   An Introduction to Twentieth Century
Music.   second edition.   Boston: Allyn & Bacon, 1967,
pp. 193-197.   Descriptive commentary.   For beginning
student.   Musical examples.
Machlis, Joseph.   Introduction to Contemporary Music.   New
York: Norton, 1961, pp. 357-363.   Descriptive and analytic commentary with musical examples.   For the beginning
student.

SCHUBERT, FRANZ, 1797-1828

Overtures

Brown, M. J.   "Schubert's Italian overtures, " Music Review

26:4 (1965), 303-307. Historical background. No discussion of the music itself.

SCHUMAN, WILLIAM, 1910-

General

Schreiber, Flora Rheta and Vincent Persichetti. William
Schuman. New York: G. Schirmer, 1954, 139p. The
American Festival Overture and Undertow discussed in
detail. Musical examples.

SCHUMANN, ROBERT, 1810-1856

General

Abraham, Gerald, ed. Schumann: A Symposium. London:
Oxford University Press, 1952, pp. 201-204; 238-244.
The Overture, Scherzo & Finale and the concert over-
tures discussed. Musical examples.
Chissel, Joan. Schumann. London: Dent, 1967, pp. 146;
152-154. Descriptive and critical commentary on the
Overture, Scherzo & Finale and the concert overtures.
Musical examples.
Walker, Alan, ed. Robert Schumann: The Man and His
Music. London: Barrie and Jenkins, 1972, pp. 288-323.
The Overture, Scherzo and Finale and the concert over-
tures discussed along with observations on Schumann's
use of the orchestra. Musical examples.

Overture, Scherzo & Finale, op. 52

Tovey, Donald Francis. Essays in Musical Analysis. London: Oxford University Press, 1969, Vol. VI, pp. 40-44.
Critical and analytic with musical examples. For the
student.

SIBELIUS, JEAN, 1865-1957

General

Abraham, Gerald, ed. The Music of Sibelius. New York:
Norton, 1947, pp. 38-90. Thorough discussion of the
orchestral and theatre works.

Layton, Robert. Sibelius. London: Dent, 1965, pp. 61-
102. The tone-poems, small orchestral pieces and
theatre music discussed. Critical and analytic. Musical
examples.
Payne, A. "The scope of Sibelius, " Music & Musicians 14
(Dec. 1965), 20-23. A look at Sibelius' orchestral technique and style as a clue to some limitations in his emotional scope. Unifying devices identified in some tone
poems and symphonies. Musical examples.
Ringbom, Nils-Erik. Jean Sibelius. Norman: University
of Oklahoma Press, 1954, 196p. Descriptive and critical
commentary. Musical examples. Use index for discussion on specific works.

Lemminkainen and the Maidens of Saari

Jacobs, R. L. "Sibelius' 'Lemminkainen and the maidens
of Saari,'" Music Review 24:2 (1963), 146-147. Analytic
commentary showing relationship to the symphonies.
Musical examples.

Tapiola

Tovey, Donald Francis. Essays in Musical Analysis. London: Oxford University Press, 1969, Vol. VI, pp. 93-95.
Critical and analytic with musical examples. For the
student.
Whittall, A. "Sibelius' Eighth symphony, " Music Review
25:3 (1964), 239-240. Critical commentary on the main
formal principle at work. No musical examples.

SMETANA, BEDRICH, 1824-1884

General

Clapham, John. Smetana. London: Dent, 1972, pp. 71-85.
Descriptive, critical and analytic remarks. Musical examples.

Má Vlast

Large, Brian. Smetana. London: Duckworth, 1970,
pp. 260-288. Background, critical and descriptive commentary with musical examples.

Moldau

Bruns, T.   "An analysis of selected folk-style themes in
the music of Bedrich Smetana and Aaron Copland, "
American Music Teacher 25:2 (1975), 8-10.   Comparison
of the type and use of folk melody used in the Moldau and
Appalachian Spring.   Musical examples.

STRAUSS, RICHARD, 1864-1949

General

Del Mar, Norman.   Richard Strauss: A Critical Commentary on His Life and Works.   New York: Free Press of
Glencoe, 1962, 3 Vols.   Thorough discussion of background with critical observations.   Musical examples.
Use table of contents to locate specific works.
Kennedy, Michael.   Richard Strauss.   London: Dent, 1976,
pp. 126-140; 195-205.   Descriptive and critical commentary.   Musical examples.

Death and Transfiguration

Longyear, R. M.   "Schiller, Moszkowkski, and Strauss:
Joan of Arc's 'Death and Transfiguration,'" Music Review
28:3 (1967), 209-217.   Influences on Strauss' tone poem
examined.   Musical examples.

Don Juan

Kerman, Joseph.   Listen.   second edition.   New York:
Worth Publishers, 1976, pp. 250-251.   Analysis with
musical examples.   For the student.
Tovey, Donald Francis.   Essays in Musical Analysis.   London: Oxford University Press, 1969, Vol. IV, pp. 154-
158.   Critical and analytic study with musical examples.
For the student.

STRAVINSKY, IGOR, 1882-1971

General

Lacy, G. M.   "Stravinsky's orchestral technique in his
Russian period, " American Music Teacher 22:5 (1973),
17-22.   Stravinsky's techniques of orchestration spot-
lighted.   Musical examples.

Tansman, Alexandre. Igor Stravinsky: The Man and His
   Music. Translated by Therese and Charles Bleefield.
   New York: Putnam, c1949, 295p. Descriptive and crit-
   ical. Light style, few musical examples.
Vlad, Roman. Stravinsky. Translated from the Italian by
   Frederic and Ann Fuller. London: Oxford University
   Press, 1967, 264p. Critical and analytic observations.
   Musical examples. Use index for discussion of specific
   works.
White, Eric Walter. Stravinsky: The Composer and His
   Works. Berkeley: University of California Press, 1966,
   608p. Thorough discussion of the works, providing back-
   ground, critical and analytic commentary. Musical ex-
   amples.

Agon

Machlis, Joseph. Introduction to Contemporary Music.
   New York: Norton, 1961, pp. 403-407. Descriptive and
   analytic commentary with musical examples. For the
   beginning student.

Le Baiser de la Fée (Fairy's Kiss)

Lang, Paul Henry, ed. Stravinsky: A New Appraisal of
   His Work. New York: Norton, 1963, pp. 47-60. Thorough discussion on analytic level, comparing Stravinsky
   and Tchaikovsky in this work. Musical examples.

Petrouchka

Deri, Otto. Exploring Twentieth-Century Music. New
   York: Holt, Rinehart, and Winston, 1968, pp. 172-182.
   Full, descriptive commentary with analytic observations.
   Musical examples.
Forte, Allen. Contemporary Tone-Structures. New York:
   Columbia University Press, 1955, pp. 128-138. Exten-
   sive analysis for the advanced student. Musical exam-
   ples.

The Rite of Spring (Sacre du Printemps)

Craft, R. "'The Rite of Spring': genesis of a masterpiece, " Perspectives of New Music 5:1 (1969), 20-36.
   Background and performance history. Some analytic remarks. No musical examples.
Hansen, Peter S. An Introduction to Twentieth Century

Music. second edition. Boston: Allyn & Bacon, 1967, pp. 48-55. Good descriptive commentary describing how Stravinsky achieves his effects. Musical examples.

Kerman, Joseph. Listen. second edition. New York: Worth Publishers, 1976, pp. 330-333. Analysis with musical examples. For the student.

Machlis, Joseph. Introduction to Contemporary Music. New York: Norton, 1961, pp. 174-177. Brief descriptive commentary with musical examples. For the beginning student.

Variations

Spies, Claudio. "Notes on Stravinsky's 'Variations,'" in Boretz, Benjamin and Edward T. Cone. Perspective on Schoenberg and Stravinsky. Princeton, N.J.: Princeton University Press, 1968, pp. 210-222. Thorough analysis with musical examples. For the advanced student.

TCHAIKOVSKY, PETER ILITCH, 1840-1893

General

Abraham, Gerald. The Music of Tchaikovsky. New York: Norton, 1946, pp. 74-103; 124-183; 184-196. Thorough review of the orchestral works, incidental music, and ballet music. No musical examples.

Evans, Edwin. Tchaikovsky. London: Dent, 1943, 234p. Descriptive and critical commentary with musical examples. Use index to locate specific works.

Evans, Edwin. Tchaikovsky. London: Dent, 1966, pp. 128-149. Overview of orchestral works with brief critical and descriptive remarks. Musical examples.

Garden, Edward. Tchaikovsky. London: Dent, 1973, 194p. Descriptive and critical commentary with musical examples. Use index to locate specific works.

Ballet Music

Evans, Edwin. Tchaikovsky. London: Dent, 1966, pp. 93-102. Overview of ballet music. Not much discussion of the music itself, focusing instead on story outlines and background. No musical examples.

VAUGHAN WILLIAMS, RALPH, 1872-1958

General

Day, James. Vaughan Williams. London: Dent, 1964,
pp. 127-136. Brief critical remarks. Musical examples.
Dickinson, A. E. F. Vaughan Williams. London: Faber &
Faber, 540p. Analytic commentary with musical examples.
Foss, Hubert. Ralph Vaughan Williams. New York: Ox-
ford University Press, 1950, pp. 167-187. Critical ob-
servations. No musical examples.
Howes, Frank. The Music of Ralph Vaughan Williams.
London: Oxford University Press, 1954, pp. 82-95.
Critical and analytic. Musical examples.
Kennedy, Michael. The Works of Ralph Vaughan Williams.
London: Oxford University Press, 776p. Descriptive com-
mentary with observations on style. Musical examples.

WAGNER, RICHARD, 1813-1883

General

Jacobs, Robert L. Wagner. London: Dent, 1965, pp. 134-
191. Observations on style and analytic remarks on the
orchestral writing. Musical examples.
Tovey, Donald Francis. Essays in Musical Analysis. London: Oxford University Press, 1969, Vol. IV, pp. 115-
132. Critical and analytic studies with musical examples.
Discusses Faust, Flying Dutchman, Meistersinger overtures and Siegfried Idyll, Tannhäuser Prelude Act III.

Tannhäuser (Venusberg Music)

Tovey, Donald Francis. Essays in Musical Analysis. London: Oxford University Press, 1969, Vol. VI, pp. 114-
116. Critical and analytic with musical examples.

Tristan and Isolde: Prelude

Friedheim, Philip. "The relationship between tonality and musical structure," Music Review 27:1 (1966), 44-53. Harmonic analysis with musical examples for advanced students.
Jackson, R. "Leitmotiv and form in the Tristan prelude,"
Music Review 36:1 (1975), 42-53. Depth analysis of the
prelude with particular emphasis on the treatment of
leitmotif. Also traces earlier appearances (before Wagner) of the so-called "Tristan Chord."

Mitchell, William J. "The Tristan Prelude: Techniques
and Structure, " in Mitchell, William J. and Felix Salzer.
The Music Forum. Vol. I, New York: Columbia Uni-
versity Press, 1967, pp. 162-203. Exhaustive analysis
with musical examples. For the advanced student.
Tovey, Donald Francis. Essays in Musical Analysis. Lon-
don: Oxford University Press, 1969, Vol. IV, pp. 124-
126. Critical and analytic study with musical examples.
For the student.
Truscott, H. "Wagner's Tristan and the twentieth century, "
Music Review 24:1 (1963), 75-85. Refutes theory that the
Tristan prelude has the basis of 12 tone music within it.
Author sees it as thoroughly tonal and holds false the
claim that 12 tone music is natural step from Wagner's
Tristan prelude.

Tristan and Isolde: Prelude and Liebestod

Kerman, Joseph. Listen. second edition. New York:
Worth Publishers, 1976, pp. 256-257. Brief analysis
with musical examples. For the student.

WEBER, CARL MARIA VON, 1786-1826

General

Saunders, William. Weber. New York: Da Capo, 1970,
pp. 168-213. Observations on style and critical remarks
with musical examples.
Warrack, John. Carl Maria von Weber. London: Hamish
Hamilton, 1968, 377p. Observations on style and critical
remarks with musical examples. See index for discussion
on specific works.

Overtures

Tovey, Donald Francis. Essays in Musical Analysis. London: Oxford University Press, 1969, Vol. IV, pp. 52-60.
Critical and analytic studies with musical examples. Discusses Euryanthe, Freischütz, and Oberon overtures.
For the student.

Preciosa

Hsu, D. M. "Carl Maria von Weber's 'Preciosa': incidental music on a Spanish theme, " Music Review 26:2 (1965),
97-103. Musical sources examined. Musical examples.

WEBERN, ANTON, 1883-1945

General

Kolneder, Walter. Anton Webern: An Introduction to His
Works. Translated by Humphrey Searle. Berkeley:
University of California Press, 1968, 232p. Analyses
with musical examples. See table of contents for discussion of specific works.
Moldenhauer, Hans, comp. Anton von Webern: Perspectives. Seattle: University of Washington Press, 1966,
191p. Analyses and critical observations by various
writers. Musical examples.

Five Pieces for Orchestra, op. 10

Kerman, Joseph. Listen. second edition. New York:
Worth Publishers, 1976, pp. 319-321. Background and
analysis with musical examples. For the student.
Machlis, Joseph. Introduction to Contemporary Music.
New York: Norton, 1961, pp. 388-390. Brief descriptive commentary with musical examples. For the beginning student.

Variations for Orchestra

Deri, Otto. Exploring Twentieth-Century Music. New
York: Holt, Rinehart & Winston, 1968, pp. 380-385.
Analysis with musical examples. For the intermediate
student.

WOLF, HUGO, 1860-1903

General

Newman, Ernest. Hugo Wolf. New York: Dover, 1966,
pp. 222-224. Brief background and critical assessment.
No musical examples.
Walker, Frank. Hugo Wolf. New York: Knopf, 1968,
522p. Background with analytic commentary and musical
examples on the larger works, such as Penthesilea.

CHAPTER V: CONCERTOS

ALBINONI, TOMASO, 1671-1750

General

Solie, John E. "Aria structure and ritornello form in the music of Albinoni," Musical Quarterly 63:1 (Jan. 1977), 31-47. Advanced discussion on recurring structural patterns in the concertos. Comparisons with Vivaldi, Torelli. Musical examples.

Talbot, M. "Albinoni: the professional dilettante," Musical Times 112 (June 1971), 538-541. Biographical background, stylistic characteristics and influence on others. No musical examples.

Talbot, M. "The concerto allegro in the early eighteenth century," Music & Letters 52:2 (1971), 163-165 The development of the concerto form in nonfugal allegros by Italian composers up to 1720, including Albinoni. Discusses analytic procedure. Advanced level discussion.

Oboe Concertos

Talbot, M. "Albinoni's oboe concertos," Consort 29 (1973), 14-22. Thorough discussion of background, style and development of the oboe concertos. Musical examples.

BACH, CARL PHILIPP EMANUEL, 1714-1788

General

Stevens, J. R. "The keyboard concertos of Carl Philipp Emanuel Bach," Current Musicology 9 (1969), 197-200. Two reviews of doctoral dissertations on the subject. The reviews cover many of the formal, stylistic and harmonic traits of the concertos under discussion. No musical examples.

Harpsichord Concertos

Crickmore, L. "C. P. E. Bach's harpsichord concertos,"
Music & Letters 39 (July 1958), 227-241. Overview of
C. P. E. Bach's achievement in this genre. Context,
stylistic traits and common formal patterns identified.
Some discussion of individual works. Musical examples.

BACH, JOHANN CHRISTIAN, 1735-1782

General

Wellesz, Egon and F. W. Sternfeld, eds. "The Concerto,"
in The New Oxford History of Music 1745-1790. (Vol.
VII, The Age of Enlightenment). London: Oxford University Press, 1973, pp. 483-485. Brief critical and descriptive remarks with musical examples. Bach's style
and output in this form mentioned. This article is part
of a larger article on the history of the Concerto form.

BACH, JOHANN SEBASTIAN, 1685-1750

General

Geiringer, Karl. Johann Sebastian Bach. New York: Oxford University Press, 1966, pp. 315-329. Descriptive
and critical commentary with musical examples. Some
discussion of Bach's place in the history of the concerto.
Hill, Ralph, ed. The Concerto. London: Penguin, 1952,
pp. 18-37. Critical and analytic commentary for the
student. Musical examples.
Spitta, Philipp. Johann Sebastian Bach. Translated from
the German by Clara Bell and J. H. Fuller-Maitland.
3 Vols. London: Novello, 1899, Vol. III, pp. 135-152.
Discussion centers around the clavier concertos and
Italian Concerto. Descriptive and critical commentary
outlining stylistic musical traits. No musical examples.
Veinus, Abraham. The Concerto. New York: Dover,
1964, pp. 53-62. General observations on the origins of
Bach's concertos and the balance between soloist and
orchestra. Less of a discussion on individual works than
an overview of Bach's achievement in the concerto form.
No musical examples.

Brandenburg Concertos

Carrel, Norman. Bach's Brandenburg Concertos. London:
Allen & Unwin, 1963, 130p. Full treatment of all the
Brandenburg Concertos including the characteristics of the
instruments used and extensive analyses. Musical exam-
ples.
Hutchings, Arthur. The Baroque Concerto. New York:
Norton, 1961, pp. 226-237. Observations on style, form,
instrumental and historical context. Musical examples.
Leichtentritt, Hugo. Musical Form. Cambridge, Mass. :
Harvard University Press, 1959, pp. 361-373. Bar-by-
bar analyses of all the Brandenburg Concertos. Best
used with score.
Nallin, Walter E. The Musical Idea. New York: Macmillan, 1968, pp. 300-303. Analytic highlights with musical
examples.
Veinus, Abraham. The Concerto. New York: Dover, 1964,
pp. 27-33. Descriptive remarks highlighting form and
instrumentation. Shows place of Bach in the development
of the concerto form. No musical examples.

Brandenburg Concerto no. 2 in F

Davie, Cedric Thorpe. Musical Structure and Design. New
York: Dover, 1966, pp. 100-101. Compact bar-by-bar
analysis. Musical examples. First movement only.
Nelson, Wendell. The Concerto. Iowa: William C. Brown,
1969, pp. 10-11. Brief remarks with musical examples.
Warburton, Annie O. Analyses of Musical Classics. Book
4. London: Longman, 1974, pp. 36-42. Full bar-by-
bar analysis. No musical examples. Needs to be used
with a score.

Brandenburg Concerto no. 5

Kerman, Joseph. Listen. second edition. New York:
Worth Publishers, 1976, pp. 101-103. Analysis with
musical examples. For the student.

Harpsichord Concerto no. 1 in D minor

Davie, Cedric Thorpe. Musical Structure and Design. New
York: Dover, 1966, pp. 104-106. Compact bar-by-bar
analysis. Musical examples. First movement only.
Leichtentritt, Hugo. Musical Form. Cambridge, Mass. :
Harvard University Press, 1959, p. 314 (2nd movement);

359-361 (1st & 3rd movements). Brief, but compact
analysis with no musical examples. Best used with score.

BALAKIREV, MILY, 1837-1910

Piano Concerto in E♭ major

Garden, Edward. Balakirev: A Critical Study of His Life
and Music. New York: St. Martin's Press, 1967,
pp. 253-259. Critical and analytic remarks with musical
examples on this little known work.

BARBER, SAMUEL, 1910-

General

Broder, Nathan. Samuel Barber. New York: Schirmer,
1954, 74-79. Descriptive and critical remarks with musical examples.

Piano Concerto, op. 38

Nelson, Wendell. The Concerto. Dubuque, Iowa: William
C. Brown, 1969, pp. 101-104. Analysis with critical
observations. Musical examples.

BARTOK, BELA, 1881-1945

General

Hill, Ralph, ed. The Concerto. London: Penguin, 1952,
pp. 327-356. Critical and analytic commentary for the
student. Musical examples.
Nordwall, Ova. "Béla Bartók and modern music," Studia
Musicologica 9:3-4 (1967), 265-280. Comprehensive
analysis of many Bartók compositions, including the concertos.
Stevens, Halsey. The Life and Music of Béla Bartók. New
York: Oxford University Press, 1953, pp. 227-255.
Thorough discussion of all the concertos in easy to read
style. Descriptive and critical with musical examples.

Piano Concertos

Meyer, J. A. "Beethoven and Bartók--a structural parallel,"

Music Review 31:4 (1970), 315-321. Traces, in detail,
Bartók's use of the scheme of Beethoven's fourth piano
concerto as a model for his own piano concertos. Musical examples.

Piano Concerto no. 1

Waldbauer, I. F. "Bartók's first piano concerto; a publication history," Musical Quarterly 51:2 (1965), 336-344.
Thorough examination of the publication history and the
errors in many of the editions. Not an analysis.

Piano Concerto no. 2

Bartók, Béla. "The Second Piano Concerto," Tempo 65
(Summer 1963), 4-7. Bartók's own analysis. Musical
examples.
Suchoff, Benjamin, ed. Béla Bartók Essays. New York:
St. Martin's, 1976, pp. 419-423. Bartók's own analysis
with musical examples.

Piano Concerto no. 3

Suchoff, B. "Some observations on Bartók's Third Piano
Concerto," Tempo C5 (Summer 1963), 8-10. Brief observations of an analytic nature. Traces possible hints
of Bartók's foreknowledge of his death during composition
of this concerto.

Violin Concerto no. 1

Mason, C. "Bartók's early violin concerto," Tempo 49
(Autumn 1958), 11-16. Background with critical and
analytic commentary. Musical examples.

Violin Concerto no. 2

Kerman, Joseph. Listen. second edition. New York:
Worth Publishers, 1976, pp. 341-346. Analysis with
musical examples. For the student.
Nelson, Wendell. The Concerto. Dubuque, Iowa: William
C. Brown, 1969, pp. 92-95. Descriptive and critical
commentary with musical examples.
Payne, E. "The theme and variation in modern music,"
Music Review 19 (May 1958), 119-124. Analytic commen-
tary with musical examples.

BEETHOVEN, LUDWIG VAN, 1770-1827

General

Deane, Basil. "The Concertos," in Arnold, Denis and Nigel
 Fortune. The Beethoven Companion. London: Faber &
 Faber, 1971, pp. 318-328. Solid discussion of all the
 concertos, showing Beethoven's growth in the form as
 well as specific critical remarks. Musical examples.
Fiske, Roger. Beethoven Concertos and Overtures. Seattle:
 University of Washington Press, 1970, 64p. Brief, but
 compact analyses of all Beethoven's concertos. Musical
 examples.
Hill, Ralph, ed. The Concerto. London: Penguin, 1952,
 pp. 119-142. Critical and analytic commentary for the
 student. Musical examples.
Tovey, Donald Francis. Essays in Musical Analysis.   6
 vols. London: Oxford University Press, 1936, vol. III,
 pp. 64-103. All the piano concertos (except the second),
 the violin concerto in D and Triple Concerto are analyzed.
 Musical examples.
Veinus, Abraham. The Concerto. New York: Dover, 1964,
 pp. 127-153. General discussion of social and historical
 factors affecting the concerto during Beethoven's time.
 Also, Beethoven's models and stylistic development are
 highlighted in individual works. No musical examples.

Piano Concerto (1815, Unfinished)

Lockwood, L. "Beethoven's unfinished piano concerto of
 1815: Sources and problems," Musical Quarterly 56:4
 (1970), 624-646. An investigation of the sketches for
 what would have been Beethoven's sixth piano concerto.
 Musical examples.

Piano Concerto no. 3 in C minor

Machlis, Joseph. The Enjoyment of Music. third edition.
 New York: Norton, 1970, pp. 291-294. Analytic over-
 view for the music student. Musical examples.
Nelson, Wendell. The Concerto. Dubuque, Iowa: William
 C. Brown, 1969, pp. 36-40. Background information
 with a brief analysis and criticism. Musical examples.

Piano Concerto no. 4

Truscott, H. "Beethoven's Fourth Piano Concerto," Music

& Dance 50 (Jan. 1960), 8-11. Descriptive and critical
remarks with observations on the innovative aspects of
this concerto. No musical examples. Also found in
Monthly Musical Record 88 (May-June 1958), 91-96.

Piano Concerto no. 5 in E♭, "Emperor"

Green, Douglass M. Form in Tonal Music. New York:
Holt, Rinehart and Winston, 1965, pp. 240-242. Close
analysis with charts, symbols and musical examples.
First movement only.
Nelson, Wendell. The Concerto. Dubuque, Iowa: William
C. Brown, 1969, pp. 40-44. Brief analysis with critical
remarks. Musical examples.

Violin Concerto, op. 61, in D major

Asher, D. "The Beethoven Violin Concerto, Opus 61--his-
tory and analysis," American String Teacher 16:4 (1966),
24-26. Background and descriptive commentary for beginning student. Not an analysis. No musical examples.
Nallin, Walter E. The Musical Idea. New York: Macmillan, 1968, pp. 210-212. Analytic highlights of the movement with musical examples. Best used with a score.
Nelson, Wendell. The Concerto Dubuque, Iowa: William
C. Brown, 1969, pp. 44-48. Brief analysis with critical
remarks. Musical examples.
Tyson, A. "The text of Beethoven's op. 61," Music & Letters 43:2 (1962), 104-114. A scholarly discussion of the
accuracy of the editions that have come down to us.
Compares Beethoven's own arrangement of the violin
concerto into a piano concerto to verify the composer's
intentions.
Tyson, A. "The textual problems of Beethoven's violin
concerto," Musical Quarterly 53:4 (1967), 482-502. Examines the four available sources for the score of op. 61
and some textually dubious passages. Later article than
above.

BERG, ALBAN, 1885-1935

Chamber Concerto

Carner, Mosco. Alban Berg. New York: Holmes & Meier,
1975, pp. 129-136. Full discussion and analysis. Musical examples.

Violin Concerto

Carner, Mosco. Alban Berg. New York: Holmes & Meier, 1975, pp. 136-144. Full discussion and analysis with musical examples.

Hansen, Peter S. An Introduction to Twentieth Century Music. second edition. Boston: Allyn & Bacon, 1967, pp. 124-216. Brief remarks on important musical features. Musical examples.

Hard, M. "Berg: Violin Concerto," Music in Education 38:370 (1974), 270-273. Detailed analysis with musical examples. Advanced.

Hill, Ralph, ed. The Concerto. London: Penguin, 1952, pp. 362-379. Critical and analytic commentary for the student. Musical examples.

Leibowitz, Rene. Schoenberg and His School. Translated from the French by Dika Newlin. New York: Philosophical Library, 1940, pp. 163-166. Advanced level analysis. Musical examples.

Machlis, Joseph. Introduction to Contemporary Music. New York: Norton, 1961, pp. 379-382. Brief, but compact analysis with musical examples. Easy-to-read style on a complex musical work.

Redlich, H. F. Alban Berg: The Man and His Music. London: John Calder, 1957, pp. 203-214. Thorough analysis with musical examples. Advanced.

Reich, Willi. Alban Berg. Translated by Cornelius Cardew. New York: Harcourt, Brace & World, 1965, pp. 178-185. Thorough analysis with musical examples.

Taylor, C. "The contemporaneity of music in history," Music Review 24:3 (1963), 205-217. Music viewed in the context of its period. Comparison of Berg's methods (in violin concerto) and Mozart's (in Symphony no. 39) to illustrate how the period affected the music. Largely a philosophic discussion on style.

Warburton, Annie O. Analyses of Musical Classics. Book 4. London: Longman, 1974, pp. 247-260. Full bar-by-bar analysis. Because there are no musical examples, it is more helpful when used with a score in hand.

BRAHMS, JOHANNES, 1833-1897

General

Hill, Ralph, ed. The Concerto. London: Penguin, 1952, pp. 187-205. Critical and analytic commentary for the student. Musical examples.

Niemann, Walter. Brahms. Translated by Catherine Alison
  Phillips. New York: Cooper Square Publishers, 1969,
  pp. 311-322. Background and descriptive commentary in
  program-note style. No musical examples.
Tovey, Donald Francis. Essays in Musical Analysis. 6
  vols. London: Oxford University Press, 1936, vol. III,
  pp. 114-147. Analysis and critical remarks on the piano
  concertos, Violin Concerto and Double Concerto for violin
  and violoncello. Musical examples.
Veinus, Abraham. The Concerto. New York: Dover,
  1964, pp. 227-234. General remarks of an evaluative
  nature. Places Brahms' contribution in historical perspective. No musical examples.

Piano Concerto no. 1, D minor, op. 15

James, Burnett. Brahms: A Critical Study. New York:
  Praeger, 1972, pp. 73-77. Descriptive commentary with
  background. Musical examples.
Nelson, Wendell. The Concerto. Dubuque, Iowa: William
  C. Brown, 1969, pp. 66-70. Background and analysis
  with musical examples.

Violin Concerto in D major

Nelson, Wendell. The Concerto. Dubuque, Iowa: William
  C. Brown, 1969, pp. 71-76. Descriptive, critical and
  analytic commentary with musical examples.
Swalin, Benjamin F. The Violin Concerto: A Study in
  German Romanticism. Chapel Hill: University of North
  Carolina, 1941, pp. 125-140. Thorough treatment, pro-
  viding background and analysis with critical observations.
  Musical examples.

BRUCH, MAX, 1838-1920

Concerto for Two Pianos, op. 88

Berkofsky, M. "Bruch Duo-Piano Concerto rediscovered,"
  Music Journal 32 (Oct. 1974) 8-9. Background informa-
  tion on this little-known work.
Mancinelli, A. "From our readers," Music Journal 33
  (March 1975), 56-58. More dialogue concerning the con-
  troversial publication history.

Violin Concertos

Swalin, Benjamin F.   The Violin Concerto: A Study in
  German Romanticism.   Chapel Hill: University of North
  Carolina, 1941, pp. 94-104.   Critical and analytic remarks on Violin Concertos nos. 1 & 2.   Musical examples.

Violin Concerto no. 1 in G minor, op. 26

Tovey, Donald Francis.   Essays in Musical Analysis.   6
  vols.   London: Oxford University Press, 1936, vol. III,
  pp. 194-197.   Background, style and form discussed with
  musical examples.

CHOPIN, FREDERIC, 1810-1849

General

Abraham, Gerald.   Slavonic and Romantic Music: Essays
  and Studies.   New York: St. Martin's Press, 1968,
  pp. 23-27.   Concentrates on the orchestral writing.
  Scoring, use of instruments and structural role of the
  orchestral part mentioned.   Musical examples.
Hill, Ralph, ed.   The Concerto.   London: Penguin, 1952,
  pp. 162-169.   Critical and analytic commentary for the
  student.   Musical examples.
Niecks, Frederick.   Frederick Chopin as a Man and Musician.   2 Vols.   London: Novello [1902], Vol. I,
  pp. 203-212.   Background, with good descriptive, critical
  and analytic commentary.   No musical examples.
Veinus, Abraham.   The Concerto.   New York: Dover, 1964,
  pp. 219-226.   Critical remarks and historical perspective.
  Not analytic.
Walker, Alan, ed.   Frederic Chopin: Profiles of the Man
  and the Musician.   New York: Taplinger, 1967, pp. 147-
  155.   Background and critical commentary with emphasis
  on Chopin's tonality.   Musical examples.
Weinstock, Herbert.   Chopin: The Man and His Music.
  New York: Knopf, 1959, pp. 195-197; 206-208.
  Brief program-note remarks on background and description of the music.   No musical examples.

Piano Concerto no. 1 in E minor

Nelson, Wendell.   The Concerto.   Dubuque, Iowa: William

C. Brown, 1969, pp. 60-62.   Mini-analysis with critical
observations. Musical examples.

Piano Concerto no. 2 in F minor, op. 21

Tovey, Donald Francis.   Essays in Musical Analysis.   6
    vols. London: Oxford University Press, 1936, vol. III,
    pp. 103-106. Critical and analytic remarks with musical
    examples.

COPLAND, AARON, 1910-

Concerto for Clarinet and String Orchestra

Smith, Julia. Aaron Copland. New York: Dutton, 1955,
    pp. 250-252. Brief remarks with some analytic insights
    and criticism. Musical examples.

Concerto for Piano and Orchestra

Smith, Julia. Aaron Copland. New York: Dutton, 1955,
    pp. 91-96. Influences, critical and analytical observa-
    tions. Musical examples.

CORELLI, ARCANGELO, 1653-1713

General

Bukofzer, Manfred F.   Music in the Baroque Era.   New
    York: Norton, 1947, pp. 222-227. Corelli's contribu-
    tion to the evolving concerto form. Some mention of
    Corelli's unique stylistic traits. Musical examples.
Harris, S. "Lully, Corelli, Muffat and the eighteenth-
    century orchestral string body," Music & Letters 54:2
    (1973), 197-202. Not an analysis, but a discussion of
    the kind of orchestra Corelli had in mind and the influ-
    ence of his work on others. No musical examples.
Hutchings, Arthur.   The Baroque Concerto.   New York:
    Norton, 1961, pp. 106-113. Examined the influences on
    Corelli as well as his impact on the concerto form.
    Musical examples.
Libby, D. "Interrelationships in Corelli," Journal of the
    American Musicological Society 26:2 (1973), 263-287.
    Very thorough analytic discussion of Corelli's stylistic
    traits and his methods of unification. Tonal and formal

patterns are examined for interrelationships.   Musical
examples.
Talbot, Michael.   "The concerto allegro in the early
eighteenth century," Music & Letters 52 (1971), 8-18;
159-172.   The development of the concerto form by
Italian composers up to 1720, including Vivaldi.   Advanced level discussion.
Veinus, Abraham.   The Concerto.   New York: Dover,
1964, pp. 13-17.   Mainly descriptive commentary with
remarks on Corelli's life and place in the development
of the concerto form.   No musical examples.

Concerti Grossi

Jander, O.   "Concerto grosso instrumentation in Rome in
the 1660's and 1670's," Journal of the American Musicological Society 21:2 (1968), 168-180.   Demonstrates that
many features of instrumentation associated with Corelli
were anticipated by Stradella.   An historical discussion.

Concerti Grossi, op. 6

Pincherle, Marc.   Corelli: His Life, His Work.   Translated from the French by Hubert E. M. Russell.   New
York: Norton, 1956, pp. 120-139.   Remarks on background, musical structure, orchestration and other important characteristics.

DELIUS, FREDERICK, 1862-1934

General

Hill, Ralph, ed.   The Concerto.   London: Penguin, 1952,
pp. 261-275.   Critical and analytic commentary for the
student.   Musical examples.
Warlock, Peter.   Frederick Delius.   New York: Oxford
University Press, 1952, pp. 122-124.   Brief, but critical
remarks on Delius' concerto output.   No musical examples.

Piano Concerto

Hughes, Gervaise.   Sidelights on a Century of Music (1825-
1924).   New York: St. Martin's, 1970, pp. 39-44.
Critical evaluation with musical examples.

Violin Concerto

Cooke, Deryck. "Delius and form: a vindication, " in Redwood, Christopher, ed. A Delius Companion. London:
John Calder, 1976, pp. 253-262. Thorough analysis of
the entire concerto. Musical examples. The same analysis also appears in The Musical Times, June and July,
1962.
Tovey, Donald Francis. Essays in Musical Analysis. 6
vols. London: Oxford University Press, 1936, Vol. III,
pp. 203-205. Brief critique and analysis with musical
examples.

DVORAK, ANTONIN, 1841-1904

General

Evans, Edwin. "The concertos, " in Fischl, Viktor.
Antonin Dvořák: His Achievement. Westport, Conn. :
Greenwood Press, 1970, pp. 89-95. Commentary on all
the concertos. No musical examples.
Hill, Ralph, ed. The Concerto. London: Penguin, 1952,
pp. 234-245. Critical and analytic commentary for the
student. Musical examples.
Robertson, Alec. Dvořák. London: Dent, 1945, pp. 111-
116. Brief overview of all the concertos with musical
examples.
Veinus, Abraham. The Concerto. New York: Dover, 1964,
pp. 237-241. General remarks of an historical and critical nature. Not analytic. No musical examples.

Violoncello Concerto in B minor

Nelson, Wendell. The Concerto. Dubuque, Iowa: William
C. Brown, 1969, pp. 80-84. Analysis with critical commentary. Musical examples.
Tischler, Hans. The Perceptive Music Listener. Englewood Cliffs, N. J. : Prentice-Hall, 1955, pp. 331-334.
Analysis with musical examples.
Tovey, Donald Francis. Essays in Musical Analysis. 6
vols. London: Oxford University Press, 1936, vol. III,
pp. 148-152. Analysis with critical commentary and
musical examples.

ELGAR, EDWARD, 1857-1934

General

Hill, Ralph, ed. The Concerto. London: Penguin, 1952,
pp. 252-260. Critical and analytic commentary for the
student. Musical examples.
Kennedy, Michael. Portrait of Elgar. London: Oxford
University Press, 1968, 324p. Background and critical
commentary with musical examples. Commentary on individual works accessible through index at end of book.
Parrott, Ian. Elgar. London: Dent, 1971, pp. 74-78.
Background and descriptive commentary with musical examples.

Violin Concerto in B minor

Tovey, Donald Francis. Essays in Musical Analysis. 6
vols. London: Oxford University Press, 1936, vol. III,
pp. 152-158. Substantial commentary with analytic remarks. Musical examples.

Violoncello Concerto in E minor

Tovey, Donald Francis. Essays in Musical Analysis. 6
vols. London: Oxford University Press, 1936, vol. III,
pp. 200-203. Descriptive, critical and analytic remarks.
Musical examples.
Young, Percy M. Elgar, O.M.: A Study of a Musician.
London: Collins, 1955, pp. 339-342. Background and
analytic remarks. No musical examples.

FALLA, MANUEL DE, 1876-1946

Harpsichord Concerto

Demarquez, Suzanne. Manuel de Falla. Translated from
the French by Salvator Attanasio. Philadelphia: Chilton,
1968, pp. 157-169. Thorough analysis. Musical examples.

FIELD, JOHN, 1782-1837

General

Branson, David. John Field and Chopin. London: Barrie

& Jenkins, 1972, pp. 57-145.   Solid chapter on all the
concertos.   Focuses on Field's influence on Chopin.
Musical examples.
Piggot, Patrick.   The Life and Music of John Field, 1782-
1837.   Berkeley: University of California Press, 1973,
pp. 145-181.   Lengthy commentary on all the concertos
with musical examples.   Focuses on influences on Field
as well as his influences on others.

GEMINIANI, FRANCESCO, 1687-1762

General

Veinus, Abraham.   The Concerto.   New York: Dover, 1964,
pp. 18-19.   Brief descriptive and critical remarks on the
music with a comparison to Corelli.   No musical examples.

GERSHWIN, GEORGE, 1898-1937

Concerto in F

Ewen, David.   A Journey to Greatness.   London: Allen,
1956, pp. 104-109.   Background and descriptive commentary.   No musical examples.
Goldberg, Isaac.   George Gershwin: A Study in American
Music.   New York: Frederick Ungar, 1958, pp. 204-217.
Extensive discussion of background and context of the
concerto with critical commentary.   Musical examples.

GOLDMARK, KARL, 1830-1915

Violin Concerto in A minor

Swalin, Benjamin F.   The Violin Concerto: A Study in
German Romanticism.   Chapel Hill: University of North
Carolina, 1941, pp. 108-113.   Critical and analytic com-
mentary with musical examples.

GRIEG, EDVARD, 1843-1907

Piano Concerto in A minor

Abraham, Gerald, ed.   Grieg: A Symposium.   Norman:

University of Oklahoma Press, 1950, pp. 26-31. Background and critical remarks. Focuses on Grieg's orchestration of the concerto and compares versions. No musical examples.
Hill, Ralph, ed. The Concerto. London: Penguin, 1952,
pp. 246-251. Critical and analytic commentary for the
student. Musical examples.
Machlis, Joseph. The Enjoyment of Music. third edition.
New York: Norton, 1970, pp. 162-164. Mini-analysis
for the student. Concise treatment with critical remarks
and musical examples.

HANDEL, GEORGE FRIDERIC, 1685-1759

General

Hutchings, Arthur. The Baroque Concerto. New York:
Norton, 1961, pp. 292-303. An overview of Handel's
concerto achievement, mentioning stylistic traits, influences on Handel as well as his influence on others.
Some comparison of Handel and Corelli included.
Lam, Basil. "The Orchestral Music," in Abraham, Gerald,
ed., Handel: A Symposium. London: Oxford University
Press, 1954, pp. 200-232. Very thorough treatment--
descriptive, critical and analytic comments on Handel's
concerto output. Style and influences mentioned as well
with many musical examples.
Lang, Paul Henry. George Frideric Handel. New York:
Norton, 1966, pp. 647-657. Background, influences and
style discussed with critical remarks. No musical examples.
Streatfeild, R. A. Handel. New York: Da Capo, 1964,
pp. 331-335. Brief overview, mentioning musical characteristics of the concertos. No musical examples.
Young, Percy M. Handel. London: Dent, 1947, pp. 120-
127. Brief but solid critical, descriptive and analytic
remarks. Musical examples.

Concerti Grossi

Rolland, Romain. Handel. Translated by A. Eaglefield
Hull. New York: Henry Holt & Co., 1916, pp. 166-181.
Extensive descriptive commentary of all the Concerti
Grossi with musical examples.

Organ Concertos--General

Fiske, R. "Handel's organ concertos--do they belong to
particular oratorios?" Organ Yearbook 3 (1972), 14-22.
Scholarly examination of the evidence of the relationship
between the oratorios and the organ concerti. Musical
examples.

Concerto for Organ, op. 7, no. 2, A major

Wollenberg, S. "Handel and Gottlieb Muffat; a newly dis-
covered borrowing," Musical Times 113 (May 1972), 448-
449. Brief, but detailed account of Handel's borrowing
of a melody from Muffat. Musical examples.

Concerto Grosso, op. 6, no. 9 in F major

Redlich, Hans F. "The oboes in Handel's op. 6," Musical
Times 109:1504 (June 1968), 530-531. Musicological dis-
cussion on the sources for the op. 6. Not an analysis.
Tischler, Hans. The Perceptive Music Listener. Engle-
wood Cliffs, N. J.: Prentice-Hall, 1955, pp. 317-319.
Analysis with musical examples.

HAYDN, FRANZ JOSEPH, 1732-1809

General

Geiringer, Karl. Haydn: A Creative Life in Music.
Berkeley: University of California Press, 1968, 434p.
Brief observations of stylistic traits common to the
concertos. Access to remarks on individual works in
index.
Hill, Ralph, ed. The Concerto. London: Penguin, 1952,
pp. 38-48. Critical and analytic commentary for the
student. Musical examples.
Wellesz, Egon and F. W. Sternfeld, eds. "The Concerto,"
in The New Oxford History of Music 1745-1790. (Vol.
VII, The Age of Enlightenment). London: Oxford University Press, 1973, pp. 472-477. Brief overview of
Haydn's concerto achievement. Focus on characteristic
musical traits and reasons why Haydn's concertos are
less popular than his other forms. Musical examples.
The article on Haydn's concertos falls within an article
on the history of the concerto form.

Trumpet Concerto in E♭

Landon, H. C. Robbins.   Haydn: Chronicle and Works.
    Vol. IV (Haydn: The Years of "The Creation," 1796-
    1800).   Bloomington: Indiana University Press, 1977,
    pp. 225-240.   Thorough critical and analytic discourse.
    Musical examples.

Violoncello Concerto in D major

Tovey, Donald Francis.   Essays in Musical Analysis.   6
    vols.   London: Oxford University Press, 1936, vol. III,
    pp. 62-63.   Brief remarks on style.   Musical examples.

JOACHIM, JOSEPH, 1831-1907

"Hungarian" Concerto for Violin in D, op. 11

Swalin, Benjamin F.   The Violin Concerto: A Study in
    German Romanticism.   Chapel Hill: University of North
    Carolina, 1941, pp. 82-87.   Critical and analytic remarks.
    Musical examples.

LISZT, FRANZ, 1811-1886

General

Beckett, Walter.   Liszt.   London: Dent, 1963, pp. 117-119.
    Brief descriptive and critical remarks with musical exam-
    ples.
Collet, Robert.   "Works for piano and orchestra," in
    Walker, Alan.   Franz Liszt: The Man and His Music.
    New York: Taplinger, 1970, pp. 258-273.   Full descrip-
    tive, critical and analytic treatment.   Musical examples.
Hill, Ralph, ed.   The Concerto.   London: Penguin, 1952,
    pp. 179-186.   Critical and analytic commentary for the
    student.   Musical examples.
Huneker, James.   Franz Liszt.   New York: AMS Press,
    1971, pp. 168-174.   Program-note variety remarks.
    Brief, no musical examples.
Searle, Humphrey.   The Music of Liszt.   Second Revised
    Edition.   New York: Dover, 1966, pp. 83-85.   Brief,
    but informative critical observations.   Musical examples.
Veinus, Abraham.   The Concerto.   New York: Dover, 1964,
    pp. 199-213.   Liszt's innovations in the concerto form,

his musical lineage traced and critical remarks on his
music included. Concise discussion of Liszt's place in
music history. No musical examples.

Piano Concerto no. 1 in E♭ major

Nelson, Wendell. The Concerto. Dubuque, Iowa: William
C. Brown, 1969, pp. 53-55. Brief analysis with critical
observations. Musical examples.

MENDELSSOHN, FELIX, 1809-1847

General

Hill, Ralph, ed. The Concerto. London: Penguin, 1952,
pp. 154-161. Critical and analytic commentary for the
student. Musical examples.
Radcliffe, Philip. Mendelssohn. London: Dent, 1954,
pp. 108-111. Brief critical remarks with musical examples.
Veinus, Abraham. The Concerto. New York: Dover, 1964,
pp. 183-191. An assessment of Mendelssohn's art in
comparison to Mozart's. Critical remarks on specific
works. No musical examples.
Werner, Eric. Mendelssohn. Translated from the German
by Dika Newlin. London: Free Press of Glencoe, 1963,
pp. 53-60, 219; 420-422. Brief, but informative critical
evaluations. Many with musical examples.

Violin Concerto

Jacob, Heinrich Edwards. Felix Mendelssohn and His
Times. Translated from the German by Richard and
Clara Winston. Westport, Conn. : Greenwood Press,
1973, pp. 304-306. Brief critical commentary. Musical
examples.
Machlis, Joseph. The Enjoyment of Music. third edition.
New York: Norton, 1970, pp. 164-166. Brief analysis
for the student. Musical examples.
Nallin, Walter E. The Musical Idea. New York: Macmil-
lan, 1968, pp. 306-309. Analytic highlights with musical
examples.
Nelson, Wendell. The Concerto. Dubuque, Iowa: William
C. Brown, 1969, pp. 56-59. Brief analysis with critical
observations. Musical examples.
Swalin, Benjamin F. The Violin Concerto: A Study in

German Romanticism. Chapel Hill: University of North
Carolina, 1941, pp. 62-74. Full treatment, providing
background, analysis and critical remarks. Musical examples.
Tovey, Donald Francis. Essays in Musical Analysis. 6
vols. London: Oxford University Press, 1936, Vol. III,
pp. 178-181. Background and analytical remarks with
musical examples.

MOZART, WOLFGANG AMADEUS, 1756-1791

General

Blom, Eric. Mozart. London: Dent, 1956, pp. 215-232.
Ample discussion of stylistic features in the concertos.
Mostly descriptive and critical commentary, intelligently
written on an intermediate level. Musical examples.
Einstein, Alfred. Mozart: His Character, His Work.
Translated by Arthur Mendel and Nathan Broder. London:
Oxford University Press, 1945, pp. 287-315. Focuses on
the piano concertos, showing influences on Mozart, stylistic traits, and achievement of balance in the concerto
form. Easy to read style by a great scholar. Musical
examples.
Hill, Ralph, ed. The Concerto. London: Penguin, 1952,
pp. 49-118. Critical and analytic commentary for the
student. Musical examples.
Landon, H. C. Robbins and Donald Mitchell, eds. The
Mozart Companion. New York: Norton, 1956, pp. 234-
279. Very thorough treatment of formal, stylistic, and
instrumental characteristics of the concertos. Shows
Mozart's stylistic growth as well as his unique contribution to the concerto form. Musical examples.
Pauly, Reinhard G. Music in the Classic Period. second
edition. Englewood Cliffs, N. J. : Prentice-Hall, 1973,
pp. 129-139. Descriptive and critical overview of
Mozart's concertos. Mentions stylistic features and
Mozart's contribution in historical context. Musical examples.
Rosen, Charles. The Classical Style: Haydn, Mozart,
Beethoven. New York: Viking, 1971, pp. 185-263.
Brilliant discussion of the concerto as a form and Mozart's
approach to it as a dramatic expression. Mentions most
of the concertos, but treats the Piano Concerto no. 20,
K. 466 at length. Historic, critical and analytic with
musical examples.

Simon, E. J. "Sonata into concerto; a study of Mozart's
first seven concertos," Acta Musicologica 31:3-4 (1959),
170-185. Description and analytic remarks on those
concertos that were adapted from sonatas. No musical
examples.
Veinus, Abraham. The Concerto. New York: Dover, 1964,
pp. 72-126. General discussion of the growth of the concerto form under Mozart, the influence of the evolving
piano on the concerto and stylistic traits of Mozart and
Beethoven. Good treatment of historical perspective. No
musical examples.

Piano Concertos--General

Girdlestone, C. M. Mozart and His Piano Concertos.
Norman: University of Oklahoma Press, 1952, 511p.
Thorough treatment of all the piano concertos individually,
as well as observations on Mozart's artistic growth and
development of the concerto form. Musical examples.
Grout, Donald Jay. A History of Western Music. New
York: Norton, 1960, pp. 466-467. General remarks on
salient musical characteristics and basic formal scheme
of the piano concertos. No musical examples.
Hutchings, Arthur. A Companion to Mozart's Piano Concertos, second edition. London: Oxford University
Press, 1951, 211p. Full treatment of all the piano
concertos individually with remarks on Mozart's form and
style. Musical examples.
Tischler, Hans. A Structural Analysis of Mozart's Piano
Concertos. New York: Institute of Mediaeval Music,
1966, 140p. Detailed, coded analyses of all the piano
concertos. Some general discussion of Mozart's style
and method as well. Musical examples.

Concerto for Clarinet, K. 622

Hacker, A. "Mozart and the basset clarinet," Musical
Times 110 (April 1969), 359-362. The evidence pointing
to the basset clarinet as the instrument Mozart had in
mind for this concerto. Musical examples.
Nallin, Walter E. The Musical Idea. New York: Macmillan, 1968, pp. 303-306. Analytic highlights with musical
examples.
Tovey, Donald Francis. Essays in Musical Analysis. 6
vols. London: Oxford University Press, 1936, Vol. III,
pp. 52-53. Brief descriptive and critical remarks.
Notes Mozart's influence on the clarinet. Musical examples.

Concerto for Flute and Harp, K. 299

Tovey, Donald Francis. Essays in Musical Analysis. 6
vols. London: Oxford University Press, 1936, vol. III,
pp. 60-62. Background and descriptive remarks with
musical examples.

Concerto nos. 1 & 2 for Flute, K. 313, 314

Tovey, Donald Francis. Essays in Musical Analysis. 6
vols. London: Oxford University Press, 1936, Vol. III,
pp. 47-51. Brief analytic remarks. Musical examples.

Piano Concerto no. 9 in E♭ major, K. 271

Cobin, M. W. "Aspects of stylistic evolution in two Mozart
concertos, K. 271 and K. 482," Music Review 31:1
(1970), 1-20. Intensive and analytic examination to show
specific factors contributing to the sense of greater ma-
turity and depth in K. 482. Quite objective, with musical examples.
Nelson, Wendell. The Concerto. Dubuque, Iowa: William
C. Brown, 1969, pp. 25-28. Brief analysis with critical
remarks. Musical examples.
Warburton, Annie O. Analyses of Musical Classics. Book
4. London: Longman, 1974, pp. 84-96. Full bar-by-
bar analysis. No musical examples. Needs to be used
with score in hand.

Piano Concerto no. 12 in A major, K. 414

Tovey, Donald Francis. Essays in Musical Analysis. 6
vols. London: Oxford University Press, 1936, vol. III,
pp. 27-30. Brief analysis with critical remarks and
musical examples.

Piano Concerto no. 15 in B♭ major, K. 450

Tovey, Donald Francis. Essays in Musical Analysis. 6
vols. London: Oxford University Press, 1936, Vol. III,
pp. 30-33. Brief analytic remarks and astute critical
observations. Musical examples.

Piano Concerto no. 17 in G major, K. 453

Tovey, Donald Francis. Essays in Musical Analysis. 6
vols. London: Oxford University Press, 1936, vol. III,

pp. 33-36. Brief analytic insights and lucid critical observations. Musical examples.

Piano Concerto no. 20 in D minor, K. 466

Davie, Cedric Thorpe. Musical Structure and Design. New
York: Dover, 1966, pp. 110-114. Compact bar-by-bar
analysis. Musical examples.
Green, Douglass M. Form in Tonal Music. New York:
Holt, Rinehart and Winston, 1965, pp. 243-244. Some
general characteristics discussed, followed by a chart-
outline summary analyzing the entire last movement. No
musical examples.
Stadlen, P. "Thoughts on musical continuity," Score 26
(Jan. 1960), 52-62. Traces Mozart's creative process
through examination of the original manuscripts. Phrases
that are today accepted as part of the natural flow of
ideas are shown as inserted afterthoughts. Musical examples.

Piano Concerto no. 21 in C major, K. 467

Machlis, Joseph. The Enjoyment of Music. third edition.
New York: Norton, 1970, pp. 269-272. Compact analysis for the music student. Musical examples.

Piano Concerto no. 22 in E♭ major, K. 482

Cobin, M. W. "Aspects of stylistic evolution in two Mozart
concertos, K. 271 and K. 482," Music Review 31:1
(1970), 1-20. Intensive and analytic examination to show
specific factors contributing to the sense of greater ma-
turity and depth in K. 482. Quite objective, with musical examples.

Piano Concerto no. 23, A major, K. 488

Green, Douglass M. Form in Tonal Music. New York:
Holt, Rinehart and Winston, 1965, p. 245. Chart-outline
analyzing entire last movement.
Nelson, Wendell. The Concerto. Dubuque, Iowa: William
C. Brown, 1969, pp. 29-31. Mini-analysis with critical
remarks. Musical examples.
Tovey, Donald Francis. Essays in Musical Analysis. 6
Vols. London: Oxford University Press, 1936, Vol. III,
pp. 37-42. Critical commentary with analytic insights.
Musical examples.

Piano Concerto no. 24, C minor, K. 491

Green, Douglass M. Form in Tonal Music. New York:
Holt, Rinehart and Winston, 1965, pp. 234-240. Very
close analysis with charts, symbols and musical examples. First movement only.
Nelson, Wendell. The Concerto. Dubuque, Iowa: William
C. Brown, 1969, pp. 31-33. Brief analysis with critical
remarks. Musical examples.
Stadlen, P. "Thoughts on musical continuity," Score 26
(Jan. 1960), 52-62. Traces Mozart's creative process
through examination of the original manuscripts. Phrases
that are today accepted as part of the natural flow of
ideas are shown as inserted afterthoughts. Musical examples.
Tischler, Hans. The Perceptive Music Listener. Englewood Cliffs, N. J.: Prentice-Hall, 1955, pp. 322-326.
Analysis with musical examples.
Tovey, Donald Francis. Essays in Musical Analysis. 6
Vols. London: Oxford University Press, 1936, Vol. III,
pp. 42-46. Brief, but solid discussion of formal principles and emotional content. Musical examples.

Piano Concerto no. 26 in D major ("Coronation"), K. 537

Reynolds, R. G. "K. 537: regression or progression?"
Music Review 35:2 (1974), 142-148. Tonal relationships
as a clue to understanding K. 537. Author feels that the
expanded tonal range in K. 537 is in keeping with the
musical trends of the time and does not reflect a lapse
in musical taste, as many critics maintain.

Violin Concerto no. 4 in D, K. 218

Nelson, Wendell. The Concerto. Dubuque, Iowa: William
C. Brown, 1969, pp. 22-25. Brief remarks on influences, form and style with musical examples.
Tovey, Donald Francis. Essays in Musical Analysis. 6
Vols. London: Oxford University Press, 1936, Vol. III,
pp. 54-56. Descriptive and critical commentary. Musical examples.

Violin Concerto no. 5 in A, K. 219

Tovey, Donald Francis. Essays in Musical Analysis. 6
vols. London: Oxford University Press, 1936, vol. III,
pp. 56-59. Remarks on authenticity, style and form.

Musical examples. Tovey refers to this concerto as
Mozart's 6th. Current numbering places the concerto as
the 5th.

NIELSEN, CARL, 1865-1931

General

Simpson, Robert. Carl Nielsen: Symphonist, 1865-1931.
London: Dent, 1952, pp. 124-135. Full discussion,
critical and analytic with musical examples.

PAGANINI, NICCOLO, 1782-1840

Violin Concertos--General

Swalin, Benjamin F. The Violin Concerto: A Study in
German Romanticism. Chapel Hill: University of North
Carolina, 1941, pp. 34-41. Critical and analytic remarks with background. Musical examples.
Veinus, Abraham. The Concerto. New York: Dover, 1964,
pp. 162-169. General discussion of Paganini's contribution to the form, rather than an analysis of individual
works. No musical examples.

PROKOFIEV, SERGEI, 1891-1953

General

Hill, Ralph, ed. The Concerto. London: Penguin, 1952,
pp. 380-386. Critical and analytic commentary for the
student. Musical examples.
Nestyev, Israel V. Prokofiev. Stanford, Calif. : Stanford
University Press, 1960, 528p. Background with descriptive and critical remarks on all the concertos. Index of
musical works in back of book provides easy access to
criticisms.

Piano Concerto no. 3 in C major

Hansen, Peter S. An Introduction to Twentieth Century
Music. second edition. Boston: Allyn & Bacon, 1967,
pp. 283-286. Brief remarks on important musical features. Musical examples.

194   CONCERTOS

Machlis, Joseph. The Enjoyment of Music. third edition.
New York: Norton, 1970, pp. 539-540. Analytic over-
view for the music student. Musical examples.
Machlis, Joseph. Introduction to Contemporary Music. New
York: Norton, 1961, pp. 281-283. Brief analytic over-
view of highlights intended for beginning music student.
Musical examples.
Nelson, Wendell. The Concerto. Dubuque, Iowa: William
C. Brown, 1969, pp. 98-100. Descriptive and critical
commentary with musical examples.

Violin Concerto no. 2

Hansen, Peter S. An Introduction to Twentieth Century
Music. second edition. Boston: Allyn & Bacon, 1967,
pp. 286-288. Brief descriptive and analytic remarks
with musical examples.

RACHMANINOFF, SERGEI, 1873-1943

General

Culshaw, John. Rachmaninov: The Man and His Music.
New York: Oxford University Press, 1950, pp. 75-95.
Descriptive, critical and analytic commentary with musical examples. Extensive discussion.
Hill, Ralph, ed. The Concerto. London: Penguin, 1952,
pp. 289-300. Critical and analytic commentary for the
student. Musical examples.
Veinus, Abraham. The Concerto. New York: Dover,
1964, pp. 253-256. General remarks, placing Rachmaninoff in historical perspective. Not analytic. No musical examples.

Piano Concerto no. 3

Yasser, J. "The opening theme of Rachmaninoff's Third
Piano Concerto and its liturgical prototype," Musical
Quarterly 55:3 (1969), 313-328. Thorough discussion
tracing liturgical and folkloric elements in the opening
theme. Musical examples.

RAVEL, MAURICE, 1875-1937

General

Demuth, Norman. Ravel. London: Dent, 1947, pp. 83-92.
Good, musical discussion of the two piano concertos.
Critical remarks and comparison of the two concerti with
musical examples.
Hill, Ralph, ed. The Concerto. London: Penguin, 1952,
pp. 307-314. Critical and analytic commentary for the
student. Musical examples.
Myers, Rollo H. Ravel: Life and Works. New York:
Thomas Yoseloff, 1960, pp. 173-180. Descriptive and
critical commentary with musical examples.
Orenstein, Arbie. Ravel: Man and Musician. New York:
Columbia University Press, 1975, pp. 202-205. Straight
descriptive commentary on a basic level. No musical examples.
Stuckenschmidt, H. H. Maurice Ravel: Variations on His
Life and Work. Translated from the German by Samuel
R. Rosenbaum. Philadelphia: Chilton, 1968, pp. 235-
238. Brief commentary on background with descriptive
remarks on the music. No musical examples.

Piano Concerto in G major

Nelson, Wendell. The Concerto. Dubuque, Iowa: William
C. Brown, 1969, pp. 89-92. Descriptive and critical
commentary with musical examples.

SAINT-SAËNS, CAMILLE, 1835-1921

General

Hervey, Arthur. Saint-Saëns. Freeport: Books for Libraries Press, 1969, pp. 101-106. Brief descriptive and
critical commentary. No musical examples.
Hill, Ralph, ed. The Concerto. London: Penguin, 1952,
pp. 206-218. Critical and analytic commentary for the
student. Musical examples.
Lyle, Watson. Camille Saint-Saëns: His Life and Art.
Westport, Conn.: Greenwood Press, 1970, pp. 83-103.
Descriptive commentary on all the concertos. On a
program-note level, with musical examples.
Veinus, Abraham. The Concerto. New York: Dover,
1964, pp. 258-260. Brief critical remarks. Not analytic. No musical examples.

Piano Concerto no. 4, C minor

Tovey, Donald Francis. Essays in Musical Analysis. 6
Vols. London: Oxford University Press, 1936, Vol. III,
pp. 189-192. Description, critique and analysis. Musical examples.

Violoncello Concerto in A minor

Tovey, Donald Francis. Essays in Musical Analysis. 6
vols. London: Oxford University Press, 1936, vol. III,
pp. 192-194. Brief critical and analytic remarks. Musical examples.

SCHOENBERG, ARNOLD, 1874-1951

General

Reich, Willi. Schoenberg: A Critical Biography. Translated by Leo Black. London: Longman, 1971, pp. 203-
204 (Violin Concerto); 211-213 (Piano Concerto). Brief
remarks on background and musical content. Some
analytic insights. No musical examples.

Piano Concerto

Hansen, Peter S. An Introduction to Twentieth Century
Music. second edition. Boston: Allyn & Bacon, 1967,
pp. 198-201. Mini-analysis of this atonal work. Musi-
cal examples.
Machlis, Joseph. The Enjoyment of Music. third edition.
New York: Norton, 1970, pp. 519-521. Analytic over-
view for the music student. Musical examples.
Machlis, Joseph. Introduction to Contemporary Music.
New York: Norton, 1961, pp. 363-365. Brief, but com-
pact analysis with musical examples. Easy to read style
on a complex musical work.
Newlin, Dika. "Secret tonality in Schoenberg's piano con-
certo," Perspectives of New Music 13:1 (1974), 137-139.
A way of viewing the concerto from a tonal standpoint.
Musical examples.

Violin Concerto

Babbitt, Milton. "Three essays on Schoenberg," in Boretz,
Benjamin and Edward T. Cone. Perspectives on Schoen-

berg and Stravinsky.   Princeton, N. J.:   Princeton, 1968,
pp. 47-50.   Very close analysis for the more advanced
student.   No musical examples.
Keller, H.   "No bridge to nowhere," Musical Times 102
(March 1961), 156-158.   Brief critical remarks.   No
musical examples.
Leibowitz, Rene.   Schoenberg and His School.   Translated
from the French by Dika Newlin.   New York: Philosophical Library, 1940, pp. 120-124.   Close analysis for the
advanced student.   Musical examples.
Perle, G.   "Babbit, Lewin, and Schoenberg: a critique,"
Perspectives of New Music 2:1 (1963), 120-132.   Very
advanced discussion of the criticism on Schoenberg's
violin concerto.   No musical examples.

SCHUMANN, ROBERT, 1810-1856

General

Hill, Ralph, ed.   The Concerto.   London: Penguin, 1952,
pp. 170-178.   Critical and analytic commentary for the
student.   Musical examples.
Lindsay, Maurice.   "The Works for Solo Instrument and
Orchestra," in Abraham, Gerald.   Schumann: A Sympo-
sium.   London: Oxford University Press, 1952, 245-249.
Critical and analytic commentary with background.   Musi-
cal examples.
Niemann, Alfred.   "The Concertos," in Walker, Alan.
Robert Schumann: The Man and His Music.   London:
Barrie and Jenkins, 1972, pp. 241-276.   Thorough treatment of all the concertos.   Musical examples.
Schauffler, Robert Haven.   Florestan: The Life and Work
of Robert Schumann.   New York: Dover, 1963, pp. 423-432.
Descriptive, critical and analytic remarks in easy-to-
understand style.   Musical examples.   Focuses on the
Piano Concerto.
Veinus, Abraham.   The Concerto.   New York: Dover,
1964, pp. 194-199.   An assessment of Schumann's art as
well as specific remarks on individual works.   Some comments on formal scheme.   No musical examples.

Piano Concerto in A minor, op. 54

Kerman, Joseph.   Listen.   second edition.   New York:
Worth Publishers, 1976, pp. 237-238.   Brief analysis
with musical examples.   For the student.

Machlis, Joseph.   The Enjoyment of Music.   third edition.
    New York: Norton, 1970, pp. 167-168.   Mini-analysis
    for the student, touching on highlights only.   Musical ex-
    amples.
Nelson, Wendell.   The Concerto.   Dubuque, Iowa: William
    C. Brown, 1969, pp. 63-66.   Analysis with critical com-
    mentary.   Musical examples.
Tovey, Donald Francis.   Essays in Musical Analysis.   6
    vols.   London: Oxford University Press, 1936, Vol. III,
    pp. 182-184.   Brief critical commentary with musical ex-
    amples.

Violin Concerto

Swalin, Benjamin F.   The Violin Concerto: A Study in
    German Romanticism.   Chapel Hill: University of North
    Carolina, 1941, pp. 76-82.   Background and analysis with
    musical examples.

Violoncello Concerto in A minor

Tovey, Donald Francis.   Essays in Musical Analysis.   6
    vols.   London: Oxford University Press, 1936, Vol. III,
    pp. 184-189.   Descriptive and critical commentary with
    musical examples.

SHOSTAKOVICH, DMITRI, 1906-1975

General

Kay, Norman.   Shostakovich.   London: Oxford University
    Press, 1971, 80p.   Critical appraisal of the concertos
    scattered throughout book.   No index to provide easy ac-
    cess to individual works, but book is small and mention
    of specific works not hard to locate.

Piano Concerto

Martynov, Ivan.   Dmitri Shostakovich: The Man and His
    Work.   Translated from the Russian by T. Guralsky.
    New York: Greenwood, 1969, pp. 51-53.   Brief descrip-
    tive and critical remarks.   No musical examples.

Violin Concerto no. 1

Ottaway, H.   "Shostakovich: some later works, " Tempo 50

(Winter 1959), 2-14.   Brief critical and analytic remarks
with musical examples.

Violin Concerto no. 2

Kay, N.   "Shostakovich's Second Violin Concerto," Tempo
83 (Winter 1967-1968), 21-23.   Brief critical and analytic
remarks.   Musical examples.
Orga, A.   "Shostakovich's new concerto," Music & Musicians 16 (Jan. 1968), 23-25+.   Good, straight analysis
with musical examples.

Violoncello Concerto, op. 107, E♭ major

McVeagh, D.   "Shostakovich's Concerto," Musical Times
101 (Nov. 1960), 701-703.   Brief critical and analytic remarks.   Musical examples.

SIBELIUS, JEAN, 1865-1957

Violin Concerto

Hill, Ralph, ed.   The Concerto.   London: Penguin, 1952,
pp, 276-281.   Critical and analytic commentary for the
student.   Musical examples.
Layton, Robert.   Sibelius.   London: Dent, 1965, pp. 103-
105.   Very brief, but valuable critical observations.   No
musical examples.
Tovey, Donald Francis.   Essays in Musical Analysis.   6
vols.   London: Oxford University Press, 1936, Vol. III,
pp. 211-215.   Critique and analysis with musical examples.
Wood, Ralph W.   "The Miscellaneous Orchestral and Theatre
Music," in Abraham, Gerald, ed.   The Music of Sibelius.
New York: Norton, 1947, pp. 67-69.   Critical remarks,
focusing on the weaknesses of the concerto.   No musical
examples.

SPOHR, LUDWIG, 1784-1859

Violin Concertos--General

Swalin, Benjamin F.   The Violin Concerto: A Study in
German Romanticism.   Chapel Hill: University of North
Carolina, 1941, pp. 8-33.   Full treatment, providing

background, analyses, and critical remarks. Musical examples.

STRAUSS, RICHARD, 1864-1949

General

Del Mar, Norman. Richard Strauss: A Critical Commentary on His Life and Works. New York: Free Press of Glencoe, 1962, 3 vols. Solid critical and analytic treatment with musical examples. Consult "List of Works Discussed" at front of each volume.

Violin Concerto in D minor, op. 8

Swalin, Benjamin F. The Violin Concerto: A Study in German Romanticism. Chapel Hill: University of North Carolina, 1941, pp. 119-121. Analysis with musical examples.

STRAVINSKY, IGOR, 1882-1971

General

Nelson, Robert U. "Stravinsky's concept of variations," in Lang, Paul Henry, ed. Stravinsky: A New Appraisal of His Work. New York: Norton, c1963, pp. 61-73. Explores Stravinsky's variation technique in the Concerto for Two Pianos and Ebony Concerto. Somewhat technical discussion with musical examples.

Tansman, Alexandre. Igor Stravinsky: The Man and His Music. Translated by Therese and Charles Bleefield. New York: Putnam's, c1949, 295p. Brief descriptive remarks on all the concertos. No musical examples.

Vlad, Roman. Stravinsky. Translated by Frederick and Ann Fuller. London: Oxford University Press, 1960, pp. 115-121. Surveys all the concertos, providing background and critical information. Musical examples.

White, Eric Walter. Stravinsky: The Composer and His Works. Berkeley: University of California Press, 1966, 608p. All the concertos discussed from a critical standpoint. Background and musical examples provided. See index in rear to gain access to discussion of individual works.

Concerto for 2 Solo Pianos

James, T. S. "Communications," Perspectives of New
Music 10:1 (1971), 358-361. Analytic remarks for the
advanced student.

TCHAIKOVSKY, PETER ILITCH, 1840-1893

General

Blom, Eric. "Works for Solo Instrument and Orchestra,"
in Abraham, Gerald. The Music of Tchaikovsky. New
York: Norton, 1946, pp. 47-73. Thorough discussion
with background and analytic commentary. No musical
examples, but some charts showing structure.
Evans, Edwin. Tchaikovsky. London: Dent, 1966, pp. 159-
168. Brief descriptive and critical remarks with background. Musical examples.
Hill, Ralph, ed. The Concertos. London: Penguin, 1952,
pp. 219-233. Critical and analytic commentary for the
student. Musical examples.
Veinus, Abraham. The Concerto. New York: Dover,
1964, pp. 243-252. General remarks of an historical
and critical nature. Not analytic. No musical examples.
Warrack, John. Tchaikovsky: Symphonies and Concertos.
Seattle: University of Washington Press, 1969, pp. 39-
56. Background with descriptive and critical remarks.
Musical examples.

Piano Concerto no. 1 in Bb minor, op. 23

Friskin, J. "The text of Tchaikovsky's B flat minor concerto," Music & Letters 50:2 (1969), 246-251. The
Dannreuther revisions of the second edition are discussed.
Not an analysis.
Nallin, Walter E. The Musical Idea. New York: Macmillan, 1968, pp. 309-312. Brief analysis with musical examples.
Newmarck, Rosa. Tchaikovsky. London: Reeves, 1908,
pp. 289-304. Analysis with musical examples.

Violin Concerto in D major

Nelson, Wendell. The Concerto. Dubuque, Iowa: William
C. Brown, 1969, pp. 77-79. Analysis with critical commentary. Musical examples.

TELEMANN, GEORG PHILIPP, 1681-1767

General

Hutchings, Arthur. The Baroque Concerto. New York:
Norton, 1961, pp. 237-251. Observations on historical
context and musical style of Telemann's concertos. Musical examples.
Petzold, Richard. Georg Philipp Telemann. Translated by
Horace Fitzpatrick. New York: Oxford University Press,
1974, pp. 69-89. Remarks on style, programmatic
qualities, and harmony, with musical examples. Comparisons made with Bach.

THOMSON, VIRGIL, 1896-

General

Hoover, Kathleen and John Cage. Virgil Thomson: His
Life and Music. Freeport, N. Y.: Books for Libraries,
1959, pp. 234-238 (Concerto for flute, strings & harp);
219-222 (Cello Concerto). Critical and analytic remarks
with musical examples.

TORELLI, GIUSEPPE, 1658-1709

General

Bukofzer, Manfred F. Music in the Baroque Era. New
York: Norton, 1947, pp. 226-229. Torelli's role in the
establishment of the baroque concerto form. Descriptive
and critical remarks on his style.
Talbot, Michael. "The concerto allegro in the early eighteenth century," Music & Letters 52 (1971), 8-18; 159-172.
The development of the concerto form by Italian composers up to 1720, including Torelli. Advanced level discussion.

VAUGHAN WILLIAMS, RALPH, 1872-1958

General

Day, James. Vaughan Williams. London: Dent, 1961,
pp. 168-174. Largely descriptive commentary with musi-

cal examples on the violin, piano, oboe and tuba con-
certos.
Dickinson, A. E. F. Vaughan Williams. London: Faber
& Faber, 1963, 540p. Analytic commentary with musical
examples.
Foss, Hubert. Ralph Vaughan Williams: A Study. New
York: Oxford University Press, 1950, 219p. Brief crit-
ical remarks with no musical examples. Good character-
ization of the individual concertos. See index of works
for access to remarks on specific works.
Howes, Frank. The Music of Ralph Vaughan Williams.
London: Oxford University Press, 1954, pp. 97-122.
Descriptive, critical and analytic remarks with musical
examples.
Kennedy, Michael. The Works of Ralph Vaughan Williams.
London: Oxford University Press, 1964, 776p. Descriptive commentary with observations on style. Musical examples.

VIVALDI, ANTONIO, 1678-1741

General

Bukofzer, Manfred F. Music in the Baroque Era. New
York: Norton, 1947, pp. 229-231. Brief, but compact
assessment of Vivaldi's part in the history of the concerto form. Stylistic features mentioned with musical
examples.
Grout, Donald Jay. A History of Western Music. New
York: Norton, 1960, pp. 371-375. General remarks on
salient musical characteristics and basic formal structure
found in the concertos. No musical examples.
Hutchings, Arthur. The Baroque Concerto. New York:
Norton, 1961, pp. 133-173. Extensive remarks on
stylistic traits and Vivaldi's contribution to the concerto
form. Much comparison with others. Musical examples.
Kolneder, Walter. Antonio Vivaldi: His Life and Work.
Translated by Bill Hopkins. Berkeley: University of
California Press, 1970, 288p. An excellent source of
critical and analytic material on all of Vivaldi's works.
Musical examples.
Palisca, Claude V. Baroque Music. Englewood Cliffs,
N. J.: Prentice Hall, 1968, pp. 149-152. Critical re-
marks on specific concertos as well as commentary on
Vivaldi's handling of the new form. Musical examples.
Pincherle, Marc. Vivaldi: Genius of the Baroque. Trans-

lated from the French by Christopher Hatch. New York:
Norton, 1962, 278p. The definitive work on Vivaldi for
many years, treating all his works and life. Good musical discussion with examples on style, form and Vivaldi's
conception of the evolving concerto form.

Veinus, Abraham. The Concerto. New York: Dover,
1964, pp. 21-26. General remarks on the special character of the music. Mainly descriptive and background
remarks. Not analytic.

Concerto in C major for Violoncello, op. 3, no. 6

Green, Douglass M. Form in Tonal Music. New York:
Holt, Rinehart and Winston, 1965, pp. 231-232. Brief,
but compact analysis with graph. Some general observations on characteristics shared by most Vivaldi first and
last movements of concertos. Last movement only.

Concerto in A minor for Violoncello, op. 3, no. 8

Green, Douglass M. Form in Tonal Music. New York:
Holt, Rinehart and Winston, 1965, pp. 228-231. Very
close analysis with elaborate graphs and musical examples. First movement only.

WEBERN, ANTON, 1883-1945

Concerto for Nine Instruments

Hansen, Peter S. An Introduction to Twentieth Century
Music. second edition. Boston: Allyn & Bacon, 1967,
pp. 226-228. Brief analysis of this nine-minute composition. Musical examples.

CHAPTER VI: CHAMBER MUSIC

BACH, JOHANN SEBASTIAN, 1685-1750

General

Geiringer, Karl. Johann Sebastian Bach. New York: Oxford University Press, 1966, pp. 302-314. Brief overview of the sonatas and trios. Musical examples.
Terry, Charles Sanford. The Music of Bach. New York: Dover, 1963, pp. 43-54. Brief review of the sonatas and trios. Musical examples.

BARBER, SAMUEL, 1910-

General

Broder, Nathan. Samuel Barber. New York: G. Schirmer, 1954, pp. 73-74. Brief remarks.

BARTOK, BELA, 1881-1945

General

Ferguson, Donald N. Image and Structure in Chamber Music. Minneapolis: University of Minnesota Press, 1964, pp. 273-292. Solid critical and analytic discussion. Musical examples.
Seiber, Matyas. "Béla Bartók's chamber music," in Béla Bartók: A Memorial Review. Oceanside, N. Y. : Boosey & Hawkes, 1950, pp. 23-35. Solid analyses of the quartets and sonatas. Musical examples.
Stevens, Halsey. The Life and Music of Béla Bartók. New York: Oxford University Press, 1953, pp. 170-226. Thorough treatment of style with analytic insights. Musical examples.

206   CHAMBER MUSIC

String Quartets

Abraham, Gerald. Slavonic and Romantic Music. New
    York: St. Martin's Press, 1968, pp. 339-349. Traces
    Bartók's style in the quartets. Analytic, with musical
    examples.
Karpati, Janos. Bartók's String Quartets. Budapest:
    Corvina Press, 1975, 279p. Thorough overview, in-depth,
    of the six string quartets. Musical examples.
Monelle, R. "Bartók's imagination in the later quartets,"
    Music Review 31:1 (1970), 70-81. Analytic and critical
    comments on the later quartets (third to sixth). Musical
    examples.
Robertson, Alec, ed. Chamber Music. Baltimore: Pen-
    guin, 1957, pp. 220-252. Thorough critical and analytic
    overview. Musical examples.
Suchoff, Benjamin, ed. Béla Bartók Essays. New York:
    St. Martin's, 1976, pp. 412-415. Brief, but highly con-
    densed formal analysis with charts. No musical exam-
    ples. Score needed.
Ulrich, Homer. Chamber Music. second edition. New
    York: Columbia University Press, 1966, pp. 355-357.
    Brief summary of the characteristics of the quartets.
    No musical examples.

String Quartet no. 2

Whittall, A. "Bartók's second string quartet," Music Re-
    view 32:3 (1971), 265-270. Analysis with musical exam-
    ples. Advanced discussion.

String Quartet no. 4

Hansen, Peter S. An Introduction to Twentieth Century
    Music. second edition. Boston: Allyn and Bacon, 1967,
    pp. 237-242. Analysis for the student. Musical exam-
    ples.
Monelle, R. "Notes on Bartók's fourth quartet," Music Re-
    view 29:2 (1968), 123-129. Analysis with musical exam-
    ples.
Travis, Roy. "Tonal coherence in the first movement of
    Bartók's Fourth String Quartet," in The Music Forum.
    Vol. II. New York: Columbia University Press, 1970,
    pp. 298-371. Advanced analysis of the first movement
    using Schenkerian concepts. Musical examples.

String Quartet no. 5

Winrow, B. "Allegretto con differencia: a study of the
'barrel organ' episode in Bartók's Fifth Quartet," Music
Review 32:2 (1971), 102-106. Shows organic relationship
of "barrel organ" episode to the whole. Musical examples.

String Quartet no. 6

Austin, William W. Music in the 20th Century. New York:
Norton, 1966, pp. 325-328. Descriptive and analytic
commentary. Musical examples.

BEETHOVEN, LUDWIG VAN, 1770-1827

General

Arnold, Denis and Nigel Fortune. The Beethoven Companion. London: Faber & Faber, 1971, pp. 197-278.
Thorough descriptive and critical overview with musical
examples.
Ferguson, Donald N. Image and Structure in Chamber
Music. Minneapolis: University of Minnesota Press,
1964, pp. 75-133. Solid critical and analytic discourse
with musical examples.
Robertson, Alec, ed. Chamber Music. Baltimore: Pen-
guin Books, 1957, pp. 94-140. Full critical and analytic
discussion of specific works. An extensive overview.
Musical examples.
Scherman, Thomas K. and Louis Biancolli, eds. The
Beethoven Companion. New York: Doubleday, 1972,
1230p. Program-note style commentary. Easy to read.
No musical examples.
Ulrich, Homer. Chamber Music. second edition. New
York: Columbia University Press, 1966, pp. 217-262.
Thorough survey of the chamber works, their background,
influences and style.

String Quartets

Cooke, D. "The unity of Beethoven's late quartets," Music
Review 24:1 (1963), 30-49. An analysis based on thematic unity of the last five string quartets. Author views
them as a single creative process. Musical examples.
Cooper, Martin. Beethoven: The Last Decade, 1817-1827.

London: Oxford University Press, 1970, pp. 349-414.
Thorough critical and analytic overview of op. 127, 130,
131, 132, 135. Musical examples.
Mann, R. "1770-1970--Beethoven's 200th year. 'Es muss
sein,'" Music Journal 28 (Oct. 1970), 36+. Critical
overview of entire string quartet output.
Marliave, Joseph de. Beethoven's Quartets. New York:
Dover, 1961, 379p. Full descriptive commentary with
musical examples. Many analytic insights.
Radcliffe, Philip. Beethoven's String Quartets. London:
Hutchinson University Library, 1965, 192p. Thorough
treatment with background and analytic insights. Musical
examples.
Riseling, Robert A. "Motivic structures in Beethoven's late
quartets," in Glowacki, John, ed. Paul A. Pisk: Essays
in His Honor. Austin: University of Texas, 1966,
pp. 141-162. Analytic discourse for the advanced student.
Musical examples.

Violin and Piano Sonatas

Robertson, Alec, ed. Chamber Music. Baltimore: Penguin, 1957, pp. 262-267. Critical remarks with musical
examples.

Grosse Fuge, op. 133

Kirkendale, W. "The 'Great Fugue,' Op. 133: Beethoven's
'Art of Fugue,'" Acta Musicologica 35:1 (1963), 14-24.
Advanced analytic discussion.
Misch, Ludwig. Beethoven Studies. Norman: University
of Oklahoma, 1953, pp. 3-13. Analysis with musical ex-
amples.

String Quartet no. 1, op. 18, F major

Warburton, A. O. "Set works for 'O' level," Music Teacher 52 (Aug. 1973), 18-19. Analysis for the student. To
be used with score.

String Quartet no. 2, op. 18, G major

Warburton, A. O. "Set works for 'O' level," Music Teacher 48 (October 1969), 19-20+. Analysis for the student.
To be used with score.

String Quartet no. 12, op. 127, E♭ major

George, Graham. Tonality and Musical Structure. New
York: Praeger, 1970, pp. 152-160. Analysis focusing
on tonality. Musical examples. Advanced.

String Quartet no. 13, op. 130, B♭ major

George, Graham. Tonality and Musical Structure. New
York: Praeger, 1970, pp. 160-171. Analysis focusing
on tonality. Musical examples. Advanced.

String quartet no. 16, op. 135, F major

Kramer, J. D. "Multiple and non-linear time in Beethoven's
opus 135," Perspectives of New Music 11:2 (1973), 122-
145. Theory that Beethoven's use of time bears strong
resemblances to modern time conceptions in music. This
is the reason for the freshness of Beethoven's music to today's ears. Advanced discussion. Musical examples.

Violin Sonata no. 9, op. 47, A major ("Kreutzer")

Nallin, Walter E. The Musical Idea. New York: Macmillan, 1968, pp. 431-434. Analysis with musical examples.

BERG, ALBAN, 1885-1935

General

Carner, Mosco. Alban Berg: The Man and the Work.
New York: Holmes & Meier, 1975, pp. 102-123. Analyses of all Berg's chamber works. Musical examples.

Chamber Concerto for Piano & 13 Wind Instruments

Reich, Willi. Alban Berg. Translated by Cornelius Cardew.
New York: Harcourt, Brace and World, 1965, pp. 143-
148. Thorough analysis by Berg himself. No musical
examples.

Lyric Suite

Bauer-Mengelberg, S. and M. Ferentz. "On eleven-interval
twelve-tone rows," Perspectives of New Music 3:2 (1965),
93-103. Advanced analytic discussion.

Ferguson, Donald N.   Image and Structure in Chamber
   Music.   Minneapolis: University of Minnesota Press,
   1964, pp. 296-301.   Brief analytic discussion.
Hansen, Peter S.   An Introduction to Twentieth Century
   Music. second edition.   Boston: Allyn & Bacon, 1967,
   pp. 210-213.   Descriptive commentary.   For beginning
   student.   Musical examples.
Redlich, H. F.   Alban Berg: The Man and His Music.
   London: John Calder, 1957, pp. 137-154.   Thorough
   analysis with musical examples.
Reich, Willi.   Alban Berg.   Translated by Cornelius Cardew.
   New York: Harcourt, Brace & World, 1965, pp. 149-152.
   Analysis.   No musical examples.

String Quartets, op. 3 and op. 10

Redlich, H. F.   Alban Berg: The Man and His Music.
   London: John Calder, 1957, pp. 49-55.   Concise analytic commentary.   Musical examples.

BLOCH, ERNEST, 1880-1959

General

Robertson, Alec, ed.   Chamber Music.   Baltimore: Penguin, 1957, pp. 215-219.   Critical remarks with musical
   examples.

String Quartet no. 2

Tischler, Hans.   The Perceptive Music Listener.   Englewood Cliffs, N. J. :   Prentice-Hall, 1955, pp. 306-311.
   Analysis with musical examples.

BRAHMS, JOHANNES, 1833-1897

General

Colles, H. C.   The Chamber Music of Brahms.   London:
   Oxford University Press, 1933, 64p.   Descriptive and
   analytic commentary for the student.   Musical examples.
Ferguson, Donald N.   Image and Structure in Chamber
   Music.   Minneapolis: University of Minnesota Press,
   1964, pp. 175-218.   Solid critical and analytic discourse
   with musical examples.

Geiringer, Karl. Brahms: His Life and Work. second
edition. New York: Oxford University Press, 1947,
pp. 224-246. Critical overview with musical examples.
Keys, Ivor. Brahms Chamber Music. London: British
Broadcasting Corp., 1974, 68p. Full background and
analyses of all the chamber works. Musical examples.
Mason, Daniel Gregory. The Chamber Music of Brahms.
New York: Macmillan, 1933, 276p. Full book-length
treatment on the chamber music. Background with de-
scriptive and analytic commentary. Musical examples.
Niemann, Walter. Brahms. Translated by Catherine
Alison Phillips. New York: Cooper Square, 1969,
pp. 256-301. Descriptive and critical overview. No
musical examples.
Pascall, R. "Ruminations on Brahms' chamber music, "
Musical Times 116 (August 1975), 697-699. Descriptive
overview with analytic insights.
Robertson, Alec, ed. Chamber Music. Baltimore: Pen-
guin, 1957, pp. 191-201. Critical and analytic remarks.
Musical examples.
Tovey, Donald Francis. The Main Stream of Music and
Other Essays. New York: Meridian, 1959, pp. 220-270.
Thorough overview of Brahms' chamber music with men-
tion of many specific works. Descriptive, critical and
analytic. For the student. Musical examples.
Ulrich, Homer. Chamber Music. second edition. New
York: Columbia University Press, 1966, pp. 299-338.
Critical overview with background and stylistic character-
istics. Musical examples.

Quartet for Piano and Strings, no. 1, op. 25, G minor

Tischler, Hans. The Perceptive Music Listener. Englewood Cliffs, N.J.: Prentice-Hall, 1955, pp. 301-306.
Analysis with musical examples.
Tovey, Donald Francis. Essays in Musical Analysis: Chamber Music. London: Oxford University Press, 1944,
pp. 185-193. Analysis with musical examples.

Quartet for Piano and Strings, no. 2, op. 26, A major

Tovey, Donald Francis. Essays in Musical Analysis: Chamber Music. London: Oxford University Press, 1944,
pp. 194-202. Analysis with musical examples.

Quartet for Piano and Strings, no. 3, op. 60, C minor

Tovey, Donald Francis. Essays in Musical Analysis: Cham-

ber Music. London: Oxford University Press, 1944,
pp. 203-214. Analysis with musical examples.

Quintet for Clarinet and Strings, op. 115, B minor

Nallin, Walter E. The Musical Idea. New York: Macmillan, 1968, pp. 434-436. Analytic sketch with musical
examples.

Quintet for Piano and Strings, op. 34, F minor

Newbould, B. "Analysis in the sixth form," Music Teacher
54 (July 1975), 16-17. Analysis with musical examples.
For the student.

Sonata for Violoncello, op. 38, F minor

Klenz, W. "Brahms, op. 38; piracy, pillage, plagiarism
or parody?" Music Review 34:1 (1973), 39-50. Similarities between the Romberg violoncello sonata and Brahms'
discussed in detail. Musical examples.

BORODIN, ALEXANDER, 1833-1887

General

Ferguson, Donald N. Image and Structure in Chamber
Music. Minneapolis: University of Minnesota Press,
1964, pp. 220-222. Brief analytic remarks.

DEBUSSY, CLAUDE, 1862-1918

General

Lockspeiser, Edward. Debussy. London: Dent, 1951,
pp. 163-181. Descriptive, critical and analytic commentary with musical examples.
Thompson, Oscar. Debussy: Man and Artist. New York:
Dover, 1965, pp. 332-340. Descriptive and critical commentary. No musical examples.

String Quartet

Ferguson, Donald N. Image and Structure in Chamber
Music. Minneapolis: University of Minnesota Press,

1964, pp. 257-259.   Brief analytic discussion.   Musical
examples.
Nichols, Roger.   Debussy.   London: Oxford University
Press, 1973, pp. 24-30.   Analytic and critical observations.   Musical examples.

DVORAK, ANTONIN, 1841-1904

General

Ferguson, Donald N.   Image and Structure in Chamber
Music.   Minneapolis: University of Minnesota Press,
1964, pp. 226-238.   Critical and analytic discourse with
musical examples.
Robertson, Alec, ed.   Chamber Music.   Baltimore: Penguin, 1957, pp. 206-214.   Critical remarks with musical
examples.
Robertson, Alec.   Dvořák.   London: Dent, 1945, pp. 172-
192.   Descriptive, critical and analytic commentary.
Musical examples.

ELGAR, EDWARD, 1857-1934

General

Kennedy, Michael.   Portrait of Elgar.   London: Oxford
University Press, 1968, 324p.   Brief critical remarks.
Musical examples.   Use index to locate discussion of
specific works.
Parrot, Ian.   Elgar.   London: Dent, 1971, pp. 79-82.
Brief critical overview.   Musical examples.
Young, Percy.   Elgar, O. M. :   A Study of a Musician.   Lon-
don: Collins, 1955, 447p.   Brief descriptive and critical
remarks.   Musical examples.   Use index to locate discus-
sion of specific works.

FAURE, GABRIEL, 1845-1924

General

Suckling, Norman.   Fauré.   London: Dent, 1946, pp. 90-
119.   Thorough critical and analytic review.   Musical
examples.
Vuillermoz, Emile.   Gabriel Fauré.   Translated by Kenneth

Schapiro.   Philadelphia: Chilton Book Co., 1960, 265p.
Brief descriptive and critical remarks.   No musical examples.

FRANCK,   CESAR,   1822-1890

General

Davies, Laurence.   Franck.   London: Dent, 1973, pp. 84-
93.   Influences, style and critical remarks.   Musical examples.
Demuth, Norman.   César Franck.   London: Dobson, n. d.,
pp. 123-142.   Thorough critical and analytic discussion.
Musical examples.
Ferguson, Donald N.   Image and Structure in Chamber
Music.   Minneapolis: University of Minnesota Press,
1964, pp. 242-257.   Critical and analytic discourse with
musical examples.
Vallas, Leon.   César Franck.   Translated by Hubert Foss.
New York: Oxford University Press, 1951, 283p.   Criti-
cal remarks.   No musical examples.

GRIEG,   EDVARD,   1843-1907

General

Abraham, Gerald, ed.   Grieg: A Symposium.   Norman:
University of Oklahoma Press, 1948, pp. 32-44.   Thorough descriptive and analytic commentary.   Musical examples.
Horton, John.   Grieg.   London: Dent, 1974, 255p.   Critical remarks with musical examples.

HAYDN,   FRANZ JOSEPH,   1732-1809

General

Ferguson, Donald N.   Image and Structure in Chamber
Music.   Minneapolis: University of Minnesota Press,
1964, pp. 30-45.   Critical and analytic discourse with
musical examples.
Geiringer, Karl.   Haydn: A Creative Life in Music.
Berkeley: University of California, 1968, 434p.   Critical
and analytic commentary with musical examples.   Use
index to locate discussion of specific works.

Hughes, Rosemary. Haydn. London: Dent, 1962, pp. 150-
169. Critical and analytic commentary for the student.
Musical examples.
Landon, H. C. Robbins. Haydn: Chronicle and Works.
Vol. III (Haydn in England, 1791-1795). Bloomington:
Indiana University Press, 1976, pp. 405-482. Thorough
treatment on all forms of Haydn's chamber music. Critical and analytic. Musical examples.
Tovey, Donald Francis. The Mainstream of Music and
Other Essays. New York: Oxford University Press,
1949, pp. 1-64. Excellent discourse on Haydn's role in
the string quartet as a medium, stylistic traits, and
specific works. Musical examples.

Baryton Trios

Wollenberg, S. "Haydn's baryton trios and the 'Gradus,'"
Music & Letters 54:2 (1973), 170-178. A study of the
influence of Fux on Haydn in these works. Musical examples.

String Quartets

Barrett-Ayres, Reginald. Joseph Haydn and the String
Quartet. New York: Schirmer Books, 1974, 417p.
Exhaustive study of style, influences and innovations with
analytic comments on specific works. Musical examples.
Cuyler, Louise. "Tonal exploitation in the later quartets of
Haydn," in Landon, H. C. Robbins, ed. Studies in
Eighteenth-Century Music. London: George Allen &
Unwin, 1970, pp. 136-150. Advanced discussion on
Haydn's daring use of tonality. Musical examples.
Geiringer, Karl. "The rise of chamber music," in The
New Oxford History of Music, Vol. 7 (The Age of En-
lightenment, 1745-1790). London: Oxford University
Press, 1973, pp. 553-563; 565-566. Brief overview
focusing on Haydn's contribution to the medium. Stylistic
traits mentioned. Musical examples.
Robertson, Alec, ed. Chamber Music. Baltimore: Pen-
guin Books, 1957, pp. 13-55. Thorough critical and
analytic review of Haydn's Quartet output. Observations
on innovations and stylistic growth. Musical examples.
Somfai, Laszlo. "A bold enharmonic modulatory model in
Joseph Haydn's string quartets," in Landon, H. C. Robbins, ed. Studies in Eighteenth-Century Music. London:
George Allen & Unwin, 1970, pp. 370-381. Advanced
discussion on Haydn's bold harmonic experiments. Musical examples.

Ulrich, Homer.   Chamber Music.   second edition.   New
   York: Columbia University Press, 1966, pp. 154-185.
   Thorough critical summation with historical background.
   Musical examples.

String Quartet, op. 9, no. 4, D minor

Keller, H.   "Today's tomorrow," Music Review 26:3 (1965),
   247-251.   Analysis with musical examples.

String Quartet, op. 20, no. 1, E♭ major

Keller, H.   "The string quartet and its relatives," Music
   Review 26:4 (1965), 340-344.   Analysis with musical examples.

String Quartet, op. 20, no. 2, C major

Keller, H.   "The string quartet and its relatives," Music
   Review 27:1 (1966), 59-62.   Analysis with musical examples.

String Quartet, op. 20, no. 3, G minor

Keller, H.   "The string quartet and its relatives," Music
   Review 27:1 (1966), 228-232.   Analysis with musical examples.

String Quartet, op. 20, no. 4, D major

Keller, H.   "The string quartet and its relatives," Music
   Review 27:3 (1966), 232-235.   Analysis with musical examples.

String Quartet, op. 54, no. 1, G major

Warburton, A. O.   "Set works for 'O' level," Music Teacher 48 (July 1969), 9-10.   Analysis for the student.   To
   be used with score.

String Quartet, op. 76, no. 3, C major ("Emperor")

Nallin, Walter E.   The Musical Idea.   New York: Macmillan, 1968, pp. 429-431.   Analytic sketch with musical
   examples.

String Quartet, op. 76, no. 5, D major

Tischler, Hans. The Perceptive Music Listener. Englewood Cliffs, N.J.: Prentice-Hall, 1955, pp. 286-290.
Analysis with musical examples.

HINDEMITH, PAUL, 1895-1963

General

Ferguson, Donald N. Image and Structure in Chamber
Music. Minneapolis: University of Minnesota Press,
1964, pp. 292-296. Brief critical and analytic remarks.
No musical examples.
Ulrich, Homer. Chamber Music. second edition. New
York: Columbia University Press, 1966, pp. 359-362.
Mainly about the quartets. A discussion of style and
idiom. No musical examples.

String Quartets

Deri, Otto. Exploring Twentieth-Century Music. New York:
Holt, Rinehart & Winston, 1968, pp. 395-410. Analysis
with musical examples.

IVES, CHARLES EDWARD, 1074-1954

General

Bader, Y. "The chamber music of Charles Edward Ives,"
Music Review 33:4 (1972), 292-299. Descriptive and
analytic overview. No musical examples.
Hitchcock, H. Wiley. Ives. London: Oxford University
Press, 1977, pp. 57-72. Analytic discussion with musi-
cal examples. Intended for student.

MENDELSSOHN, FELIX, 1809-1847

General

Ferguson, Donald N. Image and Structure in Chamber
Music. Minneapolis: University of Minnesota Press,
1964, pp. 156-163. Brief critical and analytic remarks.
No musical examples.

Horton, John. Mendelssohn Chamber Music. Seattle:
University of Washington Press, 1972, 64p. Descriptive
and analytic commentary for the student. Musical examples.
Radcliffe, Philip. Mendelssohn. London: Dent, 1954,
pp. 80-102. Brief critical overview with musical examples. Intended for student.
Robertson, Alec, ed. Chamber Music. Baltimore: Penguin, 1957, pp. 175-182. Critical and analytic remarks.
Musical examples.
Werner, Eric. Mendelssohn. Translated from the German
by Dika Newlin. New York: Free Press of Glencoe,
1963, 545p. Analytic and critical remarks with musical
examples. Use index to locate discussion of specific
works.

MOZART, WOLFGANG AMADEUS, 1756-1791

General

Blom, Eric. Mozart. London: Dent, 1952, pp. 233-252.
Brief overview, intended for student, with critical re-
marks. Musical examples.
Einstein, Alfred. Mozart: His Character, His Work.
Translated by Arthur Mendel and Nathan Broder. London:
Oxford University Press, 1945, 492p. Scholarly discourse
on influences and style. Musical examples. Use table of
contents to locate discussion of specific topics.
Ferguson, Donald N. Image and Structure in Chamber
Music. Minneapolis: University of Minnesota Press,
1964, pp. 46-74. Critical and analytic commentary with
musical examples.
Geiringer, Karl. "The Rise of Chamber Music," in The
New Oxford History of Music, Vol. 7 (The Age of En-
lightenment, 1745-1790). London: Oxford University
Press, 1973, pp. 539-545. Very brief descriptive overview of the violin sonatas, piano trios, and piano quintets.
Musical examples.
Landon, H. C. Robbins and Donald Mitchell. The Mozart
Companion. New York: Norton, 1969, pp. 90-137.
Thorough review by Hans Keller of the string quartets,
quintets, flute quartets and piano and string works. Mu-
sical examples.
Robertson, Alec, ed. Chamber Music. Baltimore: Penguin Books, 1957, pp. 60-93. The trios, quartets and
quintets explored from various musical points of view;

harmony, form, technique, use of counterpoint and
rhythm. Musical examples.
Ulrich, Homer. Chamber Music. second edition. New
York: Columbia University Press, 1966, pp. 186-216.
Thorough survey of the chamber works, their background,
influences and stylistic growth. Musical examples.

Octets for Wind Instruments

Leeson, D. N. and D. Whitwell. "Mozart's 'spurious' wind
octets," Music & Letters 53:4 (1972), 377-399. On the
authenticity of these works. Musical examples.

Quintets

Geiringer, Karl. "The Rise of Chamber Music," in The
New Oxford History of Music, Vol. 7 (The Age of En-
lightenment 1745-1790). London: Oxford University
Press, 1973, pp. 569-572. Brief overview with mention
of some outstanding examples in the form, notably K. 516.
Musical examples.

String Quartets

Dunhill, Thomas F. Mozart's String Quartets. Westport,
Conn. : Greenwood Press, 1970, 44p. Descriptive and
analytic commentary for the student. Musical examples.

Quartet for Flute, Violin, Viola and Violoncello, K. 171,
C major

Leavis, R. "Mozart's flute quartet in C, K. app. 171,"
Music & Letters 43:1 (1962), 48-52. On the authenticity
of this work. Musical examples.

Quintet for Clarinet and Strings in A major, K. 581

Kerman, Joseph. Listen. second edition. New York:
Worth Publishers, 1976, pp. 180-183. Background and
analysis with musical examples. For the student.
Tischler, Hans. The Perceptive Music Listener. Englewood Cliffs, N. J. : Prentice-Hall, 1955, pp. 291-295.
Analysis with musical examples.

Quintet for Piano, Oboe, Clarinet, Horn and Bassoon,
E♭ major, K. 452

Tovey, Donald Francis. Essays in Musical Analysis: Cham-
    ber Music. London: Oxford University Press, 1944,
    pp. 106-120. Thorough discussion with musical examples
    in an easy-to-read style.

Sinfonia Concertante, K. 364

Smith, E. "Mozart, 'Sinfonia Concertante,' K. 364,"
    Music Teacher 55 (Oct. 1976), 19-21. Analysis for the
    student. Musical examples.

String Quartet, K. 421, D minor

Mitchell, W. J. "Giuseppe Sarti and Mozart's Quartet,
    K. 421," Current Musicology 9 (1969), 147-153. Exam-
    ination of some long standing criticisms in the light of
    modern analysis. Musical examples.
Warburton, A. O. "Set works for 'O' level," Music Teach-
    er 49 (July 1970), 10+. Analysis for the student. To
    be used with score in hand.

String Quartet, K. 458, B♭ major ("Hunt")

Warburton, A. O. "Set works for 'O' level," Music Teach-
    er 52 (July 1973), 21+. Analysis for the student. To be
    used with score.

String Quartet, K. 465, C major ("Dissonant")

Vertrees, J. A. "Mozart's string quartet, K. 465; the
    history of a controversy," Current Musicology 17 (1974),
    96-114. History and discussion of criticisms directed at
    this controversial work. Musical examples.

                    RAVEL, MAURICE, 1875-1937

General

Demuth, Norman. Ravel. London: Dent, 1947, pp. 123-
    157. Overview, intended for student. The string quar-
    tet, piano trio and other chamber works receive critical
    attention. Musical examples.
Myers, Rollo H. Ravel: Life and Works. New York:

Thomas Yoseloff, 1960, pp. 180-189. Brief descriptive
and critical comments with musical examples.
Nichols, Roger. Ravel. London: Dent, 1977, 199p. Descriptive and critical commentary intended for student.
Musical examples. Use index to locate discussion of
specific works.
Orenstein, Arbie. Ravel: Man and Musician. New York:
Columbia University Press, 1975, 291p. Program-note
style treatment. No musical examples. Use index to
locate discussion of specific works.
Stuckenschmidt, H. H. Maurice Ravel. Translated from
the German by Samuel R. Rosenbaum. Philadelphia:
Chilton Book Co. , 1968, 271p. Descriptive commentary
with no musical examples. Use index to locate discussion of specific works.

String Quartet in F major

Ferguson, Donald N. Image and Structure in Chamber
Music. Minneapolis: University of Minnesota Press,
1964, pp. 260-262. Brief analytic remarks. Musical
examples.
Warburton, A. O. "Set works for 'O' level, " Music Teacher 50 (Dec. 1971), 13-15. Analysis for the student. To
be used with score.

SCHOENBERG, ARNOLD, 1874-1951

General

Ferguson, Donald N. Image and Structure in Chamber
Music. Minneapolis: University of Minnesota Press,
1964, pp. 304-309. Brief critical and analytic remarks
with musical examples.
MacDonald, Malcolm. Schoenberg. London: Dent, 1976,
pp. 131-156. Critical and analytic commentary intended
for student. Musical examples.
Payne, Anthony. Schoenberg. London: Oxford University
Press, 1968, 61p. Analytic commentary for intermediate
student. Musical examples.
Reich, Willi. Schoenberg: A Critical Biography. Trans-
lated by Leo Black. London: Longman, 268p. Descriptive and critical commentary. No musical examples.
Use index to locate discussion of specific works.
Ulrich, Homer. Chamber Music. second edition. New
York: Columbia University Press, 1966, pp. 348-352.

Brief summation of style, method and significance of the
chamber works. Musical examples.
Wellesz, Egon. Arnold Schönberg. Translated by W. H.
Kerridge. New York: Da Capo, 1969, 159p. Analytic
commentary with musical examples. For intermediate
student. Use index to locate discussion of specific works.
Whittall, Arnold. Schoenberg Chamber Music. Seattle:
University of Washington Press, 1972, 64p. Guide for
student. Surveys all the major chamber works, including
Transfigured Night. Descriptive with analytic commentary.
Musical examples.

String Quartets

Payne, A. "A note on Schoenberg's string quartets,"
Musical Times 113 (March 1972), 266-267. Brief analytic and critical remarks. No musical examples.

Second Quartet

Deri, Otto. Exploring Twentieth-Century Music. New
York: Holt, Rinehart & Winston, 1968, pp. 277-292.
Thorough analysis with musical examples.

SCHUBERT, FRANZ, 1797-1828

General

Abraham, Gerald, ed. The Music of Schubert. New York:
Norton, 1947, pp. 88-110. Solid critical overview with
musical examples.
Bie, Oscar. Schubert: The Man. New York: Dodd, Mead,
1928, pp. 123-153. Mainly descriptive commentary.
Musical examples.
Brown, Maurice J. E. Schubert: A Critical Biography.
London: Macmillan, 1961, 414p. Descriptive and criti-
cal commentary. Musical examples. Use index to locate
discussion of specific works.
Duncan, Edmondstoune. Schubert. London: Dent, 1934,
pp. 157-164. Critical commentary with musical examples.
Intended for student.
Einstein, Alfred. Schubert. Translated by David Ascoli.
London: Cassell, 1951, pp. 266-307. Critical remarks
on the three quartets. Musical examples.
Ferguson, Donald N. Image and Structure in Chamber
Music. Minneapolis: University of Minnesota Press,

1964, pp. 134-155. Critical and analytic commentary
with musical examples.
Hutchings, Arthur. Schubert. London: Dent, 1945,
pp. 109-128. Critical overview with musical examples.
Intended for student.
Robertson, Alec, ed. Chamber Music. Baltimore: Penguin, 1957, pp. 140-190. Thorough critical and analytic
overview with musical examples.
Ulrich, Homer. Chamber Music. second edition. New
York: Columbia University Press, 1966, pp. 263-298.
Critical overview with background and stylistic characteristics. Musical examples.
Whaples, M. K. "On structural integration in Schubert's
instrumental works," Acta Musicologica 40:2 (1968), 186-
195. Advanced discussion on unifying elements. Musical
examples.

String Quartets

Coolidge, R. A. "Form in the string quartets of Franz
Schubert," Music Review 32:4 (1971), 309-325. Thor-
ough analytic overview of form of the string quartets.
No musical examples.

Quartet Movement, D. 703, C minor

Bruce, R. "The lyrical element in Schubert's instrumental
forms," Music Review 30:2 (1969), 131-137. A comparison of this work to Beethoven's "Rasumovsky" quartet,
op. 59, no. 3, to show Schubert's lyrical emphasis in
contrast to Beethoven's dramatic. No musical examples.

Quartet D. 804, A minor

Tischler, Hans. The Perceptive Music Listener. Englewood Cliffs, N.J.: Prentice-Hall, 1955, pp. 296-300.
Analysis with musical examples.

String Quartet, D. 810, D minor ("Death and the Maiden")

Brown, M. J. "Schubert's D minor quartet: a footnote,"
Musical Times 111 (October 1970), 985+. A study of the
manuscript. Musical examples.

String Quartet, D. 887, G major

Gillet, J. "The problem of Schubert's G major string

quartet (D. 887), " Music Review 35:3-4 (1974), 281-292.
An interpretation on the "meaning" of this quartet. Musical examples.

String Quintet, D. 438, A minor

Kerman, Joseph. Listen. second edition. New York:
Worth Publishers, 1976, pp. 207-209. Background and
analysis with musical examples. For the student.

Trio for Violin, Violoncello, Piano, D. 898, B♭ major

Warburton, A. O. "Set works for 'O' level, " Music Teacher 48 (Nov. 1969), 15-16. Analysis for the student. To
be used with score in hand.

SCHUMANN, ROBERT, 1810-1856

General

Abraham, Gerald, ed. Schumann: A Symposium. London:
Oxford University Press, 1952, pp. 138-175. Thorough
overview with comments on background and style. Analytic insights. Musical examples.
Chissell, Joan. Schumann. London: Dent, 1967, pp. 155-
168. Critical overview intended for student. Musical
examples.
Ferguson, Donald N. Image and Structure in Chamber
Music. Minneapolis: University of Minnesota Press,
1964, pp. 164-174. Critical and analytic discourse with
musical examples.
Robertson, Alec, ed. Chamber Music. Baltimore: Pen-
guin, 1957, pp. 183-190. Critical and analytic remarks.
Musical examples.
Walker, Alan, ed. Robert Schumann: The Man and His
Music. London: Barrie & Jenkins, 1972, pp. 200-240.
Thorough analytic overview. Musical examples.

String Quartet, op. 41

Correll, L. E. "Structural revisions in the string quartets
opus 41 of Robert Schumann, " Current Musicology 7
(1968), 87-95. A study of the sketches to show Schumann's creative process. Musical examples.

Quintet for Piano and Strings, op. 44, E♭ major

Tovey, Donald Francis. Essays in Musical Analysis: Chamber Music. London: Oxford University Press, 1944,
pp. 149-154. Critical and analytic remarks with musical
examples in easy-to-read style.
Warburton, A. O. "Set works for 'O' level," Music Teacher 46 (Jan. 1967), 15+. Background and analysis for the
student. To be used with score.

SHOSTAKOVICH, DMITRI, 1906-1975

General

Kay, Norman. Shostakovich. London: Oxford University
Press, 1971, 78p. Analytic guide with special emphasis
on the twelfth Quartet. Musical examples.
Martynov, Ivan. Dmitri Shostakovich: The Man and His
Works. Translated from the Russian by T. Guralsky.
New York: Greenwood, 1947, 197p. Brief descriptive
and critical remarks. No musical examples.

SIBELIUS, JEAN, 1865-1957

General

Abraham, Gerald, ed. The Music of Sibelius. New York:
Norton, 1947, pp. 91-96. Brief critical commentary,
mainly on Voces Intimae. Musical examples.
Layton, Robert. Sibelius. London: Dent, 1965, pp. 135-
142. Brief critical overview. Musical examples.

Voces Intimae

Ringbom, Nils-Eric. Jean Sibelius. Translated from the
Swedish by G. I. C. de Courcy. Norman: University
of Oklahoma Press, 1954, pp. 97-116. Thorough analysis with musical examples.

SMETANA, BEDRICH, 1824-1884

General

Clapham, John. Smetana. London: Dent, 1972, pp. 65-70.

Critical overview with analytic commentary.   Musical examples.
Ferguson, Donald N.   Image and Structure in Chamber
Music.   Minneapolis: University of Minnesota Press,
1964, pp. 225-226.   Brief analytic remarks.
Robertson, Alec, ed.   Chamber Music.   Baltimore: Penguin, 1957, pp. 202-206.   Brief critical remarks.   Musical examples.

STRAVINSKY, IGOR, 1882-1971

General

Routh, Francis.   Stravinsky.   London: Dent, 1975, pp. 111-
114.   Brief comments on the significance of Stravinsky's
use of the chamber idiom.   No musical examples.
L'Histoire du Soldat receives some critical treatment
throughout book.
Tansman, Alexandre.   Igor Stravinsky: The Man and His
Music.   Translated by Therese and Charles Bleefield.
New York: Putnam's, 1949, 295p.   Brief descriptive
and critical commentary.   Special remarks on Soldier's
Tale.   No musical examples.   Use index to locate dis-
cussion of specific works.
Vlad, Roman.   Stravinsky.   Translated from the Italian by
Frederick and Ann Fuller.   second edition.   London:
Oxford University Press, 1967, pp. 50-66.   Critical com-
mentary with musical examples.   Includes discussion of
L'Histoire du Soldat (Soldier's Tale).
White, Eric Walter.   Stravinsky: The Composer and His
Works.   Berkeley: University of California, 1966, 608p.
Descriptive and critical commentary with musical exam-
ples.   Use index to locate discussion of specific works.

L'Histoire du Soldat (Suite) (The Soldier's Tale)

Nallin, Walter E.   The Musical Idea.   New York: Macmillan, 1968, pp. 436-440.   Analysis with musical examples.
Warburton, A. O.   "Set works for 'O' level," Music Teacher 46 (April 1967), 12+.   Background, descriptive and
analytic commentary for the student.   No musical examples.

TCHAIKOVSKY, PETER ILITCH, 1840-1893

Geńeral

Evans, Edwin. Tchaikovsky. London: Dent, 1966,
pp. 150-158. Background and critical commentary. No
musical examples.
Ferguson, Donald N. Image and Structure in Chamber
Music. Minneapolis: University of Minnesota Press,
1964, pp. 222-225. Brief analytic remarks.
Mason, Colin. "The Chamber Music," in Abraham, Gerald.
The Music of Tchaikovsky. New York: Norton, 1946,
pp. 104-113. Critical and analytic commentary with musical examples.

VAUGHAN WILLIAMS, RALPH, 1872-1958

General

Day, James. Vaughan Williams. London: Dent, 1961,
pp. 174-179. Brief remarks for the student. No musi-
cal examples.
Howes, Frank. The Music of Ralph Vaughan Williams.
London: Oxford University Press, 1954, pp. 211-226
Brief descriptive remarks with musical examples.
Kennedy, Michael. The Works of Ralph Vaughan Williams.
London: Oxford University Press, 1964, 776p. Descrip-
tive commentary with observations on style. Musical ex-
amples.

WEBERN, ANTON, 1883-1945

General

Kolneder, Walter. Anton Webern: An Introduction to His
Works. Translated by Humphrey Searle. Berkeley:
University of California Press, 1968. Analytic commentary with musical examples. Use table of contents to
locate discussion of specific works.

5 Movements for String Quartet, op. 5

Archibald, B. "Some thoughts on symmetry in early Webern: op. 4, no. 2," Perspectives of New Music 10:2
(1972), 159-163. Principle of symmetry as a unifying
device studied in this piece.

Boretz, B.   "Meta-variations, part IV: analytic fallout, "
   Perspectives of New Music 11:1 (1972), 217-223.   Highly
   technical discussion.
Ferguson, Donald N.   Image and Structure in Chamber
   Music.   Minneapolis: University of Minnesota Press,
   1964, pp. 302-304.   Discussion and analysis.   No musical examples.
Persky, S.   "A discussion of compositional choices in
   Webern's 'Fuenf Saetze fuer Streichquartett, ' op. 5, first
   movement, " Current Musicology 13 (1972), 68-74.   Advanced discussion on compositional techniques.   Musical
   examples.

Quartet for Clarinet, Violin, Saxophone and Piano

Fennelly, B.   "Structure and process in Webern's Opus 22, "
   Journal of Music Theory 10:2 (1966), 300-328.   Advanced
   analytic discussion.

String Quartet, op. 28

Huff, J. A.   "Webern's opus 28:   Serial organisation of
   time spans in the last movement, " Music Review 31:3
   (1970), 255-256.   Brief technical analysis.

String Trio, op. 20

Deri, Otto.   Exploring Twentieth-Century Music.   New
   York: Holt, Rinehart & Winston, 1968, pp. 374-376.
   Analysis with musical examples.

CHAPTER VII: SYMPHONIES

BEETHOVEN, LUDWIG VAN, 1770-1827

General

Arnold, Denis and Nigel Fortune, eds. The Beethoven Companion. London: Faber & Faber, 1971, pp. 281-313. Discusses all the symphonies. Solid, objective treatment on basic level. Musical examples.

Bekker, Paul. Beethoven. Translated and adapted from the German by M. M. Bozman. London: Dent, 1925, pp. 146-199. Discusses all the symphonies, noting Beethoven's artistic development. Highlights significant features and innovations in the symphonies. No musical examples.

Burk, John N. The Life and Works of Beethoven. New York: Random House, 1943, pp. 265-297. Individual, brief treatment of all the symphonies. Musical examples. Clear discussion of significant musical elements.

Cuyler, Louise. The Symphony. New York: Harcourt Brace Jovanovich, Inc., 1973, pp. 49-83. All the symphonies. Good, analytical treatment with musical examples. Shows formal structure clearly. Detailed, intelligent, objective.

Grove, George. Beethoven and His Nine Symphonies. third edition. New York: Dover Publications, 1962, 407p. Despite its age, a useful book for undergraduates. Full treatment of all the symphonies with musical examples. Some mention of the sketches and the creative process.

Hill, Ralph, ed. The Symphony. Harmondsworth, Middlesex, Eng.: Penguin, 1950, pp. 92-125. All the symphonies. Light, brief treatment.

La Rue, J. "Harmonic rhythm in the Beethoven Symphonies," Music Review 18:1 (Feb. 1957), 8-20. Advanced analysis focusing on rhythmic density. Musical examples.

Scherman, Thomas K. and Louis Biancolli. The Beethoven Companion. New York: Doubleday, 1972, pp. 117-939.

229

Includes critical material by Berlioz, Wagner, Debussy
and others. A compendium of remarks and observations
on the symphonies made by other famous composers.
Simpson, Robert Wilfred Levich. Beethoven Symphonies.
Seattle: University of Washington Press, 1971, 62p.
Critical and analytic guide to all the symphonies. For
the student. Musical examples.
Simpson, Robert. The Symphony. New York: Drake Publishers, 1972, pp. 104-174. Thorough stylistic and analytic overview for the student. Musical examples.
Tovey, Donald Francis. Essays in Musical Analysis. London: Oxford University Press, 1935, I, pp. 21-83.
Elevated, intelligent treatment meant for informed amateur. Objective, analytic approach to all the symphonies,
including a bar-by-bar analysis of the Ninth Symphony.

Symphony No. 1 in C major, op. 21

Hantz, E. "A pitch for rhythm: rhythmic patterns in
Beethoven's First Symphony; III (Minuetto), " In Theory
Only 1 (July 1975), 17-21. Advanced analysis focusing on
rhythmic patterns. Musical examples.

Symphony No. 2 in D major, op. 36

Pazure, R. "The development of the fourth movement of
Beethoven's Second Symphony considered as a variation of
the development of the first movement, " In Theory Only
2 (April-May 1976), 3-4. Advanced analysis with musical
examples.

Symphony No. 3 in E♭, op. 55 ("Eroica")

Bernstein, Leonard. The Infinite Variety of Music. New
York: Simon & Schuster, 1966, pp. 195-227. Analysis,
similar to Bernstein's television talks. Full discussion
with many insights. Musical examples.
Downs, Philip G. "Beethoven's 'new way' and the Eroica, "
Musical Quarterly 56:4 (Oct. 1970), 585-604. Advanced
analytic discussion focusing on Beethoven's techniques for
formal expansion. Musical examples.
Lang, Paul Henry, ed. The Creative World of Beethoven.
New York: Norton, 1970, pp. 83-102. Extensive treatment, emphasizing significance of structure and place of
this symphony in Beethoven's style. Musical examples.
Meikle, Robert Burns. "Thematic transformation in the
first movement of Beethoven's Eroica symphony, " Music

Review 32:3 (Aug. 1971), 205-218. The role of the "new"
theme introduced in the development section and its relationship to the whole. Musical examples.
Nadeau, Roland. The Symphony: Structure and Style. Boston: Crescendo, 1973, pp. 88-100. Bar-by-bar analysis
of entire symphony. Musical examples.
Nallin, Walter E. The Musical Idea. New York: Macmillan, 1968, pp. 168-169. Descriptive commentary on the
variations of final movement. Key changes, rhythms and
other musical devices employed in the variation identified.
Last movement only.
Ringer, A. L. "Clementi and the 'Eroica,'" Musical Quarterly 47:4 (1961), 454-468. Influence of Clementi on
Beethoven shown in detail. Musical examples.
Rosen, Charles. The Classical Style: Haydn, Mozart,
Beethoven. New York: Viking, 1971, pp. 392-5. Discussion of the structural implications, unifying elements
and expansion of classical sonata form as found in this
symphony. Musical examples.
Tischler, Hans. The Perceptive Music Listener. Engle-
wood Cliffs, N.J.: Prentice-Hall, 1955, pp. 347-352.
Compact analysis with musical examples.

Symphony No. 5 in C minor, op. 67

Bernstein, Leonard. The Joy of Music. New York: Simon
& Schuster, 1959, pp. 73-93. The script of Bernstein's
television shows. Shows creative process involved in ar-
riving at the "fifth" we all know. Discusses sketches.
Musical examples.
Forbes, Elliott, ed. Ludwig van Beethoven: Symphony
no. 5 in C minor. (Norton Critical Scores). New York:
Norton, 1971, 202p. The full orchestral score with crit-
ical and analytic commentary.
Kerman, Joseph. Listen. second edition. New York:
Worth Publishers, 1972, pp. 191-195. Analysis with mu-
sical examples. Intended for the student.
Machlis, Joseph. The Enjoyment of Music. third edition.
New York: Norton, 1970, pp. 279-285. Analytic over-
view for the music student. Musical examples.

Symphony No. 6 in F major, op. 68 ("Pastoral")

Kirby, F. E. "Beethoven's Pastoral Symphony as a
Sinfonia Caracteristica," Musical Quarterly 56:4 (Oct.
1970), 605-623. Shows how Beethoven remained wholly
within the objective framework of symphonic form while

superimposing an emotional content through the use of
certain pastoral or idyllic musical devices. An interesting comparison of objectivity of form and emotional content.
Nadeau, Roland. The Symphony: Structure and Style. Boston: Crescendo, 1973, pp. 193-215. Score of first movement analytically marked to show structure and thematic
treatment.
Warburton, A. O. "Set works for 'O' level," Music Teacher 47 (Nov. 1968), 13-14+. Bar-by-bar analysis for the
intermediate student. No musical examples.

Symphony No. 7 in A major, op. 92

Below, R. "Some aspects of tonal relationships in
Beethoven's Seventh Symphony," Music Review 37:1 (1976),
1-4. Concise, analytic commentary for the advanced. To
be used with score.
Cooke, Deryck. "In defence of functional analysis," Musical
Times 100 (Sept. 1959), 456-460. By way of argument
over analytic technique, Mr. Cooke analyzes Beethoven's
Symphony No. 7 in detail. Musical examples.
Machlis, Joseph. The Enjoyment of Music. third edition.
New York: Norton, 1970, pp. 287-291. Compact analy-
sis for the student. Musical examples.
Nallin, Walter E. The Musical Idea. New York: Macmillan, 1968, pp. 210-212. Brief analysis with musical ex-
amples.

Symphony No. 9 in D minor, op. 125 ("Choral")

Cooper, Martin. Beethoven, the Last Decade. London:
Oxford University Press, 1970, 277-348. Exhaustive
treatment of entire symphony. Discussion on high level
with musical examples. Also treats Beethoven's creative
process in the work, including some of his sketches for
the symphony.
Kirby, F. E. "Beethoven and the 'geselliges Lied,'" Music
& Letters 47:2 (1966), 116-125. Advanced discussion of
the choral portion of the Ninth Symphony. Specific remarks on Beethoven's intention in adding a choral movement to an instrumental work and the forms he drew upon.
Tovey, Donald Francis. Essays in Musical Analysis. London: Oxford University Press, 1935, II, pp. 1-45. Intelligent, clear treatment, including a thorough analysis.
Musical examples.
Vaughan Williams, Ralph. Some Thoughts on Beethoven's

Choral Symphony. London: Oxford University Press, 1959, pp. 1-52. Observations by a famous composer on Beethoven's Ninth. Analytical and subjective thoughts on entire symphony.

BERLIOZ, HECTOR, 1803-1869

General

MacDonald, Hugh. Berlioz Orchestral Music. Seattle: University of Washington Press, 1969, pp. 30-39. Critical and analytic commentary intended for the student.
Primmer, Brian. The Berlioz Style. London: Oxford University Press, 1973, 202p. A general discussion of Berlioz's musical characteristics. The Fantastic Symphony and other works are treated throughout the entire book. Access to discussion of specific works through index.

Symphonie fantastique

Cone, Edward T. , ed. Hector Berlioz. Fantastic Symphony: An Authoritative Score, Historical Background, Analysis, Views and Comments. New York: Norton, 1971, 305p Orchestral score accompanied by critical commentary. A Norton Critical Score for the student.
Cuyler, Louise. The Symphony. New York: Harcourt Brace Jovanovich, 1973, pp. 139-143. Brief analysis of entire symphony with musical examples.
Dickinson, A. E. F. The Music of Berlioz. London: Faber & Faber, 1972, pp. 125-138. Substantial discussion focusing on background of symphony and the creative impulse behind it. Includes analysis with musical examples.
Elliot, J. H. Berlioz. New York: Farrar, Straus and Giroux, 1967, pp. 136-140. Brief treatment, mainly of a critical rather than analytic nature.
Kerman, Joseph. Listen. second edition. New York: Worth Publishers, 1972, pp. 240-245. Analysis with musical examples. Intended for student.
Machlis, Joseph. The Enjoyment of Music. third edition. New York: Norton, 1970, pp. 111-114. Analytic overview for the student. Musical examples.
Nadeau, Roland. The Symphony: Structure and Style. shorter edition. Revised. Boston: Crescendo, 1974, pp. 115-133. Bar-by-bar analysis. Detailed and objective.

Temperley, Nicholas. "The Symphonie Fantastique and its
program," Musical Quarterly 58:4 (Oct. 1971), 593-608.
The function of Berlioz's program in this symphony, and
his reasons for supplying a program are discussed.
Tischler, Hans. The Perceptive Music Listener. Englewood Cliffs, N. J. : Prentice-Hall, 1955, pp. 353-359.
Analysis with musical examples.

BIZET, GEORGES, 1838-1875

Symphony No. 1 in C (1855)

Curtiss, Mina. Bizet and His World. New York: Knopf,
1958, pp. 38-43. Brief treatment. Not analytical. Pro-
vides background and critical commentary.
Dean, Winton. Bizet. London: Dent, 1948, pp. 100-106.
Brief analytic and critical with musical examples.
Shanet, Howard. "Bizet's suppressed symphony," Musical
Quarterly 44:4 (October 1958), 461-476. Genesis of
Bizet's only symphony and its relationship to Gounod's
symphony. Detailed comparison and speculation on why
Bizet suppressed his symphony.

BORODIN, ALEXANDER, 1833-1887

General

Abraham, Gerald E. H. Borodin: The Composer and His
Music. London: Reeves, n. d. , pp. 20-63. Lengthy
commentary, largely descriptive. Not an analysis.
Dianin, Serge. Borodin. Translated from the Russian by
Robert Lord. London: Oxford University Press, 1963,
pp. 184-228. Comprehensive discussion of Borodin's
symphonies.

BRAHMS, JOHANNES, 1833-1897

General

Browne, Philip Austin. Brahms: The Symphonies. London:
Oxford University Press, 1933, 71p. Overview for the
student. Musical examples.
Cuyler, Louise. The Symphony. New York: Harcourt
Brace Jovanovich, 1973, pp. 104-125. Good musical dis-

cussion of all the symphonies. Background and general
characteristics of the symphonies as well as a detailed
musical analysis.
Evans, Edwin. Handbook to the Chamber and Orchestral
   Music of Johannes Brahms. London: William Reeves,
   n. d. , 2 Vols. Antiquated but thorough breakdown with
   musical examples.
Harrison, Julius. Brahms and His Four Symphonies. New
   York: Da Capo Press, 1971, 312p. Background, stylistic characteristics and orchestration as well as formal
   analysis. Quite thorough.
Horton, John. Brahms Orchestral Music. Seattle: University of Washington Press, 1968, pp. 32-38; 50-61. Critical and analytic commentary intended for the student.
Niemann, Walter. Brahms. Translated by Catharine Alison
   Phillips. New York: Cooper Square, 1969, pp. 323-348.
   Background, critical and analytic commentary. No musical examples.
Smith, R. R. "Motivic procedure in opening movements of
   the symphonies of Schumann, Bruckner and Brahms,"
   Music Review 36:2 (1975), 130-134. Advanced discussion
   on motivic treatment as an important element of sonata
   form. No musical examples.
Specht, Richard. Johannes Brahms. Translated by Eric
   Blom. London: Dent, 1930, pp. 265-285. Critical commentary with some analytic remarks.

Symphony No. 3 in F major, op. 90

Machlis, Joseph. The Enjoyment of Music. third edition.
   New York: Norton, 1970, pp. 154-156. Analytic overview with musical examples.

Symphony No. 4 in E minor, op. 98

Bernstein, Leonard. The Infinite Variety of Music. New
   York: Simon & Schuster, 1966, pp. 229-262. Thorough
   critical review, with many analytic insights in an easy-
   to-read style. Musical examples. First movement only.
Cantrell, Byron. "Three B's--three chaconnes," Current
   Musicology 12 (Sept. 1971), 69-73. Advanced discussion
   of Brahms' use of chaconne in his fourth symphony. Compares with the chaconnes of Bach and Beethoven.
Hendrickson, H. "Rhythmic activity in the symphonies of
   Brahms," In Theory Only 2 (Sept. 1976), 5-12+. Advanced analysis of rhythmic structure excluding the factors of pitch, register, timbre, intensity and position in
   texture. Musical examples.

Kerman, Joseph. Listen. second edition. New York:
Worth Publishers, 1972, pp. 278-283. Analysis with musical examples. Intended for student.
Leichtentritt, Hugo. Musical Form. Cambridge, Mass. :
Harvard University Press, 1959, p. 315. Brief, but
compact statement analyzing the variations. No musical
examples. Best used with score. Fourth movement only.

BRUCKNER, ANTON, 1824-1896

General

Cooke, Deryck. "The Bruckner problem simplified," Musical Times 110 (1969), 20-22; 142-144; 362-365; 479-482.
Full discussion of the many versions. Not analytic.
Doernberg, Erwin. The Life and Symphonies of Anton
Bruckner. London: Barrie and Rockliff, 1960, pp. 113-221.
Descriptive, critical and analytic commentary. Musical
examples.
Grant, Parks. "Bruckner and Mahler--the fundamental dis-
similarity of their styles," Music Review 32:1 (Feb.
1971), 36-55. Refutes the alleged similarity of Bruckner
and Mahler by close examination of stylistic traits. Mu-
sical examples.
Moravisik, M. J. "The Coda in the Symphonies of Anton
Bruckner," Music Review 34:3-4 (1973), 241-258. De-
tailed discussion of the structural elements in Bruckner's
symphonies as seen in the Codas.
Redlich, Hans Ferdinand. Bruckner and Mahler. London:
Dent, 1955, pp. 77-105. Descriptive and critical commentary with analytic insights. Intended for student.
Musical examples.
Simpson, Robert. The Essence of Bruckner. Philadelphia:
Chilton Book Co. , 1968, pp. 29-194. Substantial analyses
of all the symphonies.
Smith, R. R. "Motivic procedure in opening movements of
the symphonies of Schumann, Bruckner, and Brahms,"
Music Review 36:2 (1975), 130-134. Advanced discussion
on motivic treatment as an important element of sonata
form. No musical examples.
Watson, Derek. Bruckner. London: Dent, 1975, 174p.
Analytic commentary intended for student. Musical exam-
ples. Consult table of contents for individual works.
Wolff, Werner. Anton Bruckner: Rustic Genius. New York:
Cooper Square Publishers, 1973, pp. 180-252. Light
analysis of the symphonies. Musical examples.

Symphony No. 4 in E♭ major ("Romantic")

Tovey, Donald Francis. Essays in Musical Analysis. London: Oxford University Press, 1935, I, pp. 69-79. Intelligent discourse, placing Bruckner in perspective. Analytic commentary on symphony with musical examples.

Symphony No. 5 in B♭ major

Pope, S. "A performer's rights," Chord and Discord 2:10 (1963), 109-123. Guide for the conductor, but many analytic insights for the student. Musical examples.

Symphony No. 6 in A major

Pope, S. "A performer's rights," Chord and Discord 2:9 (1960), 78-86. Guide for the conductor, but many analytic insights for the student. Musical examples.

Symphony No. 7 in E major

Simpson, R. "The seventh symphony of Bruckner: an analysis," Chord and Discord 2:10 (1963), 57-67. Very thorough bar-by-bar analysis with musical examples.

Symphony No. 8 in C minor

Dawson-Bowling. "Theme and Tonal Unity in Bruckner's Eighth Symphony," Music Review 30:3 (1969), 225-236. Advanced analytic discussion. Musical examples.
Leichtentritt, Hugo. Musical Form. Cambridge, Mass.: Harvard University Press, 1959, pp. 379-424. Exhaustive, intense analysis with musical examples.

CHAUSSON, ERNEST, 1855-1899

Symphony in B♭ major, op. 20

Barricelli, Jean-Pierre and Leo Weinsten. Ernest Chausson. Norman: University of Oklahoma Press, 1955, pp. 164-176. Descriptive commentary with musical examples.

CLEMENTI, MUZIO, 1752-1832

General

Plantinga, Leon. Clementi: His Life and Music. London:
Oxford University Press, 1977, pp. 120-126. Descriptive,
critical and analytic commentary with musical examples.

COPLAND, AARON, 1900-

Symphony No. 3 (1946)

Berger, Arthur. Aaron Copland. New York: Oxford Uni-
versity Press, 1953, pp. 72-82. Analytic commentary,
touching on Copland's orchestration, chord spacing and
folk idiom.
Berger, Arthur. "The Third Symphony of Aaron Copland, "
Tempo Autumn 1948, pp. 20-27. Critical and analytic
discussion.
Hansen, Peter S. An Introduction to Twentieth Century
Music. second edition. Boston: Allyn & Bacon, Inc. ,
1967, pp. 325-328. Short summary of analytic highlights.
Musical examples.
Machlis, Joseph. Introduction to Contemporary Music.
New York: Norton, 1961, pp. 487-491. Light, analytical
treatment of entire symphony. Musical examples.
Smith, Julia. Aaron Copland. New York: Dutton, 1955,
pp. 241-245. Thorough descriptive commentary on the
entire symphony. Musical examples.

D'INDY, VINCENT, 1851-1931

Symphony No. 2 in B♭ major

Cooper, Martin. French Music: From the Death of Berlioz
to the Death of Fauré. London: Oxford University Press,
1951, pp. 158-161. Comments on program and thematic
structure.

DVORAK, ANTONIN, 1841-1904

General

Clapham, John. Antonin Dvořák: Musician and Craftsman.

New York: St. Martin's, 1966, pp. 57-92. Brief analytic sketches with musical examples.
Robertson, Alec. Dvořák. London: Dent, 1947, pp. 157-
171. Descriptive commentary with musical examples.
Simpson, Robert, ed. The Symphony. New York: Drake
Publishers, 1972, Vol. I, pp. 374-378. Thorough critical and analytic overview for the student. Musical examples.

Symphony No. 9 in E minor, op. 95 (Old No. 5, "New
World")

Bernstein, Leonard. The Infinite Variety of Music. New
York: Simon & Schuster, 1966, pp. 149-169. Analysis,
similar to Bernstein's television talks, on influences,
"Americanisms," and stylistic traits. Musical examples.
Clapham, J. "The evolution of Dvořák's symphony 'From
the New World,'" Musical Quarterly 44:2 (April 1958),
167-183. Lengthy article describing the "New World
Symphony" as it emerged in Dvořák's mind. Compares
sketches with completed score, discusses choice of in-
struments and use of folk elements. Musical examples.
Cuyler, Louise. The Symphony. New York: Harcourt
Brace Jovanovich, 1973, pp. 159-161. Concentrated
analysis of entire symphony.
Fischl, Viktor, ed. Antonin Dvořák: His Achievement.
Westport, Conn.: Greenwood Press, 1970, pp. 84-89.
Descriptive commentary, mentioning some of the folk
tunes used.
Machlis, Joseph. The Enjoyment of Music. third edition.
New York: Norton, 1970, pp. 144-150. Analysis with
musical examples.
Nallin, Walter E. The Musical Idea. New York: Macmil-
lan, 1968, pp. 527-531. Brief analysis with musical ex-
amples.
Tovey, Donald Francis. Essays in Musical Analysis. Lon-
don: Oxford University Press, 1935, II, pp. 106-110.
Excellent analysis of entire symphony.

ELGAR, EDWARD, 1857-1934

General

Parrott, Ian. Elgar. London: Dent, 1971, pp. 68-73.
Brief remarks showing influences on Elgar. Musical examples.

Young, Percy M. Elgar, O. M. : A Study of a Musician.
London: Collins, 1955, pp. 326-344. Overview of all
Elgar's orchestral writing. Mainly descriptive and sub-
jective rather than analytic. No musical examples.

FRANCK, CESAR, 1822-1890

Symphony in D minor

Benjamin, W. E. "Interlocking diatonic collections as a
source of chromaticism in late nineteenth century music,"
In Theory Only 1 (Feb. -March 1976), 35-39+. Advanced
analysis. No musical examples.
Cuyler, Louise. The Symphony. New York: Harcourt
Brace Jovanovich, 1973, pp. 148-150. Brief, but effi-
cient analysis.
Davies, Laurence. César Franck and His Circle. London:
Barrie & Jenkins, 1970, pp. 237-240. Criticism and
analysis with musical examples.
Davies, Laurence. Franck. London: Dent, 1973, pp. 102-
104. Brief analysis with musical examples.
Demuth, Norman. César Franck. London: Dennis Dobson,
Ltd. , 1949, pp. 80-87. Analytic and critical commentary
with musical examples.
Martins, H. J. "Comment: the linear analysis of chromat-
icism," In Theory Only 2 (April-May 1976), 47-50. Ad-
vanced analytic discussion in reply to the W. E. Benjamin
work cited here. Musical examples.
Tovey, Donald Francis. Essays in Musical Analysis. Lon-
don: Oxford University Press, 1935, II, pp. 62-69.
Thorough analysis with musical examples.
Vallas, Leon. César Franck. Translated by Hubert Foss.
New York: Oxford University Press, 1951, pp. 209-216.
Mainly background and evaluative commentary. No musical examples.

HANSON, HOWARD, 1896-

Symphony No. 2 ("Romantic")

Hansen, Peter S. An Introduction to Twentieth Century
Music. second edition. Boston: Allyn & Bacon, Inc. ,
1967, pp. 344-346. Brief analytic synopsis of symphony.

HARRIS, ROY, 1898-

Symphony No. 3

Hansen, Peter S. An Introduction to Twentieth Century
Music. second edition. Boston: Allyn & Bacon, Inc.,
1967, pp. 330-333. Short analysis of symphony with discussion of compositional style.
Machlis, Joseph. Introduction to Contemporary Music. New
York: Norton, 1961, pp. 474-475. Brief remarks. Musical examples.

HAYDN, FRANZ JOSEPH, 1732-1809

General

Geiringer, Karl. Haydn: A Creative Life in Music.
Berkeley: University of California Press, 1968, pp. 352-
362. Overview of symphonies 92-104.
Hodgson, Anthony. The Music of Joseph Haydn: The Sym-
phonies. London: Tantivy Press, 1976, 208p. Thorough
treatment of all the symphonies. Background, criticism,
analytic remarks. Musical examples.
Hughes, Rosemary. Haydn. London: Dent, 1962, pp. 170-
193. Critical and analytic commentary for the student.
Musical examples.
Landon, H. C. Robbins. Haydn: Chronicle and Works.
Vol. III (Haydn in England, 1791-1795). Bloomington:
Indiana University Press, 1976, pp. 490-617. Thorough
discourse on the "Salomon Symphonies" (nos. 96-104) and
Sinfonia Concertante. Critical and analytic with musical
examples.
Landon, H. C. Robbins. Haydn Symphonies. Seattle: University of Washington Press, 1969, pp. 49-64. Critical
and analytic commentary intended for the student.
Pauly, Reinhard. Music in the Classic Period. second
edition. Englewood Cliffs, N. J. : Prentice-Hall, 1973,
pp. 93-99. General discussion on classicism in the symphonies with musical examples.
Sternfeld, F. W. "Instrumental masterworks and aspects of
formal design, " in The New Oxford History of Music (Vol.
VII: The Age of Enlightenment). London: Oxford University Press, 1973, pp. 615-624. Overview of Haydn's
symphonic achievement. Musical examples.
Wolf, E. K. "The recapitulations in Haydn's London Symphonies, " Musical Quarterly 52:1 (1966), 71-89. Advanced,

close examination of Haydn's musical procedures in the
recapitulations.   Musical examples.

Symphony No. 88 in G major

Kerman, Joseph.   Listen.   second edition.   New York:
     Worth Publishers, 1972, pp. 171-175.   Analysis with mu-
     sical examples intended for student.
Nadeau, Roland.   The Symphony: Structure and Style.
     shorter edition.   revised.   Boston: Crescendo Pub. ,
     1973, pp. 64-71.   Bar-by-bar analysis.

Symphony No. 92 in G major ("Oxford")

Rosen, Charles.   The Classical Style: Haydn, Mozart,
     Beethoven.   New York: Viking Press, 1971, pp. 159-163.
     Analytic comments with special emphasis on Haydn's treat-
     ment of sonata form.   Musical examples.

Symphony No. 94 in G major ("Surprise")

Johns, D. C.   "In defence of Haydn: the 'Surprise' sym-
     phony revisited, " Music Review 24:4 (1963), 305-312.
     Good straightforward analysis of entire symphony.
Machlis, Joseph.   The Enjoyment of Music.   third edition.
     New York: Norton, 1970, pp. 248-252.   Compact analy-
     sis for the student.   Musical examples.

Symphony No. 99 in E♭ major

Cuyler, Louise.   The Symphony.   New York: Harcourt
     Brace Jovanovich, 1973, pp. 30-34.   Bar-by-bar analysis.

Symphony No. 100 in G major ("Military")

Warburton, A. O.   "Set works for 'O' level, " Music Teach-
     er 48 (Aug. 1969), 11-12.   Bar-by-bar analysis for the
     intermediate student.   No musical examples.

Symphony No. 102 in B♭ major

Domek, R. C.   "Comment: Berry's remarks on tonality as
     established by means of a melody with a general reaction
     to his structural functions in music, " In Theory Only 2
     (Dec. 1976), 31-35.   Advanced analytic discussion with
     musical examples.

Symphony No. 103 in E♭ major ("Drum Roll")

Boyden, David B.   An Introduction to Music.   second edition.
New York: Knopf, 1970, pp. 74-83.   Thorough analysis
with musical examples.
Cole, M. S.   "Momigny's analysis of Haydn's Symphony No.
103," Music Review 30:4 (1969), 261-284.   A contemporary analysis (1806) of Haydn's symphony with modern
commentary.   Musical examples.
Geiringer, Karl, ed.   Franz Joseph Haydn: Symphony No.
103 in E-flat major.   New York: Norton, 1974, 116p.
Complete score with historical background, analysis,
views and comments.   A Norton Critical Score for the
student.
Nallin, Walter E.   The Musical Idea.   New York: Macmillan, 1968, pp. 517-520.   Analysis with musical examples.

HONEGGER, ARTHUR, 1892-1955

Symphony No. 5

Hansen, Peter S.   An Introduction to Twentieth Century
Music.   second edition.   Boston: Allyn & Bacon, Inc.,
1967, pp. 145-148.   Short analysis with musical examples.
Machlis, Joseph.   Introduction to Contemporary Music.   New
York: Norton, 1961, pp. 229-232.   Descriptive, program-
note style commentary with analytical observations.

IVES, CHARLES EDWARD, 1874-1954

General

Hitchcock, H. Wiley.   Ives.   London: Oxford University
Press, 1977, pp. 81-94.   Descriptive and analytic com-
mentary with musical examples.   Much discussion of the
Fourth Symphony.

Symphony No. 2

Buechner, H.   "Ives in the classroom: a teaching guide to
two compositions," Music Educators Journal 61 (Oct.
1974), 64-70.   Easy analysis for the student.   No musical examples.
Charles, Sydney Robinson.   "The use of borrowed material
in Ives' Second Symphony," Music Review 28:2 (May 1967),

102-111. Traces appearances of borrowed material and
discusses Ives' use of them as structural elements.
Sterne, Colin. "The quotations in Charles Ives' second
symphony," Music & Letters 52:1 (Jan. 1971), 39-45.
Lists tunes Ives quoted in this symphony and provides
analytic commentary.

Symphony No. 4

Cyr, Gordon. "Intervallic structural elements in Ives'
Fourth Symphony," Perspectives of New Music 9:2, 10:1
(1971), 291-303. Advanced analytic discussion.
Serebrier, J. "Ives, the most difficult ever," Music Journal 32 (Sept. 1974), 14-15+. Descriptive commentary
from the performer's viewpoint.
Stone, K. "Ives' Fourth Symphony: A Review," Musical
Quarterly 52:1 (1966), 1-16. A thorough discussion and
description, citing American melodies Ives used throughout this symphony.

MAHLER, GUSTAV, 1860-1911

General

Barford, Philip. Mahler Symphonies and Songs. Seattle:
University of Washington Press, 1970, pp. 18-64. Descriptive, critical and analytic commentary for the student. Musical examples.
Gartenberg, Egon. Mahler: The Man and His Music. New
York: Schirmer Books, 1978, pp. 251-367. Descriptive,
critical and analytic commentary on all the symphonies.
Easy-to-read style. Musical examples.
Kennedy, Michael. Mahler. London: Dent, 1974, pp. 86-
160. Critical and analytic commentary intended for the
student. Musical examples.
La Grange, Henry-Louis de. Mahler. New York: Doubleday, 1973, I, pp. 746-823. Full background with struc-
tural analyses. Musical examples. Symphonies 1-4 are
discussed here.
Mitchell, Donald. Gustav Mahler: The Wunderhorn Years.
Boulder, Colo. : Westview Press, 1975, pp. 311-332.
Extensive commentary on Third and Fourth symphonies.
Explores thematic unity and Wunderhorn spirit that pre-
vails in these two works. Musical examples.
Simpson, Robert. The Symphony. New York: Drake Publishers, 1972, Vol. II, pp. 29-51. Overview of Mahler's

symphonies, concentrating on stylistic development and significant features of the symphonies.

Symphony No. 1 in D major

Roman, Z. "Connotative irony in Mahler's 'Todtenmarsch in Callot's Manier,'" Musical Quarterly 59:2 (1973), 207-222. Discussion of the creative impulse behind the funeral march (third movement) and relationship of this work to the Songs of a Wayfarer.
Small, C. "Mahler: Symphony no. 1," Music in Education 38:369 (1974), 215-217. Brief, but concentrated analytic discussion. Musical examples.

Symphony No. 2 in C minor ("Resurrection")

Franklin, P. "Funeral rites--Mahler and Mickiewicz," Music & Letters 55:2 (1974), 203-208. Influence of the Polish Romantic poet Adam Mickiewicz on the "Totenfeier" movement.
Grant, P. "Mahler's Second Symphony," Chord and Discord 2:8 (1958), 76-85. Thorough analysis with musical examples.

Symphony No. 4 in G major

Cuyler, Louise. The Symphony. New York: Harcourt Brace Jovanovich, Inc., 1973, pp. 130-133. Concentrated musical analysis.

Symphony No. 5 in C♯ minor

Grant, P. "Mahler's Fifth Symphony," Chord and Discord 2:10 (1963), 125-137. Thorough musical analysis with many musical examples.

Symphony No. 9 in D major

Diether, J. "The expressive content of Mahler's Ninth: an interpretation," Chord and Discord 2:10 (1963), 69-107. Exhaustive analysis, focusing on Mahler's expressive devices. Cites allusions to songs and other examples of musical symbolism. On an advanced level.

Symphony No. 10 (Unfinished)

Cooke, D. "The facts concerning Mahler's Tenth Symphony,"

Chord and Discord 2:10 (1963), 3-27. Background and
analysis of Mahler's unfinished Tenth.
Cooke, D. "Mahler's Tenth Symphony," Musical Times 117
(July 1976), 563+; (Aug. 1976), 645+. Complete history
and background of the performing version of Mahler's unfinished, but sketched Tenth Symphony.

MENDELSSOHN, FELIX, 1809-1847

General

Jacob, Heinrich Eduard. Felix Mendelssohn and His Times.
Translated from the German by Richard and Clara Winston. Westport, Conn.: Greenwood Press, 1963, 356p.
Descriptive commentary with musical examples. Use
table of contents to locate discussion of specific works.
Radcliffe, Philip. Mendelssohn. New York: Farrar,
Straus and Cudahy, Inc., 1957, pp. 103-107. Brief
analytical sketches.
Werner, Eric. Mendelssohn: A New Image of the Composer and His Age. New York: The Free Press of Glencoe,
1963, 545p. Brief analyses, mainly of symphonies 3, 4,
and 5, highlighting the most significant features.

Symphony No. 4 in A major, op. 90 ("Italian")

Kerman, Joseph. Listen. second edition. New York:
Worth Publishers, 1972, pp. 286-290. Analysis with musical examples. Intended for student.
Laming, F. "Set works for 'O' level: Mendelssohn: Symphony no. 4 ('The Italian'), " Music Teacher 54 (Nov.
1975), 15-16. Analysis with musical examples.
Machlis, Joseph. The Enjoyment of Music. third edition.
New York: Norton, 1970, pp. 139-142. Analytic overview for the music student. Musical examples.
Nallin, Walter E. The Musical Idea. New York: Macmillan, 1968, pp. 524-527. Brief analysis with musical examples.
Tovey, Donald Francis. Essays in Musical Analysis. London: Oxford University Press, 1935, I, pp. 218-223.
Lucid commentary and analytic remarks. Musical examples.

MENNIN, PETER, 1923-

Symphony No. 3

Machlis, Joseph. Introduction to Contemporary Music. New York: Norton, 1961, pp. 528-530. Brief analysis for the student.

MOZART, WOLFGANG AMADEUS, 1756-1791

General

Blom, Eric. Mozart. London: Dent, 1935, pp. 189-210. Descriptive, critical and analytic commentary designed for student. Focuses mainly on the later symphonies. Musical examples.
Cuyler, Louise. The Symphony. New York: Harcourt Brace Jovanovich, 1973, pp. 40-47. Concentrated analyses of symphonies 39, 40, and 41.
Einstein, Alfred. Mozart: His Character, His Work. Translated by Arthur Mendel and Nathan Broder. London: Oxford University Press, 1945, pp. 215-236. Traces influences and deals with Mozart's stylistic traits and contributions to the symphony as a form. A general discussion on an intermediate level.
Landon, H. C. Robbins, ed. The Mozart Companion. New York: Norton, 1956, pp. 156-198. Light discussion of Mozart's evolving symphonic style.
Maycock, J. "The significance of Mozart's last symphonies," Musical Opinion 96 (Jan. 1973), 179+. Views the last three symphonies as one conception, even though they are different in character.
Pauly, Reinhard. Music in the Classic Period. second edition. Englewood Cliffs, N. J.: Prentice-Hall, 1973, pp. 99-107. General discussion on classicism in the symphonies, with musical examples.
Saint-Foix, G. de. The Symphonies of Mozart. London: Dennis Dobson Ltd., 1947, 118p. Analytic insights on all the symphonies and Mozart's stylistic growth as evidenced within the music.
Sternfeld, F. W. "Instrumental masterworks and aspects of formal design," in The New Oxford History of Music. (Vol. VIII: The Age of Enlightenment). London: Oxford University Press, 1973, pp. 629-635. Brief remarks on background and general stylistic traits. Musical examples.
Tovey, Donald Francis. Essays in Musical Analysis. Lon-

don: Oxford University Press, 1935, I, pp. 183-198.
Easy-to-read, thorough analytic commentaries on symphonies 36, 39, 40, and 41.   Musical examples.

Symphony No. 35 in D major, K. 385 ("Haffner")

Tischler, Hans.   The Perceptive Music Listener.   Englewood Cliffs, N. J. :   Prentice-Hall, 1955, pp. 344-347.
Compact analysis with musical examples.

Symphony No. 39 in E♭ major, K. 543

Taylor, C.   "The contemporaneity of music in history,"
Music Review 24:3 (1963), 205-217.   Music viewed in
context of its time.   Comparison of Berg's methods (in
the Violin Concerto) with Mozart's (in the Symphony No.
39) to illustrate how the period affected the music.
Largely a philosophical discussion on style.

Symphony No. 40 in G minor, K. 550

Berry, W. and others.   "Analysis symposium subject:
Mozart Symphony in G minor, K. 550:   Movement I," In
Theory Only 1 (Oct. 1975), 8-25+.   Advanced analysis
from different viewpoints.   Musical examples.
Broder, Nathan, ed.   Mozart: Symphony in G Minor, K.
550.   (Norton Critical Scores).   New York: Norton,
1967, 114p.   Historical background, analysis, criticism
with full musical quotation.
Kerman, Joseph.   Listen.   second edition.   New York:
Worth Publishers, 1972, pp. 186-187.   Brief analytic
summary for the student.   Musical examples.
Machlis, Joseph.   The Enjoyment of Music.   third edition.
New York: Norton, 1970, pp. 265-269.   Compact analysis, intended for the undergraduate student.   Musical examples.
Nadeau, Roland.   The Symphony: Structure and Style.
shorter edition. revised.   Boston: Crescendo Publishing,
1973, pp. 76-83.   Straight bar-by-bar analysis.
Nallin, Walter E.   The Musical Idea.   New York: Macmillan, 1968, pp. 179-182; 503-505.   Analytic highlights with
musical examples.
Smith, F. J.   "Mozart revisited, K. 550:   the problem of
survival of baroque figures in the classical era," Music
Review 31:3 (1970), 201-214.   Elevated discussion of the
use of old baroque figures in classical music to convey a
different effect than the original figure conveyed in the
baroque era.

Symphony No. 41 in C major, K. 551 ("Jupiter")

Klenz, William. "'Per aspera ad astra' or the stairway to
   Jupiter," Music Review 30 (1969), 169-210. Mozart's use
   of the main theme of this symphony in other works.
Rogers, J. E. "Pitch class sets in fourteen measures of
   Mozart's 'Jupiter' Symphony," Perspectives of New Music
   10:1 (1971), 209-231. Advanced analytic discussion. Musical examples.
Stevenson, P. "A notation of thematic structure," Music in
   Education 29:316 (1965), 273-276. Advanced analysis in
   graph showing mathematical relationships.
Wollenberg, S. "The Jupiter theme; new light on its creation," Musical Times 116 (Sept. 1975), 781-783. The
   famous "Jupiter" theme traced back to Fux as a possible
   source. Musical examples.

NIELSEN, CARL, 1865-1931

General

Simpson, Robert. Carl Nielsen: Symphonist, 1865-1931.
   London: Dent, 1952, 236p. Analytic discussion of all
   the symphonies.

Symphony No. 4, op. 29 ("Inextinguishable")

Simpson, Robert, ed. The Symphony. New York: Drake
   Publishers, 1972, Vol. II, pp. 61-71. Thorough analysis.

PISTON, WALTER, 1894-1976

Symphony No. 4

Hansen, Peter S. An Introduction to Twentieth Century
   Music. second edition. Boston: Allyn & Bacon, Inc.,
   1967, pp. 336-338. Brief overview with musical examples.
Machlis, Joseph. Introduction to Contemporary Music. New
   York: Norton, 1961, pp. 509-511. Brief analysis. Musical examples.

PROKOFIEV, SERGEI, 1891-1953

Symphony No. 1 in D major, op. 25 ("Classical")

Austin, William W.　Music in the Twentieth Century:　From
Debussy Through Stravinsky.　New York:　Norton, 1966,
pp. 451-455.　Analytical comments with remarks on
Prokofiev's style.
Elkin, Robert.　"Prokofiev's classical symphony," Music in
Education 28:310 (1964), 273-275.　Concentrated analysis
with musical examples.
Nadeau, Roland.　The Symphony:　Structure and Style.
shorter edition, revised.　Boston:　Crescendo, 1973,
pp. 169-174.　Bar-by-bar analysis.
Nestyev, Israel V.　Prokofiev.　Stanford, Calif.:　Stanford
University Press, 1960, pp. 145-148.　Descriptive commentary with remarks on Prokofiev's creative intention in
the writing of this satirical work.

Symphony No. 7, op. 131

Austin, William W.　Music in the Twentieth Century:　From
Debussy Through Stravinsky.　New York:　Norton, 1966,
pp. 468-471.　Brief but substantial commentary.

RACHMANINOFF, SERGEI, 1873-1943

General

Culshaw, John.　Rachmaninov:　The Man and His Music.
New York:　Oxford University Press, 1950, pp. 64-69.
Analytic and critical commentary on all Rachmaninoff's
symphonies.
Maycock, R.　"Rachmaninov the symphonist," Music & Mu-
sicians 21 (July 1973), 40-42+.　An assessment of
Rachmaninoff's symphonies highlighting stylistic character-
istics.　No musical examples.

Symphony No. 2 in E minor, op. 27

Rubin, D.　"Transformations of the 'Dies Irae' in Rachmaninov's Second Symphony," Music Review 23 (1962), 132-
136.　Traces variations of "Dies Irae" throughout the
symphony and elucidates its structural significance.

RIEGGER, WALLINGFORD, 1885-1961

Symphony No. 3

Machlis, Joseph. Introduction to Contemporary Music. New
York: Norton, 1961, pp. 611-613. Brief analytical commentary. Musical examples.

ROUSSEL, ALBERT, 1869-1937

Symphony No. 3 in G minor, op. 42

Machlis, Joseph. Introduction to Contemporary Music. New
York: Norton, 1961, pp. 244-246. Brief commentary.
Musical examples.

SAINT-SAËNS, CAMILLE, 1835-1921

General

Hervey, Arthur. Saint-Saëns. New York: Dodd, Mead,
pp. 82-101. Background and descriptive commentary.
No musical examples.
Lyle, Watson. Camille Saint-Saëns: His Life and Art.
Westport, Conn.: Greenwood Press, 1970. Descriptive
and analytic commentary with musical examples.

SCHUBERT, FRANZ, 1797-1828

General

Abraham, Gerald, ed. The Music of Schubert. New York:
Norton, 1947, pp. 17-87. Analytic discussion of all the
symphonies. Musical examples.
Brown, Maurice J. E. Schubert: A Critical Biography.
New York: St. Martin's, 1961, 414p. Focus is on Schu-
bert's creative process. Many analytic insights and back-
ground information. Musical examples.
Brown, Maurice J. E. Schubert Symphonies. London:
British Broadcasting Corporation, 1970, 64p. Guide to
all the symphonies. For the student.
Cuyler, Louis. The Symphony. New York: Harcourt Brace
Jovanovich, 1973, pp. 86-92. Concentrated formal analy-
sis of symphonies 8 and 9.

Duncan, Edmondstoune. Schubert. London: Dent, 1905,
    pp. 164-184. Critical and analytic commentary for the
    student. Musical examples.
Hutchings, Arthur. Schubert. London: Dent, 1945, pp. 87-
    106. Descriptive, critical and analytic commentary. Mu-
    sical examples.
Simpson, Robert, ed. The Symphony. New York: Drake
    Publishers, 1972, vol. I, pp. 188-208. Traces Schubert's
    stylistic development leading to the 8th and 9th symphonies.
Smith, Alexander Brent. Schubert: The Symphonies. Lon-
    don: Oxford University Press, 1926, 48p. Thorough ana-
    lytic discussion of both the 7th and 8th symphonies. For
    the student. Musical examples.
Tovey, Donald Francis. Essays in Musical Analysis. Lon-
    don: Oxford University Press, 1935, I, pp. 205-218.
    Short, but pointed analytic commentary on symphonies 8
    and 9.

Symphony No. 8 in B minor, D. 759 ("Unfinished")

Abraham, G. "Finishing the 'Unfinished,'" Musical Times
    112 (June 1971), 547-548. Background of the composition
    with theories on the intended last movement. Musical ex-
    amples.
Chusid, Martin, ed. Schubert: Symphony in B Minor (Un-
    finished). (Norton Critical Scores). New York: Norton,
    1967, 114p. Historical background, analysis, criticism
    with full musical quotation.
Klein, J. W. "Should one 'tamper' with a masterpiece?"
    Musical Opinion 95 (May 1972), 403-405. A response to
    Gerald Abraham's "completion" of this work and a look
    at the whole question of unfinished works.
Machlis, Joseph. The Enjoyment of Music. third edition.
    New York: Norton, 1970, pp. 301-304. Analysis with
    musical examples.
Nallin, Walter E. The Musical Idea. New York: Macmil-
    lan, 1968, pp. 188-190. Analytic highlights with musical
    examples. First movement only.
Truscott, H. "Schubert's B minor symphony," Music Review
    23:1 (1962), 1-6. Analytic remarks emphasizing the im-
    portance of tonality as a structural feature in this work.

Symphony No. 9 in C major, D. 944 ("The Great")

Brown, Maurice J. E. Essays on Schubert. New York:
    St. Martin's, 1966, pp. 30-58. Examination of the in-
    fluences and artistic development, culminating in the
    Ninth Symphony.

Reed, J. "How the 'Great' C major was written, " Music &
Letters 56:1 (1975), 18-25. Shows that many of the ideas
for this symphony were present long before it was actually written down. Disputes theory that it was written in
haste just before Schubert's death. Musical examples.
Reed, John. Schubert: The Final Years. London: Faber
& Faber, 1972, pp. 72-98. Background information on
the writing of the symphony, not an analysis.

SCHUMANN, ROBERT, 1810-1856

General

Abraham, Gerald, ed. Schumann: A Symposium. London:
Oxford University Press, 1952, 319p. Stylistic traits,
orchestration, revisions and analytic observations. Musical examples.
Chissell, Joan. Schumann. London: Dent, 1967, pp. 136-
148. Brief critical and analytic remarks. Mention made
of the problems in Schumann's orchestration. Musical examples.
Obenshain, K. "Schumann as symphonist, " American Music
Teacher 23:6 (1974), 31-33. Overview and critical assessment. No musical examples.
Schauffler, Robert Haven. Florestan: The Life and Work
of Robert Schumann. New York: Dover, 1963, pp. 396-
422. Descriptive commentary rather than formal analysis.
Musical examples.
Smith, R. R. "Motivic procedure in opening movements of
the symphonies of Schumann, Bruckner and Brahms, "
Music Review 36:2 (1975), 130-134. Advanced discussion
on motivic treatment as an important element of sonata
form. No musical examples.
Tovey, Donald Francis. Essays in Musical Analysis. Lon-
don: Oxford University Press, 1935, II, pp. 45-62.
Thorough, intelligent, musical analysis for the layman of
symphonies 1, 3, and 4. Musical examples.
Walker, Alan, ed. Robert Schumann: The Man and His
Music. London: Barrie & Jenkins, 1972, pp. 280-307.
Background and analyses of all Schumann's symphonies.

Symphony No. 1 in B♭ major, op. 38 ("Spring")

Nadeau, Roland. The Symphony: Structure and Style.
shorter edition, revised. Boston: Crescendo, 1973,
pp. 111-113. Bar-by-bar analysis.

Symphony No. 4 in D minor, op. 120

Abraham, Gerald. Slavonic and Romantic Music. New
  York: St. Martin's, 1968, pp. 281-287. Discussion of
  the three versions of this symphony. Provides an insight
  into Schumann's creative process. Musical examples.
Cuyler, Louise. The Symphony. New York: Harcourt
  Brace Jovanovich, 1973, pp. 96-103. Concentrated analy-
  sis with musical examples.
Maniates, Maria Rika. "The D minor symphony of Robert
  Schumann," in Finscher, Ludwig and Christoph-Helmut
  Mehling, comps. Festschrift für Walter Wiora. Kassel:
  Bärenreiter, 1967, pp. 441-447. Discussion of the crea-
  tive impulse behind this symphony. On a high level, but
  many easy-to-grasp analytic insights for the student.

                    SESSIONS, ROGER, 1896-

Symphony No. 1

Machlis, Joseph. Introduction to Contemporary Music. New
  York: Norton, 1961, pp. 585-586. Brief analytical remarks.

Symphony No. 2

Hansen, Peter S. An Introduction to Twentieth Century
  Music. second edition. Boston: Allyn & Bacon, Inc.,
  1967, pp. 340-342. Brief analysis with musical examples.

              SHOSTAKOVICH, DMITRI, 1906-1975

General

Gow, D. "Shostakovich's 'War' symphonies," Musical Times
  105 (March 1964), 191-193. Relationships between symphonies 7 and 8 examined. Musical examples.
Ottaway, H. "Shostakovich: some later works," Tempo 50
  (Winter 1959), 2-12. Critical and analytic discussion with
  musical examples.
Simpson, Robert. The Symphony. New York: Drake Publishers, 1972, II, pp. 199-217. An overview of the symphonies showing stylistic development. Musical examples.

Symphony No. 1 in F major, op. 10

Kay, Norman. Shostakovich. London: Oxford University
Press, 1971, pp. 100-116. Influences, stylistic traits,
and descriptive remarks. Not analytical. Musical examples.
Nallin, Walter E. The Musical Idea. New York: Macmillan, 1968, pp. 531-534. Brief analysis with musical examples.

Symphony No. 2

Lawson, P. "Shostakovich's Second Symphony," Tempo 91
(Winter 1969-1970), 14-15. Analytic and critical commentary. Musical examples.

Symphony No. 5, op. 47

Machlis, Joseph. Introduction to Contemporary Music. New
York: Norton, 1961, pp. 289-292. Descriptive commen-
tary with musical examples.
Souster, T. "Shostakovich at the Crossroads," Tempo 78
(Autumn 1966), 2-9. Full analytic and critical commen-
tary. Musical examples.

Symphony No. 7, op. 60 ("Leningrad")

Ottaway, H. "Shostakovich's 'Fascist' theme," Musical
Times 111 (March 1970), 274. Objections to the com-
monly held idea that the theme in the first movement is
meant to represent the approach of Nazi invaders. No
musical examples.

Symphony No. 14

Kay, N. "Shostakovich's Fourteenth Symphony," Tempo 92
(Spring 1970), 20-21. Brief analytic and critical commentary. Musical examples.

SIBELIUS, JEAN, 1865-1957

General

Abraham, Gerald. The Music of Sibelius. New York:
Norton, 1947, pp. 14-37. Good layman's analysis and
discussion of all the symphonies.

Gray, Cecil. Sibelius: The Symphonies. Freeport, N. Y. :
Books for Libraries Press, 1970 (originally published
1935), 77p. Good guide for amateurs through all the
symphonies.
Layton, Robert. Sibelius. London: Dent, 1965, 210p.
Analytic commentary on all the symphonies. Musical examples.
Ringbom, Nils-Eric. Jean Sibelius, a Master and His Work.
Norman: University of Oklahoma Press, 1954, pp. 132-
157. Brief, descriptive commentary of symphonies 5, 6,
7.
Simpson, Robert. The Symphony. New York: Drake Publishers, Inc. , 1972, pp. 86-130. Treats all symphonies
with emphasis on stylistic growth.
Sutton, W. "Sibelius and the symphony: a centenary tribute, "
Music in Education 29:315 (1965), 221-222. An overview,
with a characterization of Sibelius' symphonic style.

Symphony No. 2 in D major, op. 43

Machlis, Joseph. Introduction to Contemporary Music. New
York: Norton, 1961, pp. 96-99. Descriptive and analytic
comments of entire symphony with musical examples. Intended for the layman.
Nadeau, Roland. The Symphony: Structure and Style.
shorter edition, revised. Boston: Crescendo Pub. Co.
1973, pp. 160-164. Bar-by-bar analysis.

Symphony No. 5 in E♭ major, op. 82

Tovey, Donald Francis. Essays in Musical Analysis. London: Oxford, 1935, II, pp. 128-129. Analytic remarks
for the musical amateur. Musical examples.

Symphony No. 6 in D minor, op. 104

Pike, L. "Sibelius' debt to Renaissance polyphony, " Music
& Letters 55:3 (1974), 317-326. Advanced discussion on
Sibelius' use of ancient modes. Musical examples.

Symphony No. 7 in C major, op. 105

Ballantine, C. "The symphony in the twentieth century:
some aspects of its tradition and innovation, " Music Review 32:3 (1971), 226-228. Brief remarks on Sibelius'
unifying devices. Musical examples.

STRAVINSKY, IGOR, 1882-1971

General

Routh, Francis. Stravinsky. London: Dent, 1975, pp. 92-
101. Brief critical and analytic commentary for the student. Musical examples.

Symphonies of Wind Instruments

White, Eric Walter. Stravinsky: The Composer and His
Works. Berkeley: University of California, 1966,
pp. 253-260. Solid analytic commentary.

Symphony in C

Lang, Paul Henry, ed. Stravinsky: A New Appraisal of
His Work. New York: Norton, 1963, pp. 25-30. Full,
detailed analysis.
Vlad, Roman. Stravinsky. Translated from the Italian by
Frederick and Ann Fuller. Second Edition. London:
Oxford University Press, 1967, pp. 136-146. Detailed
analysis with musical examples.
White, Eric Walter. Stravinsky: The Composer and His
Works. Berkeley: University of California Press, 1966,
pp. 364-370. Background and analysis. Musical exam-
ples.

Symphony in E♭

White, Eric Walter. Stravinsky: The Composer and His
Works. Berkeley: University of California, 1966,
pp. 138-139. Brief descriptive remarks.

Symphony in Three Movements (1945)

Austin, William W. Music in the Twentieth Century: From
Debussy through Stravinsky. New York: Norton, 1966,
pp. 337-340. Concentrated discussion of unifying tonal
elements of symphony. Musical examples.
White, Eric Walter. Stravinsky: The Composer and His
Works. Berkeley: University of California, 1966,
pp. 389-397. Good analytic commentary. Musical examples.

Symphony of Psalms

Austin, William W. Music in the Twentieth Century: From

Debussy Through Stravinsky. New York: Norton, 1966,
pp. 333-335. Brief but concentrated analysis.
Burnan, J. "Stravinsky's 'Symphony of Psalms,'" Instru-
mentalist 23 (Dec. 1968), 60-62. Brief analytic and critical commentary. No musical examples.
Chittum, D. "Compositional similarities in Beethoven and
Stravinsky," Music Review 30:4 (1969), 285-290. Useful
analytic commentary of the Psalms.
Hansen, Peter S. An Introduction to Twentieth Century
Music. second edition. Boston: Allyn & Bacon, Inc.,
1967, pp. 169-173. Highlights compositional devices
employed. Musical examples.
Machlis, Joseph. Introduction to Contemporary Music. New
York: Norton, 1961, pp. 180-183. Descriptive and ana-
lytical comments for the layman.
Mellers, W. "1930: 'Symphony of Psalms,'" Tempo 97
(1971), 19-27. Full analysis with many insights to com-
poser's intentions. Musical examples.
Salzman, Eric. Twentieth Century Music: An Introduction.
Englewood Cliffs, N.J.: Prentice-Hall, 1967, pp. 52-59.
Brief but concentrated analysis with musical examples.
Stephens, H. "Stravinsky: The Symphony of Psalms,"
Music Teacher 55 (Nov. 1976), 14-15. Descriptive and
analytic commentary for the student. Musical examples.
Stravinsky, I. and Robert Craft. "A quintet of dialogues,"
Perspectives of New Music 1:1 (1962), 15-17. Stravinsky's
remarks on the Psalms.
Vlad, Roman. Stravinsky. Translated from the Italian by
Frederick and Ann Fuller. second edition. London: Ox-
ford University Press, 1967, pp. 154-164. Detailed anal-
ysis with musical examples.
Walsh, S. "Stravinsky's choral music," Tempo 81 (Summer
1967), 41-51. An overview with emphasis on Symphony of
Psalms. Musical examples.
White, Eric Walter. Stravinsky: The Composer and His
Works. Berkeley: University of California, 1966,
pp. 320-328. Solid analytic commentary.
Young, Percy M. The Choral Tradition. New York: Norton, 1971, pp. 300-304. Background and brief analysis
with musical examples.

TCHAIKOVSKY, PETER ILITCH, 1840-1893

General

Abraham, Gerald, ed. The Music of Tchaikovsky. New

York: Norton, 1946, pp. 24-46. General discussion of all Tchaikovsky's symphonies. Non-analytic. An overview of Tchaikovsky's symphonic style.

Cuyler, Louise. The Symphony. New York: Harcourt Brace Jovanovich, 1973, pp. 153-157. Short, but efficient analyses of symphonies 4 and 6.

Evans, Edwin. Tchaikovsky. New York: Farrar, Straus and Giroux, 1966, pp. 104-127. Analytic discussion of all Tchaikovsky's symphonies, with special emphasis on the fourth symphony.

Garden, Edward. Tchaikovsky. London: Dent, 1973, 194p. Critical and analytic commentary for the student. Musical examples.

Warrack, John. Tchaikovsky Symphonies and Concertos. Seattle: University of Washington Press, 1969, pp. 5-38. Analytic and critical commentary intended for the student. Musical examples.

Symphony No. 4 in F major, op. 36

Blom, Eric. Tchaikovsky: Orchestral Works. Westport, Conn.: Greenwood Press, 1970, pp. 23-41. Descriptive, critical and analytic commentary for the student. Musical examples.

Weinstock, Herbert. Tchaikovsky. New York: Knopf, 1943, 172-178. Background and critical remarks. Not analytic.

Symphony No. 5 in E minor, op. 64

Nallin, Walter E. The Musical Idea. New York: Macmillan, 1968, pp. 194-195. Analytic highlights with musical examples. Best used with a score. First movement only.

Symphony No. 6 in B minor, op. 74 ("Pathetique")

Bernstein, Leonard. The Infinite Variety of Music. New York: Simon & Schuster, 1966, pp. 171-193. Analysis, similar to Bernstein's television talks. Easy-to-read with many insights for the beginner. Musical examples.

Machlis, Joseph. The Enjoyment of Music. third edition. New York: Norton, 1970, pp. 156-158. Compact analysis for the student. Musical examples.

Tovey, Donald Francis. Essays in Musical Analysis. London: Oxford University Press, 1935, II, pp. 84-89. Intelligent analytic guide for the musical amateur.

VAUGHAN WILLIAMS, RALPH, 1872-1958

General

Day, James. Vaughan Williams. New York: Farrar,
Straus & Cudahy, 1964, pp. 137-166. Brief descriptive
overview of all the symphonies. Musical examples.
Dickinson, Alan Edgar Frederic. An Introduction to the
Music of Ralph Vaughan Williams. London: Oxford Uni-
versity Press, 1928, pp. 14-67. Descriptive and critical
commentary for the student. Musical examples.
Dickinson, A. E. F. Vaughan Williams. London: Faber &
Faber, 1963, 540p. Analytic commentary with musical
examples.
Dickinson, A. E. F. "The Vaughan Williams symphonies,"
Musical Opinion 96 (Dec. 1972), 123+. An overview,
highlighting salient features of each symphony. No musi-
cal examples.
Foss, Hubert. Ralph Vaughan Williams: A Study. New
York: Oxford University Press, 1950, pp. 90-137. De-
scriptive commentary of symphonies 1, 2 and 3. No mu-
sical examples.
Howes, Frank. The Music of Ralph Vaughan Williams.
New York: Oxford, 1954, pp. 1-81. Full analytic treat-
ment.
Kennedy, Michael. The Works of Ralph Vaughan Williams.
London: Oxford University Press, 1964, 776p. Descriptive commentary with observations on style. Musical examples.
Ottaway, Hugh. Vaughan Williams Symphonies. Seattle:
University of Washington, 1973, 64p. Excellent guide for
students.
Pakenham, Simona. Ralph Vaughan Williams: A Discovery
of His Music. London: Macmillan, 1957, 205p. Descriptive and critical commentary. No musical examples.
Schwartz, Elliot. The Symphonies of Ralph Vaughan Williams. Amherst: University of Massachusetts, 1964.
242p. Exhaustive treatment of all the symphonies.

Symphony No. 1 ("Sea Symphony")

Hurd, M. "Vaughan Williams' 'Sea Symphony'; an analysis,"
Music in Education 29:311 (1965), 27-28; 312 (1965), 83-
84. Thorough analysis with musical examples.

Symphony No. 2 ("London")

Cuyler, Louise. The Symphony. New York: Harcourt

Brace Jovanovich, 1973, pp. 191-196. Short, but efficient
musical analysis with musical examples.
Machlis, Joseph. Introduction to Contemporary Music. New
York: Norton, 1961, pp. 299-301. Analytic highlights
intended for student.

Symphony No. 5 in D major

Ottaway, H. "VW5--a new analysis, " Musical Times 105
(May 1964), 354-356. Tonal analysis, with musical examples, for the intermediate student.

Symphony No. 6

Hansen, Peter S. An Introduction to Twentieth Century
Music. second edition. Boston: Allyn & Bacon, Inc. ,
1967, pp. 306-308. "Mini-analysis, " of entire symphony
with musical examples.

WEBERN, ANTON, 1883-1945

Symphony for Chamber Orchestra, op. 21

Austin, William W. Music in the Twentieth Century from
Debussy Through Stravinsky. New York: Norton, 1966,
pp. 357-367. Analysis with musical examples.
Borris, Siegfried. "Structural analysis of Webern's Symphony op. 21, " in Glowacki, John. Paul A. Pisk: Essays in His Honor. Austin: University of Texas, 1966,
pp. 231-242. Thorough analysis with diagrams and musical examples.
Brindle, Reginald Smith. The New Music: The Avant Garde
since 1945. London: Oxford University Press, 1975,
pp. 11-12. Short paragraph, but offers key to formal
structure. Musical examples.
Deri, Otto. Exploring Twentieth Century Music. New York:
Holt & Rinehart and Winston, 1968, p. 377. Concentrated
description of formal structure.
Hansen, Peter S. An Introduction to Twentieth Century
Music. second edition. Boston: Allyn & Bacon, Inc. ,
1967, pp. 223-225. Comments on texture and form. Musical examples.
Kolneder, Walter. Anton Webern: An Introduction to His
Works. Translated by Humphrey Searle. Berkeley:
University of California Press, 1968, pp. 113-119. Anal-
ysis with musical examples.

Machlis, Joseph.   Introduction to Contemporary Music.   New
York: Norton,   1961,   pp.   391-397.   Good,   full   treatment,
treating   rather   complex   elements   in   an   easy-to-read   style.

Bibliography

Books Consulted

Abraham, Gerald, ed. Borodin: The Composer and His
    Music. London: Reeves, n. d.

_____. Grieg: A Symposium. Norman: University of
    Oklahoma, 1948.

_____. Handel: A Symposium. London: Oxford Univer-
    sity Press, 1954.

_____. The Music of Schubert. New York: Norton,
    1947.

_____. The Music of Sibelius. New York: Norton,
    1947.

_____. The Music of Tchaikovsky. New York: Dutton,
    1946.

_____. Schumann: A Symposium. London: Oxford Uni-
    versity Press, 1952.

_____. Slavonic and Romantic Music. New York: St.
    Martin's, 1968.

Arnold, Denis. Giovanni Gabrieli. London: Oxford Univer-
    sity Press, 1974.

_____. Monteverdi. London: Dent, 1963.

_____. Monteverdi Madrigals. Seattle: University of
    Washington Press, 1967.

_____, and Nigel Fortune, eds. The Beethoven Compan-
    ion. London: Faber and Faber, 1971.

263

Arundell, Dennis Drew.   Henry Purcell.   New York: Books
for Libraries, 1970.

Ashbrook, William.   The Operas of Puccini.   New York:
Oxford University Press, 1968.

Austin, William W.   Debussy: Prelude to the Afternoon of
a Faun.   (Norton Critical Scores.)   New York: Norton,
1971.

_____.   Music in the Twentieth Century: From Debussy
Through Stravinsky.   New York: Norton, 1966.

Barford, Philip.   The Keyboard Music of C. P. E. Bach.
New York: October House, 1966.

_____.   Mahler Symphonies and Songs.   Seattle: Univer-
sity of Washington Press, 1970.

Barrett-Ayres, Reginald.   Joseph Haydn and the String Quartet.   New York: Schirmer Books, 1974.

Barricelli, Jean-Pierre and Leo Weinstein.   Ernest Chausson.
Norman: University of Oklahoma Press, 1955.

Barzun, Jacques.   Berlioz and the Romantic Century.   Boston: Little, Brown & Co., 1950.

Beckett, Walter.   Liszt.   London: Dent, 1963.

Beecham, Sir Thomas.   Frederick Delius.   New York:
Knopf, 1960.

Bekker, Paul.   Beethoven.   Translated and adapted from the
German by M. M. Bozman.   London: Dent, 1925.

_____.   Richard Wagner: His Life in His Work.   Trans-
lated by M. M. Bozman.   New York: Books for Libraries Press, 1970.

Béla Bartók: A Memorial Review.   New York: Boosey &
Hawkes, 1950.

Berger, Arthur.   Aaron Copland.   New York: Oxford University Press, 1953.

Bernac, Pierre.   Francis Poulenc: The Man and His Songs.

Translated by Winifred Radford.   New York: Norton,
1977.

Bernstein, Leonard.   The Infinite Variety of Music.   New
York: Simon and Schuster, 1966.

_____. The Joy of Music.   New York: Simon and
Schuster, 1959.

Biancolli, Louis, ed.   The Mozart Handbook: A Guide to
the Man and His Music.   Cleveland: World Publishing
Co. , 1954.

Bidou, Henri.   Chopin.   Translated by Catherine Alison
Phillips.   New York: Knopf, 1927.

Bie, Oscar.   Schubert: The Man.   New York: Dodd, Mead,
1928.

Blom, Eric.   Beethoven's Pianoforte Sonatas Discussed.
New York: Da Capo, 1968.

_____. Mozart.   London: Dent, 1935.

_____. Tchaikovsky Orchestral Works.   Westport:
Greenwood Press, 1970.

Bogianchino, Massimo.   The Harpsichord Music of Domenico
Scarlatti.   Translation from Italian by John Tickner.
Roma: Edizioni de Santis, 1967.

Bonavia, F.   Verdi.   London: Oxford University Press,
1930.

Boretz, Benjamin and Edward T. Cone.   Perspectives on
Schoenberg and Stravinsky.   Princeton: Princeton University Press, 1968.

Bowers, Faubion.   The New Scriabin: Enigma and Answers.
New York: St. Martin's Press, 1973.

Boyden, David B.   An Introduction to Music.   Second edition.   New York: Knopf, 1970.

Branson, David.   John Field and Chopin.   London: Barrie
& Jenkins, 1972.

Brenet, Michael. Haydn. Translated by C. Leonard Leese. London: Oxford University Press, 1926.

Brindle, Reginald Smith. The New Music: The Avant-Garde Since 1945. London: Oxford University Press, 1975.

Broder, Nathan. Samuel Barber. New York: G. Schirmer, 1954.

Brown, David. Mikhail Glinka: A Biographical and Critical Study. London: Oxford University Press, 1974.

Brown, Maurice J. E. Essays on Schubert. New York: St. Martin's, 1966.

_____. Schubert: A Critical Biography. London: Macmillan, 1961.

_____. Schubert Symphonies. London: British Broadcasting Corporation, 1970.

_____. Schubert's Variations. London: Macmillan, 1954.

Browne, Philip Austin. Brahms: The Symphonies. London: Oxford University Press, 1933.

Budden, Julian. The Operas of Verdi. New York: Praeger, 1973.

Bukofzer, Manfred F. Music in the Baroque Era. New York: Norton, 1947.

Burk, John N. The Life and Works of Beethoven. New York: Modern Library, 1943.

Burley, Rosa and Franck C. Carruthers. Edward Elgar: The Record of a Friendship. London: Barrie & Jenkins, 1972.

Calvocoressi, M. D. Modeste Mussorgsky. London: Rockliff, 1956.

_____. Mussorgsky. London: Dent, 1946.

_____. Mussorgsky. London: Dent, 1974.

_____. Mussorgsky: The Russian Musical Nationalist.
Second Edition, Revised. London: Kegan, Paul, 1919.

Capell, Richard. Schubert's Songs. New York: Macmillan,
1957.

Cardus, Neville. Gustav Mahler: His Mind and His Music.
London: Gollancz Ltd., 1965.

Carner, Mosco. Alban Berg: The Man and the Work. New
York: Holmes & Meier, 1977.

_____. Puccini: A Critical Biography. New York:
Knopf, 1959.

Carrell, Norman. Bach's Brandenburg Concertos. London:
Allen & Unwin, 1963.

Chissel, Joan. Schumann. London: Dent, 1967.

Clapham, John. Antonin Dvořák: Musician and Craftsman.
New York: St. Martin's, 1966.

_____. Smetana. London: Dent, 1972.

Coates, Henry. Palestrina. London. Dent, 1948.

Colles, H. C. The Chamber Music of Brahms. London:
Oxford University Press, 1933.

Cone, Edward T., ed. Hector Berlioz. Fantastic Symphony: An Authoritative Score, Historical Background, Analysis, Views and Comments. (Norton Critical Scores).
New York: Norton, 1971.

Cooper, Martin. Beethoven: The Last Decade, 1817-1827.
London: Oxford University Press, 1970.

_____. Georges Bizet. London: Oxford University
Press, 1938.

Cortot, Alfred. French Piano Music. Translated by Hilda
Andrews. London: Oxford University Press, 1932.

Cowell, Henry & Sidney. Charles Ives and His Music.
New York: Oxford University Press, 1955.

Culshaw, John. Rachmaninov: The Man and His Music. New York: Oxford University Press, 1950.

Curtis, Alan. Sweelinck's Keyboard Music. London: Oxford University Press, 1969.

Curtiss, Mina. Bizet and His World. New York: Knopf, 1958.

Cuyler, Louise. The Symphony. New York: Harcourt, Brace, Jovanovich, 1973.

Dale, Kathleen. Nineteenth-Century Piano Music: A Handbook for Pianists. London: Oxford University Press, 1954.

Davie, Cedric Thorpe. Musical Structure and Design. New York: Dover, 1966.

Davies, Laurence. César Franck and His Circle. London: Barrie & Jenkins, 1970.

_____. Franck. London: Dent, 1973.

_____. Paths to Modern Music: Aspects of Music from Wagner to the Present Day. London: Barrie & Jenkins, 1971.

_____. Ravel Orchestral Music. Seattle: University of Washington Press, 1970.

Dawes, Frank. Debussy's Piano Music. (BBC Music Guides). London: British Broadcasting Corporation, 1969.

Day, James, Vaughan Williams. London: Dent, 1964.

Dean, Winton. Bizet. London: Dent, 1948.

_____. Handel and the Opera Seria. London: Oxford University Press, 1970.

_____. Handel's Dramatic Oratorios and Masques. London: Oxford University Press, 1959.

Deane, Basil. Albert Roussel. London: Barrie and Rockliff, 1961.

_____. Cherubini. London: Oxford University Press,
1965.

Del Mar, Norman. Richard Strauss: A Critical Commentary on His Life and Works. New York: Free Press of
Glencoe, 1962.

Demarquez, Suzanne. Manuel de Falla. Translated from
the French by Salvator Attanasio. Philadelphia: Chilton,
1968.

Demuth, Norman. César Franck. London: Dennis Dobson,
1949.

_____. Ravel. London: Dent, 1947.

Dent, Edward J. Mozart's Operas: A Critical Study. Second Edition. London: Oxford University Press, 1947.

_____. The Rise of Romantic Opera. Cambridge:
Cambridge University Press, 1976.

Deri, Otto. Exploring Twentieth-Century Music. New
York: Holt, Rinehart and Winston, 1968.

Dianin, Serge. Borodin. Translated from the Russian by
Robert Lord. London: Oxford University Press, 1963.

Dickinson, Alan Edgar Frederic. Beethoven. London:
Nelson, 1941.

_____. An Introduction to the Music of Ralph Vaughan
Williams. London: Oxford University Press, 1928.

_____. The Music of Berlioz. London: Faber & Faber,
1972.

_____. Vaughan Williams. London: Faber & Faber,
n. d.

Doernberg, Erwin. The Life and Symphonies of Anton
Bruckner. London: Barrie and Rockliff, n. d.

Donington, Robert. Wagner's 'Ring' and Its Symbols. London: Faber & Faber, 1974.

Duncan, Edmondstoune. Schubert. London: Dent, 1934.

Dunhill, Thomas F. Mozart's String Quartets. Westport: Greenwood Press, 1970.

Edwards, H. Sutherland. Rossini and His School. London: Sampson, Low, Marston & Co. , n. d.

Einstein, Alfred. Gluck. Translated by Eric Blom. London: Dent, 1936.

_____. The Italian Madrigal. Translated by Alexander H. Krappe, Roger H. Sessions, and Oliver Strunk. Princeton: Princeton University Press, 1949.

_____. Mozart; His Character, His Work. Translated by Arthur Mendel and Nathan Broder. New York: Oxford University Press, 1945.

_____. Music in the Romantic Era. New York: Norton, 1947.

_____. Schubert: A Musical Portrait. New York: Oxford University Press, 1951.

Elliot, J. H. Berlioz. Revised Edition. London: Dent, 1967.

Eösze, Laszlo. Zoltan Kodaly: His Life and Works. London: Collet's, 1962.

Evans, Edwin. Handbook to the Pianoforte Works of Johannes Brahms. London: William Reeves, n. d.

_____. Historical, Descriptive and Analytic Account of the Entire Works of Johannes Brahms. London: William Reeves, 1912.

_____. Tchaikovsky. London: Dent, 1966.

Ewen, David. A Journey to Greatness: The Life and Music of George Gershwin. London: Allen, 1956.

Fellowes, Edmund H. William Byrd. London: Oxford University Press, 1936.

Ferguson, Donald N. Piano Music of Six Great Composers. New York: Books for Libraries, 1947.

Finck, Henry T.   Grieg and His Music.   New York: Dodd,
Mead, 1922.

_____.   Massenet and His Operas.   New York: John
Love, 1910.

Finscher, Ludwig and Christoph Hellmut Mahling, eds.
Festschrift für Walter Wiora zum 30. Dezember 1966.
Kassel: Bärenreiter, 1967.

Fischer-Dieskau, Dietrich.   Schubert's Songs.   Translated
from the German by Kenneth S. Shitton.   New York:
Knopf, 1977.

Fischl, Viktor, ed.   Antonin Dvořák: His Achievement.
Westport: Greenwood, 1970.

Fiske, Roger.   Beethoven Concertos and Overtures.   Seattle:
University of Washington Press, 1970.

Fontaine, Paul.   Basic Formal Structures in Music.   New
York: Appleton-Century-Crofts, 1967.

Forbes, Elliot, ed.   Ludwig van Beethoven.   Symphony no.
5 in C minor: An Authoritative Score.   The Sketches,
Historical Background, Analysis, Views and Comments.
(Norton Critical Scores).   New York: Norton, 1971.

Forkel, Johann Nikolaus.   Johann Sebastian Bach.   London:
Constable & Co. , 1920.

Forte, Allen.   The Compositional Matrix.   New York:
Music Teachers National Association, 1961.

_____.   Contemporary Tone-Structures.   New York:
Columbia University Press, 1955.

Foss, Hubert.   Ralph Vaughan Williams.   New York: Oxford University Press, 1950.

Friedlaender, Max.   Brahms' Lieder.   Translated by C.
Leonard Leese.   London: Oxford University Press, 1928.

Fuller-Maitland, John A.   The '48':   Bach's Wohltemperirtes
Clavier.   New York: Books for Libraries Press, 1970.

Gal, Hans.   Franz Schubert and the Essence of Melody.
London: Gollancz, 1974.

Garden, Edward. Balakirev. New York: St. Martin's, 1967.

_____. Tchaikovsky. London: Dent, 1973.

Gartenberg, Egon. Mahler: The Man and His Music. New York: Schirmer Books, 1978.

Gatti, Carlo. Verdi: The Man and His Music. Translated from the Italian by Elisabeth Abbott. New York: Putnam's Sons, 1955.

Geiringer, Karl. Brahms: His Life and Work. Second Edition. New York: Oxford University Press, 1947.

_____. Haydn: A Creative Life in Music. Berkeley: University of California Press, 1968.

_____. Johann Sebastian Bach. New York: Oxford University Press, 1966.

George, Graham. Tonality and Musical Structure. New York: Praeger, 1970.

Gilman, Lawrence. Debussy's Pelléas et Melisande. New York: G. Schirmer, 1907.

Girdlestone, Cuthbert. Jean-Philippe Rameau: His Life and Work. New York: Dover, 1969.

_____. Mozart and His Piano Concertos. Norman: University of Oklahoma Press, 1952.

Glowacki, John, ed. Paul A. Piske: Essays in His Honor. Austin: University of Texas, 1966.

Goldberg, Isaac. George Gershwin: A Study in American Music. New York: Frederick Ungar, 1958.

Gounod, Charles. Mozart's Don Giovanni: A Commentary. Translated from the Third French Edition by Windeyer Clark and J. T. Hutchinson. New York: Da Capo Press, 1970.

Grace, Harvey. The Organ Works of Bach. London: Novello, n. d.

Gray, Cecil. The Forty-Eight Preludes and Fugues of J. S.
Bach. London: Oxford University Press, 1952.

Green, Douglass M. Form in Tonal Music. New York:
Holt, Rinehart and Winston, 1965.

Grout, Donald Jay. A History of Western Music. New
York: Norton, 1960.

Grove, George. Beethoven and His Nine Symphonies. Third
Edition. New York: Dover Publications, 1962.

Hadden, J. Cuthbert. Haydn. London: Dent, 1934.

Hansen, Peter S. An Introduction to Twentieth-Century
Music. Second Edition. Boston: Allyn & Bacon, 1967.

Harding, James. Gounod. New York: Stein and Day, 1973.

_____. Massenet. London: Dent, 1970.

_____. Rossini. London: Faber & Faber, 1971.

Harrison, Julius. Brahms and His Four Symphonies. New
York: Da Capo Press, 1971.

Harrison, Max. The Lieder of Brahms. London: Cassell,
1972.

The Haydn Yearbook. Bryn Mawr: Presser, 1962.

Hedley, Arthur. Chopin. London: Dent, 1974.

Henderson, W. J. Richard Wagner: His Life and His
Dramas. Second Edition. Revised. New York: Putnam's, 1923.

Hervey, Arthur. Saint-Saëns. New York: Books for Libraries Press, 1969.

Heseltine, Philip. Frederick Delius. New York: Oxford
University Press, 1952.

_____, and Cecil Gray. Carlo Gesualdo, Prince of
Venosa. Westport: Greenwood, 1971.

Heyworth, Peter, ed. Berlioz, Romantic and Classic:

BIBLIOGRAPHY

Writings by Ernest Newman. London: Gollancz, 1972.

Higgins, Thomas, ed. Chopin: Preludes, op. 28 (Norton Critical Scores). New York: Norton, 1974.

Hill, Ralph, ed. The Symphony. Harmondsworth: Penguin, 1950.

Hitchcock, H. Wiley. Ives. London: Oxford University Press, 1973.

Hodgson, Antony. The Music of Joseph Haydn: The Symphonies. London: Tantivy Press, 1976.

Holland, Arthur Keith. Henry Purcell: The English Musical Tradition. New York: Books for Libraries, 1970.

Hollander, Hans. Leos Janáček: His Life and Work. Translated by Paul Hamburger. London: John Calder, 1963.

Holst, Imogen. Gustav Holst: A Biography. Second Edition. London: Oxford University Press, 1969.

_____. The Music of Gustav Holst. London: Oxford University Press, 1968.

Hoover, Kathleen and John Cage. Virgil Thomson: His Life and Music. New York: Books for Libraries, 1970.

Horton, John. Brahms Orchestral Music. London: British Broadcasting Corp. , 1968.

_____. César Franck. London: Oxford University Press, 1948.

_____. Grieg. London: Dent, 1974.

_____. Mendelssohn Chamber Music. Seattle: University of Washington Press, 1972.

Howes, Frank. The Music of Ralph Vaughan Williams. London: Oxford University Press, 1954.

Hughes, Gervase. Sidelights on a Century of Music (1825-1924). New York: St. Martin's, 1970.

Hughes, Rosemary. Haydn. London: Dent, 1962.

Hughes, Spike. Famous Mozart Operas. Second Revised Edition. New York: Dover, 1972.

Hull, A. Eaglefield. A Great Russian Tone Poet: Scriabin. New York: AMS Press, 1970.

Huneker, James. Chopin: The Man and His Music. New York: Scribner's, 1900.

_____. Franz Liszt. New York: AMS Press, 1971.

Hussey, Dynely. Verdi. London: Dent, 1948.

Hutchings, Arthur. The Baroque Concerto. New York: Norton, 1961.

_____. A Companion to Mozart's Piano Concertos. Second Edition. London: Oxford University Press, 1951.

_____. Delius. London: Macmillan, 1949.

_____. Schubert. London: Dent, 1964.

Jacob, Heinrich Eduard. Felix Mendelssohn and His Times. Translated from the German by Richard and Clara Winston. Westport: Greenwood Press, 1973.

Jacobs, Robert L. Wagner. London: Dent, 1965.

James, Burnett. Brahms: A Critical Study. New York: Praeger, 1972.

Jefferson, Alan. Delius. New York: Octagon Books, 1972.

_____. The Lieder of Richard Strauss. London: Cassell, 1971.

Johnson, Robert Sherlaw. Messiaen. Berkeley: University of California Press, 1975.

Karpati, Janos. Bartók's String Quartets. Budapest: Corvina Press, 1975.

Kay, Norman. Shostakovich. London: Oxford University Press, 1971.

Keller, Hermann. The Organ Works of Bach. Translated
from the German by Helen Hewitt. New York: Peters,
1967.

_____. The Well-Tempered Clavier by Johann Sebastian
Bach. Translated by Leigh Gerdine. New York: Norton,
1976.

Kelley, Edgar Stillman. Chopin the Composer. New York:
Schirmer, 1913.

Kennedy, Michael. Mahler. London: Dent, 1974.

_____. Portrait of Elgar. London: Oxford University
Press, 1968.

_____. Richard Strauss. London: Dent, 1976.

_____. The Works of Ralph Vaughan Williams. London:
Oxford University Press, 1964.

Kerman, Joseph. Listen. Second Edition. New York:
Worth Publishers, 1976.

Keys, Ivor. Brahms Chamber Music. London: British
Broadcasting Corporation, 1974.

King, A. Hyatt. Mozart in Retrospect: Studies in Criticism
and Bibliography. London: Oxford University Press,
1955.

Kirkpatrick, Ralph. Domenico Scarlatti. Princeton, N. J. :
Princeton University Press, 1953.

Kolneder, Walter. Anton Webern: An Introduction to His
Works. Translated by Humphrey Searle. Berkeley: University of California Press, 1968.

_____. Antonio Vivaldi: His Life and Work. Translated
by Bill Hopkins. Berkeley: University of California
Press, 1970.

Kolodin, Irving. The Interior Beethoven. New York:
Knopf, 1975.

Krause, Ernst. Richard Strauss: The Man and His Work.
London: Collet's, 1964.

Krenek, Ernst. Exploring Music. Translated by Margaret
Shenfield & Geoffrey Skelton. New York: October House,
1966.

La Grange, Henry-Louis de. Mahler. New York: Doubleday, 1973.

Landon, H. C. Robbins. Essays on the Viennese Classical
Style: Gluck, Haydn, Mozart, Beethoven. London: Barrie & Rockliff, 1970.

_____. Haydn: Chronicle and Works. Bloomington:
Indiana University Press, 1976.

_____. Haydn Symphonies. Seattle: University of Wash-
ington Press, 1969.

_____. The Mozart Companion. New York: Norton,
1969.

_____. Studies in Eighteenth-Century Music. New York:
Oxford University Press, 1970.

Lang, Paul Henry, ed. The Creative World of Beethoven.
New York: Norton, 1971.

_____. George Frideric Handel. New York: Norton,
1966.

_____, ed. Stravinsky: A New Appraisal of His Work.
New York: Norton, 1963.

Large, Brian. Smetana. London: Duckworth, 1970.

Larsen, Jens Peter. Handel's Messiah. New York: Norton, 1957.

Layton, Robert. Sibelius. London: Dent, 1965.

Leibowitz, Rene. Schoenberg and His School. Translated
from the French by Dika Newlin. New York: Da Capo
Press, 1970.

Leichtentritt, Hugo. Musical Form. Cambridge: Harvard
University Press, 1959.

Liebich, Louise. Claude-Achille Debussy. London: John
Lee, 1918.

Liebner, Janos. Mozart on the Stage. New York: Praeger,
1972.

Liess, Andreas. Carl Orff. Translated by Adelheid and
Herbert Parkin. London: Calder and Boyars, 1966.

Lincoln, Harry, ed. The Computer and Music. Ithaca:
Cornell University Press, 1970.

Lockspeiser, Edward. Debussy. London: Dent, 1951.

_____. Debussy: His Life and Mind. New York: Mac-
millan, 1962.

Long, Marguerite. At the Piano with Debussy. Translated
by Olive Senior-Ellis. London: Dent, 1972.

Longyear, Rey M. Nineteenth Century Romanticism in
Music. Englewood Cliffs, N.J.: Prentice-Hall, 1969.

Lyle, Watson. Camille Saint-Saëns. Westport, Conn.:
Greenwood, 1970.

MacDonald, Hugh. Berlioz Orchestral Music. London:
British Broadcasting Corp., 1969.

MacDonald, Malcolm. Schoenberg. London: Dent, 1976.

MacDonald, Ray S. Puccini: King of Verismo. New York:
Vantage Press, 1973.

Machlis, Joseph. The Enjoyment of Music. Third Edition.
New York: Norton, 1970.

_____. Introduction to Contemporary Music. New York:
Norton, 1961.

Maisel, Edward M. Charles T. Griffes. New York: Da
Capo, 1972.

Mann, William. The Operas of Mozart. New York: Oxford University Press, 1977.

_____. Richard Strauss: A Critical Study of the Operas.
London: Cassell & Co., 1964.

Marek, George R. Richard Strauss: The Life of a Non-
Hero. New York: Simon & Schuster, 1967.

Marliave, Joseph de. Beethoven's Quartets. New York:
Dover, 1961.

Martin, George Whitney. Verdi: His Music, Life and
Times. New York: Dodd, Mead, 1963.

Martynov, Ivan. Dmitri Shostakovich: The Man and His
Work. New York: Greenwood Press, 1969.

Mason, Daniel Gregory. The Chamber Music of Brahms.
New York: Macmillan, 1933.

Matthews, Denis. Beethoven Piano Sonatas. (BBC Music
Guides) Seattle: University of Washington Press, 1969.

_____, ed. Keyboard Music. New York: Praeger,
1972.

Mellers, Wilfrid. Francois Couperin and the French Classical Tradition. New York: Roy Publishers, 1951.

_____. Music in a New Found Land. New York: Knopf,
1965.

Meyer, Leonard B. Emotion and Meaning in Music.
Chicago: University of Chicago Press, 1956.

Misch, Ludwig. Beethoven Studies. Norman: University of
Oklahoma Press, 1953.

Mitchell, Donald. Gustav Mahler: The Wunderhorn Years.
Boulder, Colo. : Westview Press, 1975.

Moberly, R. B. Three Mozart Operas: Figaro, Don Giovanni, The Magic Flute. New York: Dodd, Mead, 1968.

Moldenhauer, Hans, comp. Anton von Webern: Perspectives.
Seattle: University of Washington Press, 1966.

Montagu-Nathan, M. Rimsky-Korsakoff. New York: Duffield and Co. , 1917.

Moore, Robert Etheridge. Henry Purcell and the Restora-
tion Theatre. Westport, Conn. : Greenwood Press, 1974.

Moser, Hans Joachim. Heinrich Schütz: His Life and Work.
Translated from the Second Revised Edition by Carl F.
Pfatteicher. St. Louis: Concordia, 1959.

Murdock, William.   Brahms.   New York: Sears Publishing,
n. d.

The Music Forum.   New York: Columbia University Press,
1967.

Myers, Rollo.   Emmanuel Chabrier and His Circle.   London: Dent, 1969.

_____.   Ravel: Life and Works.   New York: Thomas
Yoseloff, 1960.

Nadeau, Roland.   The Symphony: Structure and Style.
Shorter Edition: Revised.   Boston: Crescendo Publishing, 1974.

Nallin, Walter E.   The Musical Idea.   New York: Macmillan, 1968.

Nelson, Wendell.   The Concerto.   Iowa: William C. Brown,
1969.

Nestyev, Israel V.   Prokofiev.   Translated from the Russian
by Florence Jonas.   California: Stanford University
Press, 1960.

The New Oxford History of Music.   London: Oxford University Press, 1957.

Newman, Ernest.   Gluck and the Opera: A Study in Musical
History.   London: Gollancz, 1964.

_____.   Hugo Wolf.   New York: Dover, 1966.

_____.   Richard Strauss.   New York: Books for Li-
braries, 1969.

_____.   A Study of Wagner.   New York: Putnam's, 1899.

_____.   Wagner as Man and Artist.   London: Dent,
1914.

Newmarch, Rosa.   Tchaikovsky.   London: Reeves, 1908.

Nichols, Roger.   Debussy.   London: Oxford University
Press, 1973.

_____.   Messiaen.   London: Oxford University Press, 1975.

_____. Ravel. London: Dent, 1977.

Niecks, Frederick. Frederick Chopin as a Man and Musician. 2 vols. London: Novello, 1902.

Niemann, Walter. Brahms. Translated from the German by Catherine Alison Phillips. New York: Knopf, 1929.

Orenstein, Arbie. Ravel: Man and Musician. New York: Columbia University Press, 1975.

Orrey, Leslie. Bellini. New York: Farrar, Straus and Giroux, 1969.

Osborne, Charles. The Complete Operas of Verdi. New York: Knopf, 1970.

Ottaway, Hugh. Vaughan Williams Symphonies. Seattle: University of Washington Press, 1973.

Pakenham, Simona. Ralph Vaughan Williams: A Discovery of His Music. London: Macmillan, 1957.

Palisca, Claude V. Baroque Music. Englewood Cliffs, N. J. : Prentice-Hall, 1968.

Palmer, Christopher. Delius. Portrait of a Cosmopolitan. New York: Holmes & Meier, 1976.

Parrot, Ian. Elgar. London: Dent, 1971.

Patterson, Annie. Schumann. London: Dent, 1934.

Pauly, Reinhard G. Music in the Classic Period. Second Edition. Englewood Cliffs, N. J. : Prentice-Hall, 1973.

Payne, Anthony. Schoenberg. London: Oxford University Press, 1969.

Perry, Rosalie Sandra. Charles Ives and the American Mind. Ohio: Kent State University Press, 1974.

Petzold, Richard. Georg Philipp Telemann. Translated by Horace Fitzpatrick. New York: Oxford University Press, 1974.

Peyser, Joan. Boulez. New York: Schirmer Books, 1976.

Piggot, Patrick. The Life and Music of John Field: 1782-
1837. Berkeley: University of California Press, 1973.

_____. Rachmaninov Orchestral Music. London: British
Broadcasting Corporation, 1974.

Pincherle, Marc. Corelli: His Life, His Work. Translated from the French by Hubert E. M. Russell. New
York: Norton, 1956.

_____. Vivaldi: Genius of the Baroque. Translated
from the French by Christopher Hatch. New York: Norton, 1962.

Pirro, Andre. J. S. Bach. Translated from the French by
Mervyn Savill. New York: Orion Press, 1957.

Plantinga, Leon. Clementi: His Life and Music. London:
Oxford University Press, 1977.

Poulton, Diana. John Dowland: His Life and Works.
Berkeley: University of California Press, 1972.

Powers, Harold, ed. Studies in Music History: Essays for
Oliver Strunk. Princeton: Princeton University Press,
1968.

Primmer, Brian. The Berlioz Style. London: Oxford University Press, 1973.

Prunières, Henry. Monteverdi: His Life and Work.
Translated from the French by Marie D. Mackie. New
York: Dover, 1972.

Radcliffe, Philip. Beethoven's String Quartets. London:
Hutchinson University Library, 1965.

_____. Mendelssohn. London: Dent, 1957.

_____. Schubert Piano Sonatas. Seattle: University of
Washington Press, 1971.

Raphael, Robert. Richard Wagner. New York: Twayne,
1969.

Raynor, Robert M. Wagner and Die Meistersinger. London: Oxford University Press, 1940.

Redlich, H. F. Alban Berg: The Man and His Music.
London: John Calder, 1957.

_____. Bruckner and Mahler. London: Dent, 1955.

_____. Claudio Monteverdi: Life and Works. London:
Oxford University Press, 1952.

Redwood, Christopher, ed. A Delius Companion. London:
John Calder, 1976.

Reed, John. Schubert: The Final Years. London: Faber
& Faber, 1972.

Reese, Gustav. Music in the Renaissance. Revised Edition. New York: Norton, 1959.

Reich, Willi. Alban Berg. Translated by Cornelius
Cardew. New York: Harcourt, Brace & World, 1965.

_____. Schoenberg: A Critical Biography. Translated
by Leo Black. London: Longman, 1968.

Reti, Rudolph. Thematic Patterns in Sonatas of Beethoven.
New York: Macmillan, 1967.

Riedel, Johannes. Music of the Romantic Period. Iowa:
William C. Brown, 1969.

Riesemann, Oskar von. Moussorgsky. Translated from the
German by Paul England. New York: Knopf, 1929.

Ringbom, Nils-Erik. Jean Sibelius. Norman: University
of Oklahoma Press, 1954.

Robertson, Alec, ed. Chamber Music. Baltimore: Penguin
Books, 1957.

_____. The Church Cantatas. New York: Praeger,
1972.

_____. Dvořák. London: Dent, 1945.

_____. Requiem: Music of Mourning and Consolation.
New York: Praeger, 1968.

Rolland, Romain. Handel. Translated by A. Eaglefield
Hull. New York: Holt, 1916.

Rosen, Charles. Arnold Schoenberg. New York: Viking Press, 1975.

————. The Classical Style. New York: Viking Press, 1971.

Routh, Francis. Stravinsky. London: Dent, 1975.

Sadie, Stanley. Beethoven. London: Faber & Faber, 1967.

————. Mozart. New York: Grossman Publishers, 1970.

Saint-Foix, G. de. The Symphonies of Mozart. London: Dennis Dobson, 1947.

Salzman, Eric. Twentieth Century Music: An Introduction. Englewood Cliffs, N. J. : Prentice-Hall, 1967.

Sams, Eric. Brahms Songs. Seattle: University of Washington Press, 1972.

————. The Songs of Hugo Wolf. London: Methuen & Co. , 1961.

————. The Songs of Robert Schumann. New York: Norton, 1969.

Saunders, William. Weber. New York: Da Capo, 1970.

Schauffler, Robert Haven. Florestan: The Life and Work of Robert Schumann. New York: Dover, 1963.

————. The Unknown Brahms. New York: Dodd, Mead, 1936.

Scherman, Thomas K. and Louis Biancolli, eds. The Beethoven Companion. New York: Doubleday, 1972.

Schmitz, E. Robert. The Piano Works of Claude Debussy. New York: Duell, Sloan & Pearce, 1950.

Schrade, Leo. Monteverdi: Creator of Modern Music. New York: Norton, 1950.

Schreiber, Flora and Vincent Persichetti. William Schuman. New York: G. Schirmer, 1954.

Schwartz, Charles. Gershwin: His Life and Music. New York: Bobbs-Merrill, 1973.

Schwartz, Elliott. The Symphonies of Ralph Vaughan Williams. Amherst: University of Mass., 1964.

Schweitzer, Albert. J. S. Bach. 2 Vols. English translation by Ernest Newman. London: Breitkopf & Härtel, 1911.

Searle, Humphrey. The Music of Liszt. Second Revised Edition. New York: Dover, 1966.

Simpson, Robert Wilfred Levich. Beethoven Symphonies. Seattle: University of Washington Press, 1971.

_____. Carl Nielsen: Symphonist, 1865-1931. London: Dent, 1952.

_____. The Essence of Bruckner: An Essay Towards the Understanding of His Music. Philadelphia: Chilton Book Co., 1968.

_____. The Symphony. New York: Drake Publishers, 1972,

Sitwell, Sacheverell. Mozart. New York: Appleton, 1932.

Smith, Alexander Brent. Schubert: The Symphonies. London: Oxford University Press, 1926.

Smith, Julia. Aaron Copland. New York: Dutton, 1955.

Sourek, Otakar. Antonin Dvořák. Westport, Conn.: Greenwood Press, 1970.

Specht, Richard. Johannes Brahms. Translated by Eric Blom. London: Dent, 1930.

Spitta, Philipp. Johann Sebastian Bach. Translated from the German by Clara Bell and J. A. Fuller-Maitland. New York: Dover, 1951.

Stevens, Halsey. The Life and Music of Béla Bartók. New York: Oxford University Press, 1953.

Streatfeild, R. A. Handel. New York: Da Capo Press, 1964.

Stuckenschmidt, H. H. Maurice Ravel: Variations on His
Life and Work. Philadelphia: Chilton, 1968.

Suchoff, Benjamin, ed. Béla Bartók Essays. New York:
St. Martin's, 1976.

_____. Guide to Bartók's Mikrokosmos. Revised Edi-
tion. London: Boosey & Hawkes, 1971.

Suckling, Norman. Fauré. London: Dent, 1951.

Swalin, Benjamin F. The Violin Concerto: A Study in
German Romanticism. Chapel Hill: University of North
Carolina, 1941.

Tansman, Alexandre. Igor Stravinsky: The Man and His
Music. Translated by Therese and Charles Bleefield.
New York: Putnam, 1949.

Templier, Pierre-Daniel. Erik Satie. Translation by Elena
L. French and David S. French. Cambridge: MIT Press,
1969.

Terry, Charles Sanford. The Music of Bach: An Introduction. New York: Dover, 1963.

Thompson, Oscar. Debussy: Man and Artist. New York:
Dover, 1965.

Tischler, Hans. The Perceptive Music Listener. Englewood Cliffs, N. J. : Prentice-Hall, 1955.

_____. A Structural Analysis of Mozart's Piano Con-
certos. New York: Institute of Medieval Music, 1966.

Tobin, John. Handel's Messiah. London: Cassell, 1969.

Tobin, Joseph. Mozart and the Sonata Form. New York:
Da Capo, 1971.

Tovey, Donald Francis. A Companion to Beethoven's Pianoforte Sonatas. London: The Associated Board of the
Royal Schools of Music, 1931.

_____. Essays in Musical Analysis. London: Oxford
University Press, 1937.

_____. The Main Stream of Music and Other Essays. New York: Meridian, 1959.

Toye, Francis. Giuseppe Verdi: His Life and Works. New York: Knopf, 1931.

_____. Rossini: A Study in Tragi-Comedy. New York: Norton, 1963.

Tusler, Robert L. The Style of Bach's Chorale Preludes. New York: Da Capo, 1968.

Tyson, Alan, ed. Beethoven Studies. New York: Norton, 1973.

Ulrich, Homer. Chamber Music. Second Edition. New York: Columbia University Press, 1966.

Vallas, Leon. César Franck. Translated by Hubert Foss. New York: Oxford University Press, 1951.

Vaughan Williams, Ralph. Some Thoughts on Beethoven's Choral Symphony. London: Oxford University Press, 1959.

Veinus, Abraham. The Concerto. New York: Dover, 1964.

Vlad, Roman. Stravinsky. Translated from the Italian by Frederick and Ann Fuller. Second Edition. London: Oxford University Press, 1967.

Vuillermoz, Emile. Gabriel Fauré. Translated by Kenneth Schapin. Philadelphia: Chilton, 1969.

Walker, Alan, ed. The Chopin Companion. New York: Norton, 1966.

_____. Franz Liszt: The Man and IIis Music. New York: Taplinger, 1970.

_____. Frederic Chopin. New York: Taplinger, 1967.

_____. Robert Schumann: The Man and His Music. London: Barrie and Jenkins, 1972.

Walker, Frank. Hugo Wolf: A Biography. New York: Knopf, 1968.

Walsh, Stephen. The Lieder of Schumann. London: Cassell, 1971.

Walton, Charles W. Basic Forms in Music. New York: Alfred Publishing Co. , 1974.

Warburton, Annie O. Analyses of Musical Classics. London: Longman, 1974.

Warrack, John. Carl Maria von Weber. London: Hamish Hamilton, 1968.

_____. Tchaikovsky: Symphonies and Concertos. Seattle: University of Washington Press, 1969.

Watkins, Glenn. Gesualdo: The Man and His Music. Chapel Hill: University of North Carolina, 1973.

Watson, Derek. Bruckner. London: Dent, 1975.

Weinstock, Herbert. Chopin: The Man and His Music. New York: Knopf, 1959.

_____. Tchaikovsky. New York: Knopf, 1943.

_____. Vincenzo Bellini: His Life and His Operas. New York: Knopf, 1971.

Wellesz, Egon. Arnold Schoenberg. Translated by W. H. Kerridge. New York: Da Capo Press, 1969.

Werner, Eric. Mendelssohn. Translated from the German by Dika Newlin. London: Free Press of Glencoe, 1963.

Werner, Jack. Mendelssohn's Elijah. London: Chappell & Co. , 1965.

Westrup, J. A. Bach Cantatas. London: British Broadcasting Corporation, 1966.

_____. Purcell. London: Dent, 1960.

White, Eric Walter. Benjamin Britten: His Life and Operas. Berkeley: University of California Press, 1970.

_____. Stravinsky: The Composer and His Works. Berkeley: University of California Press, 1966.

Whittaker, W. Gillies. The Cantatas of Johann Sebastian
    Bach: Sacred and Secular. London: Oxford University
    Press, 1959.

Whittall, Arnold. Schoenberg Chamber Music. Seattle:
    University of Washington Press, 1972.

Williams, C. F. Abdy. Bach. London: Dent, 1934.

Wörner, Karl H. Schoenberg's Moses and Aaron. Trans-
    lated by Paul Hamburger. London: Faber & Faber,
    1963.

Wolff, Werner. Anton Bruckner, Rustic Genius. New York:
    Cooper Square Publishers, 1973.

Young, Percy M. The Choral Tradition. New York: Nor-
    ton, 1971.

_____. Elgar, O. M. : A Study of a Musician. London:
    Collins, 1955.

_____. Handel. London: Dent, 1961.

_____. The Oratorios of Handel. London: Dennis Dob-
    son, 1949.

Periodicals Consulted

Acta Musicologica. Basel, Switzerland
American Choral Review. New York
American Music Teacher. Cincinnati, Ohio
American Record Guide. Melville, New York
American String Teacher. Terre Haute, Indiana
Bach. Berea, Ohio
Choir. London
Choral Journal. Tampa, Florida
Chord and Discord. New York: Bruckner Society of Amer-
    ica
Clavier. Evanston, Illinois
Consort. Wiltshire, England (Dolmetsch Foundation)
Current Musicology. New York: Columbia University
Diapason. Chicago
Early Music. London: Oxford University Press
Hi-Fi/Musical America. New York

High Fidelity. Great Barrington, Mass.
In Theory Only. Ann Arbor: University of Michigan
The Instrumentalist. Evanston, Illinois
Journal of Aesthetics and Art Criticism. Philadelphia:
    Temple University
Journal of Music Theory. New Haven, Conn.
Journal of Research in Music Education. Baltimore, Mary-
    land
Journal of the American Musicological Society. Philadelphia:
    University of Pennsylvania
Monthly Musical Record. London
Music (A. G. O.). New York: American Guild of Organists
Music and Dance. Melbourne, Australia
Music & Letters. London: Oxford University Press
Music and Musicians. London
Music Educators Journal. Reston, Virginia
Music in Education. London
Music Journal. Southampton, New York
Music Review. Cambridge, England
Music Teacher. London
Musical Opinion. Bournemouth, England
Musical Quarterly. New York: G. Schirmer
Musical Times. London: Novello
NATS. Chicago
The New Yorker. New York
Opera. London
Opera Journal. Mississippi: University of Mississippi
Opera News. New York
Organ. Bournemouth, England
Organ Yearbook. Amsterdam: Knuf
Perspectives of New Music. Annandale-on-Hudson, New
    York
Piano Quarterly. Wilmington, Vermont
Proceedings of the Royal Music Association. Birmingham,
    England
Radford Review. Radford, Virginia
Die Reihe. Bryn Mawr: Presser
Saturday Review. New York
Score. London
Stereo Review. New York
Studia Musicologica. Budapest, Hungary
Studies in Romanticism. Boston
Symphony News. Vienna, Virginia
Symposium. Syracuse: Syracuse University
Tempo. London: Boosey & Hawkes
Yale Review. New Haven: Yale University

COMPOSER INDEX

ALBICASTRO, Henricus (see under Concertos)
ALBINONI, Tomaso (see under Concertos)

BACH, Carl Philipp Emanuel (see also under Concertos,
   Solo Works)
Rondo espresivo for piano 1
Solfegietto 1
BACH, Johann Christian (see under Concertos)
BACH, Johann Sebastian (see also under Chamber Music,
   Concertos, Orchestral Music, Solo Works, Vocal)
Art of the Fugue 3
Brandenburg Concerto no. 2 171
Brandenburg Concerto no. 5 171
Cantata no. 79 100
Cantata no. 131 101
Cantata no. 140 101
Chorale Preludes 3
Christmas Oratorio 101
English Suites for Harpsichord 3
Fantasy and Fugue in G minor, organ, S. 542 3
French Suite no. 5, G major, Harpsichord 3
Goldberg Variations 4
Harpsichord Concerto no. 1 in D minor 171
Invention no. 1, C major 4
Invention no. 6, E major 4
Jesu, Meine Freude, Motet 101
Magnificat 101
Mass in B minor 101
Musical Offering 102
Partita no. 1 for harpsichord, B♭ major, S. 825 4
Partita no. 2, violin unaccompanied: Chaconne, D minor,
   S. 1004 5
Partita no. 3, violin unaccompanied: Gavotte en Rondeau,
   S. 1006 5
Passacaglia and Fugue, organ, C minor, S. 582 5

St. Matthew Passion 102
Sonatas and Partitas for violin, unaccompanied 3
Suite for Orchestra no. 1, C major, S. 1066 140
Suite for Orchestra no. 3, D major, S. 1068 140
Suite no. 3 for violoncello unaccompanied; Sarabande, C
    major, S. 1009 5
Suite no. 6 for violoncello unaccompanied, D major,
    S. 1012 5
Well-Tempered Clavier (Book I):
    Preludes 1 & 2 6
    Fugue no. 1, C major 6
    Prelude no. 2, C minor 6
    Fugue no. 2, C minor 7
    Fugue no. 8, E♭ minor 7
    Prelude and Fugue no. 8, E♭ minor 7
    Prelude no. 10, E minor 7
    Prelude and Fugue no. 21, B♭ major 7
Well-Tempered Clavier (Book II):
    Fugue no. 3, C minor 7
    Fugue no. 5, D major 7
    Fugue no. 6, D minor 8
    Fugue no. 9, E major 8
    Fugue no. 12, F minor 8
BALAKIREV, Mily (see also under Concertos, Orchestral
    Music, Solo Works)
    Piano Concerto in E♭ major 172
BARBER, Samuel (see also under Chamber Music, Concer-
    tos, Orchestral Music, Solo Works, Vocal Music)
    Piano Concerto, op. 38 172
    Piano Sonata, op. 26 9
BARTOK, Béla (see also under Chamber Music, Concertos,
    Operas, Orchestral Music, Solo Works, Vocal Music)
    Bluebeard's Castle 56
    Cantata Profana 102
    Concerto for Orchestra 141
    Fifteen Hungarian Peasant Songs 9
    Mikrokosmos 9
    Music for Strings, Percussion and Celesta 141
    Piano Concertos nos. 1, 2, 3 172, 173
    String Quartets nos. 2, 4 206
    String Quartet no. 5 207
    String Quartet no. 6 207
    Violin Concertos nos. 1, 2 173
BEETHOVEN, Ludwig van (see also under Chamber Music,
    Concertos, Operas, Orchestral Music, Solo Works,
    Symphonies, Vocal Music)
    Bagatelle no. 2, op. 126, G minor 11

COMPOSITION TITLE INDEX